Women Global Political Movement

Women Global Political Movement

Anju Bindra

MANGLAM

MANGLAM PUBLICATIONS

DELHI-110053 (INDIA)

Published by :
MANGLAM PUBLICATIONS
L-21/1, Street No. 5, Shivaji Marg, Near Kali Mandir,
J.P. Nagar, Kartar Nagar, West Ghonda, Delhi-110053
Phone : 011-22945677, (M.) 9968367559, 9868572512
E-mail: manglam.books2007@rediffmail.com
manglam.publications2007@rediffmail.com

Women Global Political Movement

First Edition 2009

ISBN 978-93-80013-22-0

PRINTED IN INDIA

Published by Ravindra Kumar Yadav for Manglam Publications, Delhi-110053 Laser Typesetting at M.K. Computers, Delhi- 53, Printed at Sachin Printers, Moujpur Delhi- 53

Preface

This issue of Feminist Studies offers two distinct clusters of work: on Middle Eastern women. But it also discusses themes that cross these regional divides and extend to China and Latin America as well. These shared concerns include the ways that history and national politics shape, constrain, distort, and nurture feminist politics; the intersections of memoir and biography with larger cultural and social developments; and the role of the visual arts in expressing, framing, and furthering radical visions. Several authors trace the complicated trajectory of radical, revolutionary, and feminist visions and politics within and across national and personal histories. The art and poetry included here also speak forcefully to the complex interplay among culture, politics, history, and memory.

Is it inevitable that men will always be the dominant sex? Is it also inevitable that we always will live in a world of conflict, war and poverty? Steven Goldberg put forward a powerful argument for this in his book, *The Inevitability of Patriarchy*. His reasoning largely focused on hormones. Men naturally have more testosterone than women. This hormone not only makes men physically stronger than women, it also makes them more aggressive and competitive. This competitive behaviour Goldburg says, will always make men strive harder than most women to gain the high-status roles in any society. He claims this means that men will always outnumber women in most positions of power in our world. To be fair, this is the situation in our world today, and has always been the case throughout recorded history.

— *Author*

Contents

1

Why Men are Not Feminists

It's a strange fact that when Feminists used to take to the streets agitating for sexual equality, you rarely see men marching along with them. You can find both sexes protesting about worker's rights, race equality, and the rights of homosexuals, but Feminism? If you find men involved they always seem to want to keep quiet about it. The only man I heard openly advocating Feminism was the English poet Robert Graves. Yet he was criticised by many Feminists because they claimed his brand of Feminism was not about equality, but that women should rule the world.

Feminism is about the equality of the sexes and this makes perfect sense to most women. From the time of Mary Wollstonecraft's *A Vindication Of The Rights Of women* in 1792, until now, women have written countless book on sex equality. Yet we don't find many male authors writing about Feminism, unless it is about why it can't work. (like *The Inevitability of Patriarchy*). Nor do we find many men protesting on the street about this either. Men either make jokes about Feminism and political correctness or claim that Feminism has gone too far and men now are being discriminated against! Or they just keep quiet about the whole subject.

In my personal experience I have found that Feminists themselves regard many men who voice any sympathy about Feminism with deep suspicion. Most Feminists groups have a very strict rule about not allowing men into their groups. Which is a strange rule for a group that advocates, equality, political correctness and anti-discrimination. Though I can understand why they don't want men in their groups. There is admittedly the problem of some, big I am, turning up and lecturing them on why Feminism won't work, or attempt to take over. This was the experience of Feminists during the 1970s. They then allowed men into their groups, but even very sympathetic and well-intended men still tended to dominate the conversation and compete with women within the group. For this reason most Feminist groups ended up banning men.

The most famous case of this was the Greenham Common Peace Camp. In 1981 a group of 36 women started a protest against the deployment of cruise missiles at an American Air Base, at Greenham Common. This began a mass protest of both men and women but soon the women started to ban men from their camps around the site. Some camps placed a complete ban on men while others only allowed men to join them to protest during the daytime. This was given as one of the reasons why the Greenham Common protest was so successful, because men didn't interfere with the unity of the women.

Yet the very fact of banning men undermines the Feminist ideal of sexual equality. Because it is a admission by Feminists that they cannot make equality with men work, even in just Feminist meetings and protest movements. So if they are willing to acknowledge that they cannot create equality with men in groups that actually advocate sexual equality. Now do they expect to do the same in all other aspects of life?

So why is sexual equality strongly advocated by women but men show little interest? The obvious reason would be that women have something to gain through sexual equality. Whist men have something to lose. That is to say, men would lose dominance over women. While women have progressed from a position of servitude to that of equal opportunities in the West at least. This is true in all aspects of life. If you are a serf, slave or live in poverty, then equality sounds like a really great idea. If on the other hand, you are a wealthy member of the ruling elite, then of course, equality is a very dangerous, stupid and totally impracticable idea. Perhaps this argument might be a bit too hard on men. After all it was 100% male governments in the early 20th century who voted to give women equal voting rights. It was also male dominated legislative chambers who voted to pass equal opportunity laws for women in the 1960s and 70s. So it does seem that the majority of men in the Western world are not actually opposed to Feminism, and secretly many men seem to support it. Yet even men who will support Feminist women, do not seem that enthusiastic about sexual equality. The problem might be that equality is a totally alien concept to the masculine mind.

For many men the whole of life is a big competitive game. In fact some men do talk about, "the game of life". The only trouble with treating life as one big game is that there will always be winners and losers. Which doesn't seem to be a problem if you are a winner, but a real problem if you happen to be a loser. If you happen to come from a wealthy family and have gone to university and have a well paid job, like a lawyer. Then you are not going to see a problem with treating life as just one big game, because you are on the winning team. It is of interest that many people who do live in poverty are contemptuously referred to as losers by some of the well off. They will even go as far as to claim that it is people's own fault if they live in poverty. Forgetting that in a world of winners and losers, you cannot have winners without losers.

In fact in any competitive game the losers always far outnumber winners. We can see this in any sporting competition you might have hundreds of individuals or teams enter it, but in the end you can only have one winner. So in a competition like the football World Cup it was started with hundreds of teams seeking qualification, but all finally got defeated and knocked out, except for the single winner. The same is true of the game of life, the poor and powerless far outnumber the rich and powerful.

Men have dominated our world for the last five thousand years. Yet if we go through every society ruled by men, what we don't find is any form of equality. Even political movements that have set out with the firm intention to create equality have totally failed in this. If we go back to the English Civil War of 1642-8 between the King Charles 1 and Parliament, it was started because of the dictatorial behaviour of Charles 1 who wanted to dissolve

Parliament and rule alone. This created a bitterly fought war, (the worst internal war in English history) and guess what happened? Cromwell, the commander-in-chief of the Parliament forces became dictator and it was HE who ended up dissolving Parliament! Which was supposed to be what the Civil war was all about. The idealists of the time agitated to create an equal society, but they soon ended up in jail or on the scaffold. (Even equal rights between men and women were briefly discussed before Cromwell took control). The dictatorship of Cromwell was so bad that within a few years after his death, Charles 2 the son of the hated Charles 1, was invited back to rule England.

Egalitarianism was also the aim of the French Revolution in the 18th century, yet again all they created was a dictatorship and a reign of terror ruled by people like Robespierre and later Napoleon. Who was so competitive that he tried to conquer the world. The same was to happen in the communist revolutions of the 20th century where brutal dictators like Stalin and Mao Tse-tung took power. All these revolutions ended up creating tyrants, far worse than the ones they replaced. So the lesson here was that violent revolution is probably the worse possible way to try and create equality. Because all you do is to replace one group of very competitive men with another group of competitive men. What is more, the new rulers are likely to be also very violent men, because this was the way they obtained power.

The exception to this rule is the American Revolution. Where although the commander-in-chief of the revolutionary army George Washington did also became the President. Fortunately unlike Cromwell he didn't lose sight of why the revolution was fought. In his term of office he showed he believed in Democracy and wasn't interested in becoming a dictator. Another exception was Marshell Tito who although he was an extremely ruthless and violent partisan leader during World War Two. When he became dictator of Yugoslavia he turned out to be a reasonably enlightened leader. He was able to keep the Balkans in peace while he was in power, but unfortunately when he died the whole country split apart into violence. So it is possible for men of violence to become reasonable enlighten rulers but unfortunately they are a small minority.

Men themselves have seen that our very unequal world is a problem, and have attempted to do something about it through political movements like Communism, Socialism and Democracy. Unfortunately in all these systems only Democracy has worked. Though even with Democracy it took a long time to find a way to make it possible. The ancient Greeks and Romans tried it out, but it created so many disputes, it was finally given up as impossibility. So people switched back to dictatorship and kingship. Men have for a long time been searching for better ways to rule their societies. It is a sign of progress that Democracy was finally made to work in modern times after it was abandoned two thousand years ago in ancient Greece and Rome.

The problem with the failure of Communism and Socialism as well as the failure of Democracy in ancient times is that it takes away all hope of creating a just and equal society. Capitalists claim that competition is essential to motivate men. Some even go, as far to claim, "greed is good". This is perfectly true from the viewpoint of a wealthy businessman. From the viewpoint of those living in poverty, greed is a source of frustration, envy and even hatred. So it means that in positive way greed can motivate men to work hard to achieve their desires. Or in a negative way it can motivate men towards hatred, envy, crime and violent revolution. Also greed is not the best motivation for political leaders, as it is more likely to make them corrupt, or to become conquers of other nations. While competitive desires seem to motive politicians to want power for its own sake. That is to say they have become a winner, (the champion politician of their country) and the exercise of power is all they are interested in.

Yet we cannot just blame dictators and world leaders for all the ills of the world. They are ordinary competitive men who just happen to get to the top of the heap. All men, it seems, like nothing better to do than to be involved in competitive games with each other. If they are not playing competitive games with other men, then they like to watch them, as we can see with the great popularity of sport on TV. Because of this, it is men's competitive instinct that has made capitalism such a success in our world. One of the reasons why Communism and Socialism failed was that it didn't allow competitiveness in industry.

Resulting in communist industry stagnating and becoming very inefficient, while in the Western world industry was made very efficient and progressive by the competition between industrial companies. Democracy is also only possible because of competition between political parties for power. That is the upside of competition but it also has a terrible downside.

Rulers of countries have for centuries competed with each other so vigorously that they have gone to war with each other. Conquers like Alexander the Great, Julius Caesar, Genghis Khan, Napoleon and Hitler have conquered and destroyed many countries and caused the deaths of millions of people. Just so they can proudly say, "wow, look how many countries I've conquered". In fact their attitude doesn't seem to be much different to say a famous tennis player who has won the grand slam, and wants to be remembered as the greatest tennis player of all time. The difference is that the only harm a great sporting hero causes is the bruised egos of some of his opponents. With a great conqueror we are talking about widespread death, destruction and suffering of millions of people. So for five thousand years of human history, competition between countries and rulers has led to countless wars and acts of genocide. This became so bad in the 20th century that whole cities were destroyed in the Second World War through aerial bombing. As well as the many instances of genocide practised in Nazi Germany, Cambodia, The Balkans and Rwanda. Also in the Cold War between NATO counties and the Soviet Union both sides armed themselves with enough nuclear weapons to destroy the planet many times over.

The competition between the USSR and the USA became really crazy during the Cold War. In the 1950s and early 60s, there was competition about who could produce the biggest nuclear explosion. The Soviet Union won this one. A hydrogen bomb test conducted by the Soviet Union in 1961 detonated with an explosive force of 50 megatons, or 3300 times the power of the Hiroshima and Nagasaki bombs, which were "only" 1-1.5 kilotons. The winning Soviet explosion was so large that it punched through atmosphere above it, right into outer space. It frightened both sides so much they decided to give up on this, one-up-man-ship game, as scientists on both sides informed their leaders that a bigger explosion might do permanent damage to the biosphere. There was also a concern that nuclear testing in the atmosphere was producing radiation fall out. Even though the politicians of the time claimed, "that there was no scientific proof that fall out from nuclear bombs was harmful to humans." How many times since have we the public receive reassurances like this? Anyway you can't let little problems like the radiation poisoning of whole countries, get in the way of being able to proudly say, "we built the biggest bomb in the world". Can you?

Then there was the space race where both sides spent billions of dollars just to get the first man on the moon. As well as a competition about who had the most nuclear missiles. At the end of the Cold War the USSR had 39,000 nuclear warheads while USA had "only" 24,000. Why both sides needed so many nuclear weapons was never made clear. It was just another case of the competitive spirit among men getting completely out of hand. Yet because of it, for four decades from the 1950s to the 1980s people all over the world lived in fear of a Third World War that would wipe out the whole human race.

There was even one case where a defect in the defence computer of the Soviet Union, told its operators that they were under missile attack from the USA. Fortunately the man in charge knew that the computer wasn't reliable and waited for confirmation from other sources, before he would give the order to launch a counter strike. He was then thrown out of the military for disobeying orders! Still it was better than being court marshalled and then shot, as would normally happen in the USSR. I suppose the only consolation he had, was that he is the only man ever; who can claim he single-handedly saved the world. It is total insanity that because of fierce competition between the super powers, we came that close to committing global suicide. The Americans indirectly admitted to this insanity by naming their nuclear strategy M.A.D (Mutually Assured Destruction).

This then means that men's competitive instinct rules out completely any chance of men creating an equal society or overcoming the suffering of poverty. Because it is natural for men to compete with each other about, "who is boss around here"? We live in a "winner takes it all" world where the rich and powerful want more and more power and wealth and the poor get nothing. USA is the most competitive capitalist country in the world; this undoubtedly makes it the most dynamic and go-ahead state in the world. The downside of this ferocious competition is that 0.5% of the population of the USA own as much as the bottom 90%. It is no wonder the rich and wealthy like capitalism so much. It is these individuals that own all TV stations, film companies and newspapers, so it is natural for them to use the media to sing the praises of capitalism as much as they can. USA is the richest country in the world yet 45 million of its people live below the poverty line and over 40% have no medical cover.

To add insult to injury the rich don't even pay taxes. In most Western countries an entire industry has been created to help the rich to minimise their payment of taxation. So successful has this industry become that accountants make a mockery of taxation laws and use myriad of personal allowances, pension rights, deductible expenses and reinvestment allowances to allow their rich clients not to pay taxation. As one American millionairess once remarked, "Only poor people pay taxes".

The rich also put their money in overseas accounts, well away from the reach of the taxman. The point is that this means that it is only the poor and middle class have to pay the taxes, to keep the infrastructure of individual countries going, as well as to pay for the trillion dollar arms industry. The reason why this happens it that this wealthy rule the world, and so can make up their own rules and laws to suit themselves. It is also the big advantage of globalisation, as it makes it so much easier for the super rich to dodge taxation.

We live in a world where, it seems "nice guys come last". The fact is that you are unlikely to be the leader of a country, a religion or international business by being a compassionate, caring and loving person. The only exception to this I know is Nelson Mandela, he became president of South Africa because the previous white minority government was under pressure to give in to majority rule. Fortunately because Nelson Mandela the leader of the biggest party was a genuine forgiving and caring man, it was easy for the white politicians to hand power over to him. So we had a non-violent hand over of power to majority rule. Had Nelson Mandela been a different sort of person, the white minority in power may of wanted to fight it out, like they did in Zimbabwe. This was because they had to deal with a very different sort of leader in Robert Mugabe, who has since become another brutal dictator.

So it is possible for a caring and compassionate politician to make a positive difference to our world. Unfortunately Nelson Mandela is more the exception that proves the rule. Most politicians get to these positions of power through being ruthless, aggressive and devious. Political leaders even make claims that they are very tough and ruthless to get votes. Then we wonder why we live in an unjust and uncaring world. The point is that because we live in a world where only the most competitive, ruthless and Machiavellian people get to the top, it is no wonder that equality seems totally impossible in our world.

So where does this leave Feminism? Nowhere unfortunately. Today in the Western world we have laws to enforce equal opportunity. Now note the phrasing here, it says equal OPPORTUNITY not sex EQUALITY. Yes, by law women can in theory be equal to men, the catch is, women have to play the man's game and behave like competitive men.

This is the problem identified by Feminists themselves. Over more than a generation after the first equal opportunity laws were passed in the Western world, women on average are still paid far less then men, while the vast majority of the top jobs are still in the hands of men. If we look at this problem worldwide we find that women only own 1% of the world's wealth. This means that 99% of world's wealth is still owned by men. It makes you realise that the great progress that women seem to have made over the 20th century for equality, is still very much an illusion. Perhaps the only thing you can say about it that it is better than perhaps the 0001% that existed in the 19th century. Where women by law had few rights to own any property and didn't even have the right to vote. The problem for Feminists is that if women want to get top jobs they have to act like a Margaret Thatcher and become totally ruthless and uncaring. It seems only a small minority of women want to do this.

The solution given by Feminists is that we have to change the whole structure of society, because every social system in the world was created by men, for men. So they reflect men's competitive instincts and strengths. This then means if we have Democracy we have to have ferocious competition between political parties for power.

If we don't have this, Democracy is eroded to the degree that it doesn't matter which party you vote for, the policies are the same. (Which is true in both the UK and the USA today). The same is true for the capitalist system. Capitalism only works while there is again ruthless competition between companies. If one company becomes too successful it will take over its competitors or put them out of business.

Then it becomes a monopoly with no competition. Or if you are only left with a few large companies they will start to wonder why they need to compete with each other, when it is so much easier to co-operate. So they form a secret cartel and we soon have price fixing and complacency. This has happen in all the older industries. In the first half of the 20th century there were hundreds of car and aircraft companies competing with each other for customers. At the end of the 20th century there are only two large companies in the world that make commercial airlines and only a handful of car manufacturers, who are all in each other's pockets.

This then means that if the Feminists have their way and ruthless competition is eliminated, then men would be at a serious disadvantage, because without competition men do seem to lose interest in what they are doing. This is clearly demonstrated in communist countries where industries stagnated because of the lack of competition. Communists only did well in competing or fighting against the USA, as we can see in Vietnam, where a third world country defeated a super power. (Though admittedly they were well armed by the Soviet Union).

This was also true in the space race. In fact during most of the 1950s and 60s the USSR was far ahead of USA in putting the first satellite, the first man, the first woman and the first space station in space. They only missed out on the main prize of putting the first man on the moon, and since then have lagged far behind. Now, without the competition between the Soviet Union and America, space exploration has stagnated.

So it seems competition is essential for men to be efficient. The problem is that competition can lead to possible global suicide, as we saw in the Cold War. It also creates a world of winners and losers, where the majority of the people of the world are losers in that they live in poverty. While the small minority of winners keep all the wealth of the world in their greedy hands. Another problem is that in a competitive world everyone is so busy looking after number one and no one is looking where they are going. This can create unbelievable cock-ups.

In 1960 the oil producing countries of Iran, Iraq, Kuwait, Saudi Arabia and Venezuela got together to form a cartel called OPEC because they wanted to prevent the trend of falling oil prices. Later on other oil producing counties also joined. Then in 1973 Egypt and Syria attacked Israel to try and regain all the territory they had lost in the previous Six-Day War of 1967. At first the war went well for the Arab states and Israel appealed to USA for more weapons. President Nixon acceded to this request and publicly proposed a $2.2 billion military aid package for Israel. This greatly angered the Arab countries that decided to use the power of OPEC as an oil weapon.

OPEC imposed an oil embargo on USA and Europe and agreed a $3.00 a barrel price rise. In the end this didn't make any difference and Israel won the war. Yet as a result of the greatly increased oil price OPEC countries found themselves awash with so much money, they didn't know what to do with it. Some of them bought brand new toys like the latest weapons that arms dealers could supply them, and what was left over they invested in international banks. Now this was to cause a big problem because the banks didn't know what to do with the surplus money either, until someone had the bright idea of loaning the money to poor third world countries. The theory being that developing countries would be able to invest in projects to industrialise their countries. That was the theory; the reality was a total disaster.

Most third world countries are ruled by corrupt dictatorships, so the money that was lent, went into buying arms, and starting a third world arms race. Which suited countries like Britain, as arms are its biggest export earner.

As well as the USA because it is, the biggest arms exporter in the world. Money was also squandered on large inappropriate projects. Which again suited many Western governments, as it was Western engineering companies that built dams and other grandiose schemes the politicians thought up.

Also unfortunately much of the money simply ended up in the pockets of corrupt officials. The only exception to this for a while was India, which was ruled at the time by Indira Gandhi. Although she took the opportunity to borrow from the World Bank she was prudent enough to make sure she was able to pay back later everything she borrowed. Unfortunately she was assassinated in 1984 and her son Rajiv Gandhi became leader. He didn't have any of his mother's prudence and borrowed heavily and soon found he was unable to pay the money back, plunging India into debt.

The result was that all these third world countries were unable not only to pay back the original debt but unable to pay back the INTEREST on the debt. The IMF and World Bank stepped in and demanded that these countries started to go over to planting cash crops like cotton for export money and not crops to feed their own people.

They also demanded cut backs on government spending. The result was these governments cut back on health care and education for the people. (You couldn't seriously expect them to cut back on far more important things like arms, bribes and high salaries for important government officials, could you?)

Which was a disaster because without proper education for the people, there is no way a developing country can catch up with the developed world. Also without proper health care, and using land to grow cash crops for export, there has been an increase in the mortality rate of people in the third world through disease and starvation. The scale of this tragedy can been seen by the following statistics. Internationally, 815 million people worldwide go hungry. We live on a planet where 55% of the 12 million child deaths each year are caused by malnutrition. And it's getting worse. According to the United Nations, the poorest countries are worse off now, than they were 30 years ago.

The irony of this is that if any third world country wants to have a fight with its neighbour or have a civil war, guns and a limitless supply of ammunition are readily available. Yet money for education, heath care is in short supply for these countries, but then you got to get your priorities right haven't you? You cannot deny men the fun of playing with exciting toys like machine guns; tanks and flamethrowers can you?

Yet we have to be fair about this, men in the last few hundred years have made progress. Back in the 18th century it was commonplace for criminals to be flogged, tortured and executed for minor offences. People would die of starvation in the streets of major European cities and slavery was still practised. All this extreme brutality has slowly been banned in the West by exclusively male governments. This means that men in power are capable of compassion for their fellow human beings.

It means that men do have a choice. They are more than capable of being extremely brutal, as we have seen in so many cases of torture, violence and genocide even in our world of today. Yet this is not true of all men and we can find many examples of men who are capable of caring for others. Philanthropists like William Wilberforce (1759-1833) and Granville Sharp (1735-1813) who devoted their lives to abolishing slavery or John Barnardo (1845-1905) who set up homes for destitute children. Are examples of this. Yet a man doesn't have to be a wealthy philanthropist to be caring of others. Many ordinary men are caring of others. Unfortunately not enough of the loving and compassionate people get into positions of power to create a peaceful and caring world.

So what causes men to become extremely brutal while others devote their lives to caring for others? The simplistic answer is that some men are good while others are evil. Which explains nothing and this explanation does more harm than good. A better explanation comes from evolutionary theory, the study of early humans and primate studies. This science tells us where we come from and why we are like we are. Unfortunately these studies have also been distorted through sexual bias by male academics, who are blinded to the role of women and the feminine in the evolution of the human species. A more balanced approach would give us a far deeper insight to the human condition.

This is something I will explore in the following chapters. Showing that if we are aware of the masculine bias in evolutionary theory, history and early human studies. We can discover why men have created a world of conflict, violence and suffering and what can be done to change this.

2

The Selfish Gene, (And Other Feeble Excuses Made up by Men)

Back in the 1960s at when the women's Liberation Movement was going strong, women libbers were claiming that men and women were exactly the same. They claimed this for two reasons-

1. Men previously were claiming that women were not as intelligent as men. In fact in the 19th century male scientists "proved" that women had smaller brains then men. The idea that perhaps these male scientists might be a little biased never crossed anyone's mind. After all scientists are above human failings like emotions, bias and prejudice. These super humans can see the facts logically and clearly without human emotions. So of course they cannot possibly make a mistake, can they? They were also claiming that women were too emotional to make sensible decisions. After all women would get too emotional to make rational decisions like ordering hundreds of thousands of men to die in the face of machine gun fire. Or use gas warfare, as a more efficient way to kill and blind people. Like they did in the First World War.
2. In the 1960s the fashionable scientific theory then was that it was our upbringing that made us what we are. So Feminists seized on this and claimed it was only cultural bias in the way we brought up children that made the sexes different. Great theory, but somehow in practice it didn't work out like this. Feminist mothers and schoolteachers worked hard at treating little boys and

> girls exactly the same. So little Johnny was given a doll to play with, which he immediately took apart, or used as a football. While little Mary was given a train set, which she didn't know what to do with. No matter what Feminist mothers did, they found that the majority of little girls still liked playing with dolls and the majority of little boys still liked playing with toy guns.

Since then it has become clear that the sexes are very different. Scientists have discovered that the brains of men and women are not the same and are wired up very differently. Also the latest fashionable scientific theory is that, "it's all in the jeans". Genetics has taken over as the "theory of everything" to do with human and animal life. This then means a man cannot behave like a woman or a woman behave like a man, unless they have the genes within them to make them that way.

So is that it? Is it impossible for men and women to be different because it is programmed in our genes? Will this mean that men always want to compete and fight each other and try to blow up the world with nuclear bombs? And will women always be nice and kind and end up at the bottom of the heap in our competitive world? Well not quite. In the "nature verse nurture" debate there is surprisingly a third possibility. That both our genes AND the way we were brought up could influence our behaviour. We could even be influenced by the way we choose to think. (Which is a very revolutionary idea that politicians and marketing people don't want to hear). After all we are supposed to be the most intelligent creatures on this earth, aren't we? Well you would think so, but from the crazy way we run our world, a case could be made that we are the most stupidest animal on this earth. After all although we are very clever monkeys, we seem to use to use our brains to mostly find better ways to inflict, pain, hate, violence and suffering on each other. We are so intelligent that we can produce a space ship that can fly to the moon. Yet we are unable to find a solution to far more important problems like world poverty. To quote UN statistics.

Why are we so stupid that we have all our priorities so completely wrong? In that we put our best brains and trillions of dollars into finding better ways to kill each other. Yet in comparison we put hardly any intellectual or material capital into making this world a better place for ALL people to live in. We are also supposed to have free will. (Though not if the politicians can help it). Yet few of us seem to use it and we follow the herd like sheep. In fact throughout history people who are slightly different from the norm are persecuted and have even been murdered for this, "crime".

The biggest problem with the nature v nurture debate is that it is also very political. In no way should political leanings get in the way of scientific inquiry, but then, science is practised by human beings. So it means that the belief that it is, "all in the jeans" is a powerful argument for conservatism. Which means that human nature is the way it is because it has been programmed in our genes. Which in turn justifies the status quo, which is war, capitalism and poverty. Those who advocate nurture are looking for social change and are mostly feminists, pacifists or left wing activists. So in means in recent years the scientific beliefs that it is only genes that determine our behaviour has been used as a very powerful argument for the forces of conservatism. Though as I will explain later in this book this argument is a two edged sword.

The Selfish Gene theory by Richard Dawkins is presented as a very powerful argument for conservatism and capitalism to the degree it has become a standard textbook in American universities. As it claims that the only purpose in life is for gene to reproduce themselves, and we all compete with each other to ensure it is our genes that produce the next generation.

Reproduction is the most important instinct all animals have. To the degree it will take precedence over personal survival. As in the case of the octopus. When the mother lays her eggs she will slowly starve to death looking after her eggs until they hatch. Some female insects die when they lay their eggs and the first meal the larvae has, when they hatch, is the body of their own mother. In the case of some species of spiders, the female eats the male after they have mated, (apparently sex gives her a appetite). The praying mantis also has similar habits. While the male is mating, the female have been observed to eat his head, yet the headless body will continue to mate. Which is a confirmation of what many women say about men.

"Their brains are in the end of their penis' ".

Although these instincts seem to be brutal, it still makes sense because if any species of animal is to endure, then it has to ensure its offspring will survive to adulthood.

This then is why in most species of animals the mother has very powerful maternal instincts. In the evolutionary theories invented by neo-Dawinists they always focus on the power and strength of the males. Yet the most important factor in the survival of any species is the behaviour of females. To be fair the Selfish Gene theory does acknowledge the role of the mother.

He is willing to accept that except for some species of birds, it is females who have most to do with ensuring the next generation will survive and go on to reproduce again. Whist for many species the male has very little to do with helping their offspring and in some cases will hinder and sabotage the efforts of the mother to protect and care for her young. Yet Dawkins seem to see this as a clever strategy by males in putting all his efforts into passing on his genes to as many females as possible.

So what is the role of the male in survival of the species? In most species of birds the male bird behaves like "a new man" in that they help to make nests, and sit on eggs and feed the chicks. This is not the case in most mammals, which is what we are. Male lions have been witnessed killing cubs whom he hasn't fathered. Lionesses do most of the hunting in prides but the male lion will use his larger size to bully the lionesses away to feed first, or even steal the food completely from the lionesses. In spite of the fact, it is far more important for the survival of the pride, and his own off spring, that lionesses take priory in feeding, if she has to suckle young or is pregnant. In many mammals the only job the male does is to impregnate the females.

Of course we human males are not like this, are we? If we get a girl pregnant we always stick by her and help look after the kid, don't we? Well, some of us do. A very large number of young men leave girls who get pregnant and refuse to pay maintenance.

After all, the child might not be his! And anyway it wasn't his idea to have children! She should have taken the pill or something. Why can't she just get an abortion? I mean he had nothing to do with it, did he? All he wanted was a bit of fun and certainly not being saddled with a screaming brat, the rest of his life.

In most species of mammals the females are more than capable of feeding and protecting her young herself. Even in herd animals except in the case of buffaloes and cattle the males don't get involved in protecting the young, and will run off like everyone else if approached by a predator. So if males don't do much in caring and protecting of the young, what do they do? It seems what they do best, is fight each other.

Fighting seems to be the common pastime among most types of male animals. We have animals like stags, bulls and rams that every spring goes in for bashing their heads together. Or giraffes who also use their head as a weapon as they swing it on their long neck. Which makes boxing, and the damage that can be done to the brain by being punched in the head, seem quite sane and sensible. So why do male animals go in for head banging and inflicting damage to each other? According to evolutionists it has something to do with the male sex drive.

In the "survival of the fittest" theory, it is important that only the strongest male animals mates with the females. So the instinct for males to fight each other is a test of strength to ensure that only the strongest will pass on their genes to the next generation. Though this theory doesn't always work out in practice. Studies done on the coyote show that although male coyotes will fight each other for the privilege of mating, the females will not always pick the winner. Some females have been observed driving off the winner and mating with the loser. Clearly this is a case where coyotes need someone to teach them how the theory of evolution works.

If we take all the knowledge we have on the observation of animals in the wild and apply it to human behaviour we can see a similarity. It was once normal for non-Christian kings and tribal chiefs to have more than a hundred wives and hundreds of children. Which makes sense, in evolutionary theory, because he would be the alpha male in the community. So would have a desire to pass on his genes to as many offspring as possible. In this way, he is not behaving much differently from a stag or lion who have a harem of females and tries to mate with all of them.

Many alpha males in the animal world have territories, which they fight for against other males. Again we see similar behaviour among humans. Kings, and tribal chiefs, would also have territories that he would claim as his, and fight other kings or chiefs who trespass on his borders. It is even possible to make out a case for genocide using this argument. Lions will kill cubs that are not his when he takes over a pride. So it would also be "normal" for conquerors to kill and wipe out those who are not the same race as themselves. Which is what happened when Europeans invaded the Americas and Australia, where the native people were slaughtered and very nearly wiped out.

So that's all right then. It is "normal" for men to fight each other, have wars between countries and even practice genocide. Which is great if you are a psychopath and enjoy killing other people. You can kill as many other people as you like, and it's all right, because it is all about the survival of the fittest! If you are the sort of person who is a bit of a wimp, because you actually care about others, then there is a real problem with these theories.

In recent years neo-Darwinism has used genetics to back up theories of the selfish gene. According to his theory the whole of life is basically selfish. Now this as a purely erudite theory confined to ivory towers of the academic world. Unfortunately such theories tend to leak out into real life. Where it tells people it is perfectly all right to be selfish. Then we have social Darwinism, which can be used to justify all sorts of selfish and brutal behaviour. It was taken to the extreme by the Nazis who used the concept of the "survival of the fittest" as one of their justifications for practising genocide on Jews, Slavs and Gypsies.

The problem is that men who do take a very masculine point of view invent these theories. We hear about, "man the mighty hunter" theories where at one time scientists claimed that it was Stone-Age hunters that caused the extinction of Mammoths and other giant animals of the Ice-Age. Now this theory has changed and it is accepted that it was rapid climate change that caused this mass extinction. At one time when male palaeontologists found the sites of human settlements in the Stone Age they would concentrate on flints used in hunting. It was only when female palaeontologists also began to excavate these sites that they began to notice other stones that would have been used to grind up seeds. (Stones that male scientists had previously discarded as being of no importance). So we can see that the masculine attitudes of male scientists and academics can greatly influence their theories and what they discover.

As men are naturally competitive and think that the whole of life is a game of winners and losers. It would make sense that men see evolutionary theory the same way. They would concentrate on any competition they see like a predator going after a grazing animal, and totally ignore any example of co-operation. Like the way bees and plants work together, in that the plant gives the bees pollen, while the bee fertilised other flowers by transporting the pollen from flower to flower. Or plants producing fruit for animals to eat, then the fruit has seeds inside them that are planted in the ground when the animal defecates. Or birds that feed off the hides of large grazing animals, who allow them to do this, as the bird get rid of troublesome insects. There are as many observations in the wild of life co-operating with each other, as there are of life competing against each other. Also in any competition, no forms of life can afford to become winners. Predators that become too successful can end up making extinct the animals they feed on, and in turn will become extinct through starvation.

Neo-Darwinian theories tell us that male animals have an instinct to impregnate and pass on his genes to as many females as possible. This then makes sense of young men's desires to "sow their wild oats". It also makes sense of why many young men have a very cavalier attitude towards birth control. Where many men claim that, "having sex with a condom is like having a shower in a raincoat." I know when I was a young man in the 1960s I was told of a trick to fool young women. Apparently these young men would cut the bottom off condoms. Then in the half-light of having sex in the back of a car the girl would see him put on the condom ring, not realising that the bottom half was missing. The problem with this was that illegitimate children were still a very big issue in the 1960s and abortion was still illegal. I do wonder about the tragedies caused by tricks like this with young pregnant girls being thrown out of their homes to fend for themselves, for "disgracing" their parents. But then as explained to me, "any girl who has sex before marriage is only a whore or slut". So that's all right.

Its strange how people never worked out the inconstancy of this? It was a taboo then that young women didn't have sex before marriage, but the attitude also was there was something seriously wrong with a young man who was still a virgin by the time he was 18. With whom were young men supposed to have sex with? Prostitutes, "sluts" and "whores" of course. These women made young men feel like "real men" and were rewarded by being treated with contempt and derision.

These sorts of attitudes are even more tragic in Africa. Many young men in Africa refuse to use condoms, which allows Aids to flourish in that continent. Causing deaths to millions of people. But not to worry, these young men have found the prefect solution to the Aids problem. Apparently if you have sex with a virgin, it cures Aids. Yea really! What is more, the younger the girl the better it works. You don't say! So of course it means men with Aids are perfectly justified in raping pre-adolescent girls. I mean you wouldn't want to stop men from being cured of Aids would you? All right it didn't work the first few times they tried it, but perhaps they haven't done it enough times. Or the girls weren't young enough, but keep at it and it will eventually work. Won't it?

In the meantime, what about the young girls being given Aids by these men before they are even teenagers? There is a deafening silence about this, but then as evolutionists will explain, men have a powerful instinct to pass on his genes to as many women as possible. So the poor boys can't help it. There, there. (Though it has to be admitted that condoms as not as easy to obtain in the African bush as they are in any Western town or city. Also recent research shows that Aids also may be carried by contaminated needles when vaccinating the population for other diseases).

The irresponsible attitude of many men is also fuelling the Aids epidemic in the West. It seem there is a type of man who has the mentality of a psychopath and will use their penis as a genuine killing weapon. In that, they are aware they have Aids or HIV and yet will knowingly infect other men and women and will get very offended if it is suggested they use a condom.

The very irresponsible attitude of many men towards women, children and other men puts doubt on another theory invented by academic men about the Stone Age. The theory was that, not only was man, "the great white hunter", (even in pictures of Stone-Age men in Africa he was painted as white up until very recently), he was a good husband as well. The man went out killing Mammoths and presumably carried it to the cave on his back to feed his family. He also protected his wife and children by fighting off Sabre Tooth Tigers and Giant Wolves. (What a man). The reasoning why Stone Age man would do this is because he had this instinct to pass on his genes so he needed to protect his women and children to do so.

This attitude doesn't seem to have been passed down to many modern men, who do their best to get out of paying child support. Also this theory assumes that men in the Stone Age were married or pair bonded. Marriage, and pair bonding, is an idea invented by religions like the Christian Church, (The Muslims allow men to have many wives as did the Chinese up until the communist take-over). The Church also need laws, taboos and social censor to enforce marriage. If marriage or pair bonding was natural for us, the Church wouldn't needs to force us to marry and stay faithful. (Which large numbers of people don't do). The reason religions enforce customs that women remain faithful to one man, is that it is the only way a man can be sure that the children of women he lives with are his.

With the break down of marriage in recent years we find men who are happy to live with and support women with children who are not his. Clearly this in another case where these men need to be re-educated about their desire to pass on their genes. Perhaps if they are taught neo-Darwinian they will, "naturally" kill the children their partners previously had with another man and then force her to become pregnant with this sperm.

Now anyone reading this book might get the impression I disagree with Darwin's theory of evolution. I am not against the theory that says that one species of animal evolved from another. That has been proven in the fossil record. The problem is the means by which this happened. Theories like, "the survival of the fittest", "nature red in tooth and claw", or "the selfish gene" are just reflections of a very competitive, masculine point of view. If a man is competitive, aggressive and selfish in his attitude then he will naturally want to claim that the whole of life is like this, as it justifies his belligerent behaviour. In much the same way as a bigoted and intolerant priest will want to claim that god is very judgmental and punitive, for the same reason.

"The survival of the fittest" and "selfish gene" theories are not the only shows in town. There is another theory around that doesn't go against evolutionary theory but takes it from a completely different point of view. This is called the Gaia hypothesis.

3

The Theory of One

When Dawkins presented his selfish gene theory one section of the population very much disagree with this theory and that was the homosexual community. The foundation of the Dawkins's theory is that all genes are programmed to want to reproduce themselves. This means our basic instincts are to, "go forth and multiply". That is of course, unless you are gay. Homosexual relationships do not produce children. This has caused a big problem for the selfish gene theory, more so when some scientists have claimed to have found "gay genes". Because of this, supporters of Dawkins have made claims that homosexuality is not caused by genetics. Even fundamentalist Christian have since become supporters of the selfish gene theory as it more or less "proves" that homosexuality is unnatural.

The problem with this is that homosexuality is that it is not exclusive to humans. Same-sex activity has been observed in 450 species of birds and mammals. This includes the macho lion, where males have been observed to sodomise each other. So does this mean that, "The king of the beasts", is a queen after all? In species as diverse as the Japanese macaques, the mountain sheep, the giraffes and flamingo homosexuality is more commonplace than heterosexual behaviour.

Unfortunately zoologist and ethnologists have kept quiet about this because even today animal homosexual behaviour is not seen as "natural". This is why in wild life films, although they like to show the violence of animals killing each other or having heterosexual sex, homosexual behaviour is still censored.

The point is that it doesn't matter if homosexuality is caused by genes, environment or choice. If people and animals are involved in same sex relationship to the degree it interferes with their ability or desire to reproduce. Then it undermines the theory that the only purpose of life is to reproduce it's genes.

Then there is the problem that not all heterosexual people want to multiply. With the freedom that Feminism has given women some have made a deliberate decision not the have children. While other women who have problems in reproduction are happy to adopt children. If passing on their genes were the most important instinct in people, then these women would have no interest in bringing up other people's children. The same is true for men, not all men get to become fathers and many men today are happy being stepfathers. So do we then condemn these people as unnatural perverts because like homosexuals they don't have a powerful desire to reproduce?

This is true for other species of animals. It is true that some male lions will kill the young of pride he hasn't fathered, but not all lions do this. Other lions have been observed to accept cubs fathered by other males in the pride. So it is not a hard and fast rule that all males are obsessed by wanting to pass on their genes. This is true of females as well. Yes female animals have been observed to ignore young that have be orphaned. Yet there are many other cases of females mothering young that are not hers. There have even been cases of mothers of one species caring for the young of another species. As in the case of wild-children where human children have been cared for by female animals. So it seems that there are many humans and animals that are not conforming to Dawkins's theory. Perhaps we need to employ animal trainers for wild animals to train males to murder young that are not theirs and train females to ignore any young that is not hers. To make the theory work.

If there is a real problem with the selfish gene theory what is the alternative?

Mystics have for centuries claimed we are all one mind, one spirit. This concept has never caught on as it seems to go against all our personal experiences of competition and conflict with others. So is seen by ordinary people as to be a unrealistic fantasy. Then a scientist called James Lovelock developed a scientific theory that claimed the whole of life on this Earth is simply ONE ORGANISM. Which at first sight seem incredible but his theory answers many mysteries about the nature of life.

Back in the 1960s James Lovelock was employed by NASA to find ways a space craft could discover if there was life on Mars. So he started by examining the atmosphere of Mars to see it that would give a clue to signs of life. To understand this better he decided to examine the atmosphere of Earth and compared it with Mars. What he discovered was that the atmosphere on Mars was very stable and inert. Unlike Earth which had an unstable and dynamic atmosphere, because life itself was continually changing the gases within it. He then realised that you don't have to send a spacecraft to Mars to find out if it had life. You could do it by simply examining its atmosphere. Which is not what his bosses in NASA wanted to hear, because they needed a reason to convince politicians to fund a space mission to Mars. This resulted in him and NASA parting company, but he continued to develop his ideas further. As his studies of the Earth's atmosphere presented him with a number of scientific puzzles.

Every school child knows that there is a cycle where animals convert oxygen into carbon dioxide while plants convert carbon dioxide back into oxygen once again. But Lovelock took this concept even further, he looked at a mystery that no one had addressed, and that was although life began 3 - 4 billion years ago, the temperature of the Earth has changed very little in that time. The problem with this is that the sun 3 billion years ago was 30% colder, than today and has since been steadily heating up. The answer seems to be that 3 billion years ago the Earth's atmosphere had more carbon dioxide in it. Even though the sun was cooler the CO2 created a greenhouse effect and so keeping the temperature the same as it is today. Since then the levels of carbon dioxide have slowly fallen to keep the temperature of the Earth stable. So that's all right, problem solved.

Then Lovelock went on to ask a further question. How was it possible for the carbon dioxide to decrease over a period of 3-4 billion years AT EXACTLY THE SAME RATE THE SUN WAS

WARMING UP. This is a real a problem, when you realise that by just making the Earth a few degrees colder can bring on an ice age. Also it only needs 10 degree increase or decrease in the earth's temperature to make the vast majority of life extinct. So how has the Earth kept in the very narrow range of temperatures to make life on Earth possible? There was no answer to this and to say it was just a lucky fluke was stretching credibility a bit too far.

Then Lovelock came across other amazing coincidences. At present 21% of the atmosphere is oxygen. Now oxygen is a very dangerous and volatile gas. If it was to increase to 25% (only 4% higher) and a fire was to start, through a lightening strike, it would be impossible to put it out. Even green and wet vegetation will continue to burn causing all vegetation on the earth to quickly burn up. Yet lower levels of oxygen would seriously effect the energy efficiency of animals.

This means the oxygen levels on the Earth are about the most effective we need for life, without it increasing to a dangerous level. Yet life is continually taking oxygen out of the atmosphere and putting it back again. So how does life get it so right? In that it doesn't take too much oxygen out of the atmosphere thereby reducing the efficiency of animal respiration, or get it too high and create a worldwide disaster. What is more, life has been able to do this delicate balancing act for billions of years.

Lovelock realised that as it was life itself producing both carbon dioxide and oxygen and it was life that was regulating temperature and oxygen levels of the Earth, within the parameters to make life on earth possible. He was to find many more coincidences like this. Life also needs a chemical balanced world that is either too acid or too alkaline. Which is what we find on Earth, unlike both Venus and Mars who have environments that are too acid to support life. It seems that Earth has many forms of microorganisms that are working away to keep our world chemically neutral. He presented all his ideas in a scientific meeting about the origins of life but his ideas went down like a lead balloon. Only two scientists took a interest in his ideas, one being Lynn Margulis who had a background in Life science and was able to later help him to present and develop his ideas even further.

It took about 20 years for the scientific community to take his ideas seriously. (After all only theories that nature is very savage, brutal and selfish make sense. The idea that all life works in harmony, is the stuff of fairy tales) As the evidence piled up in favour of Lovelock, many scientists are now very reluctantly accepting his hypothesis, though he still gets his detractors, and guess who is one of his biggest critic? It is not a surprise to learn it is Richard Dawkins. A man, who tries to prove that life is basically selfish, is not going to be sympathetic to any idea that the whole of life is one organism.

Though Dawkins himself even admits that many species of animal do co-operate with each other for their mutual benefit, like the aphids who live in ants nests. The aphids get the benefit of being protected by the ants while the ants milk the aphids for food. Yet in when discussing life that helps each other he prefers to see it in terms of manipulation. He would rather use the word "bearers" instead of "carers" when writing about animals who care for the young. Hinting perhaps that bearers are suckers or losers. While the idea that any form of life could possibly give or help others because they love and care for them is completely ignored.

Another criticism of the Gaia hypothesis is that there is no very large brain laying around the place directing life and telling it what to do. Yet this problem is the same we have about social insects like Ants, Termites and Bees. They live in complex societies with different insects having very different roles, (like workers, queens, drone and soldiers). Yet what makes these nests and hives work is a mystery because these insects have minuscule brains and no obvious leader. (The queen is seen as the leader, but her role in directing what goes on in the nest is still a mystery). The Gaia hypothosis just treats the whole of life on this planet as a far bigger and more complex version of a beehive, with different species of animals, plants and microorganisms all having different roles in keeping the planet going. This is similar to the concepts of the Collective Unconscious that was put forward by the psychologist Carl Jung. Who discovered that the unconscious minds of his patients were remarkably similar. This means, we don't have to have an enormous brain lying around somewhere, to make the Gaia theory work. The whole of life can be the brain and intelligence of the planet.

If this is true then what is the role of human beings? After all we seem to be busy destroying the earth with thousands of species of animals and plants becoming extinct through the actions of men. Also we now have global warming where we are heating up the planet. Yet the planet has even got a bigger crisis than the meddling of a naked ape. As pointed out earlier the sun is slowing heating up, and life counteracts this by taking carbon dioxide out of the atmosphere. The problem is now carbon dioxide is down to just 0.03% of the atmosphere. So it doesn't take a genius to work out that the planet will not be able to take much more CO2 out the atmosphere if the sun continues to warm up. So the strategy of using carbon dioxide as a means of regulating the temperature of the earth is coming to a end, as there is only a small amount of this gas left. This means life has to devise a new system in which to do this.

So perhaps the creation of a clever monkey like humans with hands that can manipulate the environment, is part of this new strategy. Hopefully we will in time produce technology that can keep our planet cool, as the sun heats up. Or we can transport life from our planet to others planets or moons or even other stars with planetary systems.

Admittedly at present we are not doing well, in that we are heating up the planet through industrial pollution. Yet even this may be part of the plan. In that an environmental catastrophe caused by global warming may make us human being realise the importance of looking after the planet. We now have the technological power to destroy the Earth, which we might do through thoughtless and irresponsible action. Because we still have a attitude of wanting to plunder and exploit the environment for our selfish gain. Once we wake up to the fact that to damage and destroy the world is to also to destroy ourselves. Then we may change our attitude and use our science and technology to save Gaia instead of trying to attack her.

Now an intellectual argument between Lovelock and Dawkins is not going have much effect on the lives of normal people. It only happens when these ideas are taken from the ivory towers of academic debate and are used by people like politicians and businessmen. We can see this clearly with the ideas of Social Darwinism that has been popularised by people like Andrew Carnegie. Which advocates competitive individualism and a market economy unregulated by government. I also have to say the Nazis used Social Darwinism as a justification for the genocide of "inferior" races. This then means that academic debate on the nature of life can be used as political tools in the hands of politicians.

So how have the theories of Lovelock and Dawkins been used? Clearly Dawkins' ideas are just another support for Social Darwinism, and conservative politics. While Lovelock's ideas have been taken up by the New Age movement. Though Lovelock himself is clearly not a New Ager in that he was a scientific adviser to Margaret Thatcher in the 1980s. He advocated then that Britain builds far more nuclear power stations and not worry about radiation contamination. He claimed that we receive enough radiation poisoning from the Sun so a little more is not going to harm us. (This was the position of many scientists until very recently. Then it was discovered that life has as much radiation poisoning from the Sun as it can cope with and even a small increase will greatly escalate the amount of cancers and other illnesses.)

So what effect has the Gaia hypothesis had on the public? Not a lot it seems, perhaps the idea that we are all one mind and one organism is too boring. Concepts like, "nature red in tooth and claw" is far more exciting and dramatic. While the Selfish Gene theory and Social Darwinism gives us license to behave as selfishly and badly as we like. If we were to think in terms that we are all One, we would have all the problems of caring about others and worrying about things like world poverty. Not a good idea. If we go down that route, we might think we need to take a more responsible attitude to the planet and all the life forms that live on it. When it's far, far easier to ignore all this and dull our minds with drink, drugs and consumer goods, to escape the suffering we create for others and ourselves.

The Gaia hypothesis also reflect many ideas in mysticism that we are all one mind, one spirit, but ideas like this only appeal to a minority of people. The problem for Gaia is that Oneness is a very feminine concept in much the same way as Social Darwinism is very masculine. So masculine competition is the foundation of Social Darwinism, while Gaia is about all of life co-operating with each other for the good of the whole. Feminists and other women see co-operation as being very feminine and the ideal they all want to achieve. Something they see as completely impossible while we live in a male dominated society.

Also the idea that life is dominated by masculine principles is the same as the concept, that a male god created our world. So it means neo-Darwinist and patriarchal religions like Judaism, Christianity and Islam have in one way a similar view of the world. While the Gaia theory says that the whole of life is dominated by the feminine. (So it is of interest that it was named after a Goddess). This means that a person's individual bias of wanting to live in either a masculine or feminine world, can greatly influence the religion or scientific theory they want to belong or subscribe to.

We all live in a masculine world that Feminists have pointed out is created by men for men. Just by reading history or reading today's newspapers we can see clearly how a masculine world operates. Where the three Cs, conflict, confrontation and competition is the name of the game. The problem is that the masculine world is the only world we know. Read any history books and you don't find it describing societies ruled by women, neither do you find equal societies. It is true that there are Ancient Greek and Roman stories of the Amazons but they are just myths, aren't they? So it is natural for us to assume that the masculine, patriarchal society is normal and natural.

Likewise if you read books about pre-history and the Stone Age you will also get the impression that men have always been the dominant sex. Which is used as a powerful argument against Feminism in books like *The Inevitability of Patriarchy*. Because if it was always the case that men were the dominant sex, even as far back as a million years ago, then we have to see Feminism as just a passing phase, a social experiment that will inevitably fail. Because the natural assertiveness of men will in the end win through and women will lose, and once again to be confined to the job of homemakers for their lords and masters. So it is only going to be a matter of time before we go back to a natural world, "where men are men and women love them for it". Right?

Now the foundation of this powerful argument is that women have never ruled society. If we find that this is not the case and women did once rule the world, and rule communities even today in many parts of the world, then the foundations of this argument is destroyed. Women ruling the world? Surely not! You show me a history book that says this! Well yes, in official history you will never find any reference to that very taboo word matriarchy. Matriarchy has been a taboo, in our world for the last two thousand years and more. Even today it is a very controversial subject within academic circles. There are many books about matriarchal or matrifocal societies and other books tell you that pre-history matriarchal is a myth. Yet there is a lot of evidence around that says that it did once exist. As we can see from the following examples

4

Matriarchal Societies

In 1540 Francisco de Orellana led an expedition to the Amazon river and was the first European to do an extensive exploration of it. He reported finding along the riverbank large cities, towns and villages. He also somehow managed to communicate with the natives who told him women ruled them and they even showed him statues of these female rulers.

Then the Spanish managed to upset the natives and the first peaceful exchanges soon turned to open hostility. Where they were being to be attacked by the natives whenever they came to a village or town. He reported that female warriors led these attacks. When he got back to Spain the river he sailed on was named the Amazon after the stories Orellana told about these female warriors.

Yet 20 years later when the next European expedition explored the river they found no trace of the fabulous cities reported by Orellana or the Amazon warriors. As a result Orellana was to be labelled by historians a liar, and his stories of marvellous cities, female rulers and Amazon warriors exaggerated fantasies. This was to be confirmed in more modern time when it was realised that the soil in the rail-forests is very poor for growing crops. At present farmers are destroying the Amazon forest by the slash and burn method.

They cut down a large area, then burn it and plant crops. Yet after a few years the soil is so depleted that crops no longer can be grown. So they have to go on to cut down another area and do the same thing.

For this reason modern experts claimed that an ancient civilisation to exist in the Amazon basin was impossible because all civilisations in the past have relied on intensive farming for food. So it seems to be that Orellana was clearly a liar because there was no evidence of any kind to support his stories.

Then very recently archaeologists began to find large earth mounds in the Amazon forests. It occurred to some of them that these mounds might be artificial and they began to dig in them and quickly found large amounts of pottery and other man made artefacts. Not only this, some of these fragments suggested they come from very large pots, far too large to be carried around by anyone. This then means that these mounds were the remains of ancient settlements. As the archaeologists explored further they found ancient roads, linking these mounds demonstrating a complex infrastructure of an ancient civilisation. If this was so, how did they feed themselves? Because, as previously mentioned, without intensive farming they could not feed a large population.

The archaeologists then noticed the soil in the mounds was very different to the normal soil of the rain forest. It was reasoned, that this ancient civilisation must have found a way to fertilise this normally barren soil. Tests were done on it and it was discovered the soil was full of charcoal. What become clear was this ancient civilisation used the slash and burn method, but instead of burning the vegetation they cooked the wood instead. (This is the method of making charcoal all over the world). The charcoal was then able to retain the nutrients in the wood. Not only that, this charcoal rich soil was full of bacteria, which fed the plants growing in it. So impressive are the trials that have been done on this soil. (In experimental plots, adding a combination of charcoal and fertiliser into the rain-forest soil boosted yields by 880% compared with fertiliser alone.) This has now been hailed as a solution to the world's hunger problem. It seems that this ancient civilisation found solutions to the problems of poor soil that modern science with all its sophisticated chemical fertilisers was unable to find.

This soil has been found in many other areas along the Amazon River. With ancient artificial artefacts within it wherever found.

Showing a large civilisation and in all in the places where Orellana claimed he saw these cities and towns. So what happened to this ancient civilisation?

Scientists can only speculate, but it is known that the Europeans brought with them diseases that were unknown to the native population, like small pox and influenza. Not having any immunity to these diseases the native population was decimated. It means that the Orellana expedition brought to the native population these diseases, which would have wiped out most of them out very quickly. The civilisation collapsed and the jungle soon overgrew the cities and town. So by the time the next Europeans came to the same area all they would have seen was virgin jungle. The few survivors were then forcefully converted into Christianity and all knowledge of their ancient ways and stories ruthlessly destroyed. Though I have to say that it is not usual for civilizations to be wiped out by disease, civilization generally collapse through nature disasters like years of famine or conquest and genocide. Orellana questioned a native who told him that these female rulers had gold. We all know how gold mad the conquistadors were and with this knowledge reaching Spain they would want to come back to plunder this gold. Orellana did come back but was killed and his leaderless expedition returned to Spain, but it is likely that another expedition did go to the Amazon. If they had destroyed the Amazon civilization, plundered their gold and committed genocide they may not of wanted the world to know about this, so this expedition may have been written out of history.

This then means that Orellana has been vindicated. Though archaeologists as far as I know haven't been able to confirm that women ruled this ancient civilisation. Yet as everything else he reported has now been confirmed as correct, we can probably accept that was true as well.

The concept that women once ruled the world in ancient times is nothing new. A scholar called J.J Bachofen in the 19th century started it. He brought together all the evidence of matriarchy in ancient times then available, and very mildly suggested a matriarchal age in the past. He was strongly criticised for this by other scholars who dismissed and discredited his work. Yet in spite of this, his work was to inspire scholars like James Frazer who wrote his famous book, *The Golden Bough*, and more recently Joseph Campbell. It also influenced Karl Marx and Friedrich Engels who publicly praised Bachofen's work. As well as the psychologist Carl Jung who developed from it the theory that the ancient Great Mother, is a very important archetype in the collective unconscious. Other scholars in the early 20th century also wrote about matriarchy like Robert Briffault, who had pointed out that anthropologists then were very biased in their field studies. As they assumed that in all the Stone-Age cultures they studied they were all male dominated, and ignored any evidence when this wasn't the case. This didn't go down well with the academic community and again he was very heavily criticised. Yet his work was to inspire the anthropologist Bronislaw Malinowski who also found Stone Age communities they didn't fit the "normal patriarchal model. As did Margaret Mead who again was greatly criticised for making observations about societies that didn't fit into the patriarchal norm. Another anthropologist Eva Meyerowitz was to find evidence of matriarchal rule up to recent times in African tribes. While Evelyn Reed, in articles, lectures and her book, "Sexism and Science" was to savagery attack anthropologists for their sexual bias against women.

Jane Harrison another scholar also suggest matriarchy in ancient Greece, but managed to escape criticism by not being too explicit. Unlike Dr Margaret Murray a respected Egyptologist also received heavy criticism for writing that Witchcraft was an ancient Goddess religion that has survived up to the middle ages. These arguments were kept mostly within academic circles. Then in the 1940s the poet Robert Graves wrote his book, *The White Goddess*, which was the first attempt to bring this argument to the general public. Even though it was a very complex book. At about the same time Erich Fromm was bringing together the works of Freud, Marx and Bachofen. Where he pointed out that communism and socialism could cnly work in a matriarchy. Then on the wave of the Feminist movement of the 1960s and 70s Feminist scholars like Merlin Stone and Barbara G. Walker also continued to dig deep into ancient history to find more evidence of matriarchy in ancient times. After the Second World War archaeologists started to make finds supporting the idea that there was a matriarchal age in the past. This evidence was again dismissed by academics but Feminist writers began to write about it. Like Elizabeth Gould Davis who was brave enough to directly claim that women did once rule the world, and Riane Eisler who kept strictly to Feminist dogma of equality.

Yet we don't have to go to pre-history to find matriarchal societies, the shocking fact is that they exist in today's world. The biggest is the The Minangkabau people in Western Sumatra which numbers about 4 million people and is the largest and most stable Matriarchal community in the world today. There are also matriarchal communities in China, Tibet and Malaya, which is kept quiet as government officials find this an embarrassment. In Southern India there is a region called Keralal, which again is matriarchal and has a reputation of being a well run, stable and prosperous area. There is evidence of matriarchal communities that survived in Africa up until colonial times and even American Indian tribes that are still Matriarchal. The Basque people of France and Spain were matriarchal in historic times, but the Inquisition and the medieval witch-hunts finally destroyed this way of life.

There are legends that the Czech people were matriarchal up until the sixth or seventh century. Where it seems that after Libuse, the last matriarchal ruler, had died there was a patriarchal take over. In this legend the women fought back led by two women warriors called Vlasta and Sarka. After a very long and vicious war the men finally won and imposed patriarchy on the women. I have been informed that there are over 150 matriarchal communities all over the world, but we never hear about this in either the mainstream or alternative media.

Yet many Feminists are uncomfortable about this concept for three reasons.

Feminism is about equality; so many Feminists just see matriarchy as being the flip side of patriarchy. That is to say instead of men ruling the world, it is women doing it instead. Feminism has achieved a lot through just pointing out the unfairness and injustice of sexual bias in laws and customs. Which has resulted in men standing aside and allowing women to achieve equal opportunities in Western society. Start talking about matriarchy and this totally undermines the foundation of Feminism. As men can then claim that Feminism is not about equality but just "the thin end of the wedge" of female dominance. (Many men see it this way already, and don't really believe Feminists when they say, "we only want equality.")

Read any Feminist books, they are mostly about the horrors of patriarchy, and why it is wrong for men to dominate women. If there was an age in the past where women dominated men, then women will be as just a bad as men. (According to the women's Liberation Movement of the 1960s men and women are exactly the same. So if we accept this theory there shouldn't be a problem. Men have dominated women over the last five thousand years, so if women are like men, they will naturally want, "their turn").

There is also a fear of male violence among Feminists. Men in the past, and in Islamic countries today have dominated women through violence. In the 19th century in the West men were legally entitled to beat their wife with sticks if she misbehaves, and social custom encouraged this. (You weren't a "real" man if you couldn't dominate and beat up your wife). Yet over the last hundred years men in the West men seem to have seen the error of their ways through an appeal to fairness and equality. Start talking about matriarchy and women dominating society and men might get angry with women and perhaps use violence to take back everything women have gained over the last 100 years.

I can't say I would personally agree with this last reason, though I can understand women being frightened of male violence. Because just 4 hundred years ago the Church was still carrying on a murderous campaign of slaughtering millions of Witches, (mostly women). Also even today women are publicly executed and flogged in places like Iran, Afghanistan and Pakistan for minor infringements of Islamic law. Yet society in industrial countries has changed. After the Second World War the American military decided to interview all the returning troops to see if they could learn anything from their experiences. Most of these soldiers claimed that in the war they didn't kill anyone and only fired over the heads of the enemy. It seems only a small minority admitted to killing anyone. Which is not exactly the sort of image we have of GI soldiers in Hollywood films.

The Japanese military had similar problems. Japan ranks with Southern Ireland and Switzerland as being one off the most non-violent and crime free, countries in the world. Yet in the Second World War Japanese soldiers were even worse than German and Russian troops for brutality. So how did this happen?

It seems in the 1930s and 40s the Japanese military completely brutalised their troops. Older recruits at the beginning of their training beat up the new recruits. Then in the second year of training they were forced to do the same to the new intake. Later on many were made to kill prisoners of war, either as live dummies in bayonet practise or cutting off their heads. This total brutalisation made it possible for Japanese soldiers to kill without pity. Yet it is of interest that the Japanese military had to go this far into brutalisation to turn their troops into killers.

In very brutal societies as many third world countries, it seems men are so brutalised that they are far more likely to use violence against women to retain male dominance. Where men are less brutalised as in most industrial countries, then they are far less likely to resort to violence. Though I have to say the brutalisation of men in the West seems mostly to come from very violent films and video games. In that it helps to make violence acceptable to many young men. (Perhaps the makers of these films hope it will turn our young men into, "real "macho" men" who will put women back in their place).

Scientific studies have shown that boy and men who have been subjected to violence or fierce competition do have greatly increased testosterone levels. This can be increased to a level where sportsmen will commit horrific violence on the sporting field. A case in point is Australian Rugby. In the 1990s Australian rugby players developed what was called the pile-driver tackle. Where a group of players would lift a player of the opposing side off his feet and then drop him on his head. Neck injuries are the most horrendous injury you can get in rugby, where injured players have been left paralysed from the neck down. Also a pile-driver tackle has the potential to kill a player. So rugby laws had to be made to quickly stop this practice. Yet the question that was never asked is why were players willing to do it in the first place? They must also be aware of the physical damage that can happen by doing a pile-driver tackle. They also must be aware of the fact if they do it to the opposing side it will in turn be done to them. Yet reason and common sense didn't come into it and a law had to be made to outlaw his practise. This begs the question that if a loophole was found in the law that players could legally take a gun on the field of play and shoot opposing players to win the game. Would they do this?

So it means that when the testosterone levels are high in sportsmen they are willing to commit terrible injuries on the players of the opposing side. Surprisingly even watching competitive sport can increase the testosterone levels of men. So it seems that violent and competitions do make men even more violent. The less brutal and competitive a society is the less violent men become. This might be the answer to a very puzzling archaeological mystery and controversy.

5

A World Without War and Violence (You Must Be Joking!)

On Thursday 31 January 2002 at 9.00pm in Britain BBC Two the scientific TV program Horizon. Called, "The Lost Pyramids of Caral", the subject matter was archaeology (http://www.bbc.co.uk/science/horizon/2001/caral.shtml)

Now to anyone who didn't have an interest in science this program passed by unnoticed. Yet what this program was about is a very big shift in the understanding of our past and the true nature of human beings. To the degree that historians in the future will have to re-write history and sociologists will have to rethink all their theories about human nature. In fact what was discovered could bring about a colossal social, religious and political change in our future. Once the information about what was discovered fillers down to ordinary people.

As previously pointed out, most books about our ancestors in the Stone, Bronze and Iron age portray them as very brutal and violence people. It also seems that the further you go back in time the more violence and savage people seem to be. For this reason it was assumed that people who lived in prehistoric times were even more barbaric than the people in historic times. This has been the prevailing view by most archaeologists, anthropologist and palaeontologists up until very recently.

Now to most people academic theories are irrelevant to their normal daily lives, but the belief that we descended from savage barbarians effects us all. Because it assumes we are all deep down just violent brutes in modern clothing, and have to be kept in line through strict laws, moral codes and brutal punishment. This belief influences the nature of our religions, political systems and laws. It also has a unconscious effect on the way we treat others, because if we are to believe that the true nature of humans is barbaric. Then we learn to fear other people and assume the worst in them. Creating a vicious cycle of fear and hatred for other people.

This belief is not much different from the Christian belief that all people are born into sin. The implication of this belief, is that people can only be saved by obeying the very strict rules and moral code of the Christian religion. When scientists replaced priests as the "wise men" of our society all they done was to continue this belief in another form. In that we are no longer born into sin but we are given instead the equal negative belief that deep down we are all savage brutes.

This belief was spelt out on this Horizon program by Prof. C.C. Lamberg-Karlovsky of Harvard University, who said-

"I frankly find it difficult to conceive of the emergence of urbanisation complexity civilisation in the absence of degrees of conflict, or the presence of, warfare."

In other words he was saying it is natural for human beings to live in conflict, and he couldn't imagine any civilisation that didn't generate violence and war.

Proof of this belief was found by Dr Tom Pozorski of the University of Texas-Pan American and his wife Sheila who had previously discovered what was then thought to be the oldest city in South America. In the Casma Valley they had discovered one of the largest pyramids in the world, in fact it was so large that previous explorers had assumed it was just a hill. Wood on the site was carbon dated to 1500 BC and this at the time it made it the oldest city in the America. In the excavation they discovered carvings of warriors who were killing and mutilating their victims. To quote, Jonathan Haas of Field Museum, Chicago-

"Heads have blood flowing from their eyes and blood flowing from their mouths and then you have body parts so you'll have just the leg and you'll have a torso or you'll have feet and you'll have crossed hands".

So this find seems to confirm everything archaeologists believed about the early civilisations. That they were created by warlords who ruled by fear and created the first cities as fortresses against conquest by other warlords. This theory seemed to be validated until Dr Ruth Shady if the University of San Marcos, Lima, was to make a discovery that was to turn everything archaeologists believed about early civilisations, on its head.

Like Tom Pozorski she began to dig around what was thought to be hills in a place called Caral in Peru only to discover they were pyramids. As she and her team began to excavate the site she was puzzled the fact that there was no pottery on the site, (pottery is nearly always found in ancient civilisations) and finding only stone tools. This suggested this site was so ancient that it existed before the invention of pottery and metal. This was confirmed when some bags made of reeds found on the site were carbon dated. They were dated to 2600 BC so Caral was nearly five thousand years old making it as nearly as old as the first civilisation in Egypt, and was a thousand years older than any other civilisation in South America. This was to cause a sensation in the archaeological world and archaeologists from North America came to visit the site.

Jonathan Haas, "the world's leading expert on the warfare theory" began to search around for evidence of warfare. To his surprise he couldn't find any fortifications or any means the city could have defended itself. He began to look further afield to look for battlements in the hills around Caral and then in mountain passes where invading armies would have to travel though, but came up with nothing. Meanwhile Ruth Shady couldn't find any weapons of war or any carvings of violence in her excavations; so all this lack of evidence was undermining the warfare theory. To the degree Jonathan Haas had to admit-

"You seemed to really have the beginnings of that complex society and I'm able to look at it right at the start and I look for the conflict and I look for the warfare, I look for the armies and the fortifications and they're not there. They should be here and they're not and you have to change your whole mind-set about the role of warfare in these societies and so it's demolishing our warfare hypothesis. The warfare hypothesis just doesn't work."

It seems that archaeologists now accept that it was irrigation and not warfare is what started the first civilisations.

Another realisation about Caral is that what was true of this civilisation was also true for nearly the whole of South America at the time. Trading goods were found from the Amazon jungle at the other side of the Andes Mountains as well as from the coast. The picture that emerged was that Caral was the centre of a vast trading network. So if the people of Caral felt so safe that they didn't bother to look for ways to defend themselves. The same must of been true for most of South America, because in no way was Caral just an isolated city cut off from the rest of the world. It suggests that Caral lived in an age where warfare was completely unknown. The evidence is that the first civilisations in South America lived in peace for about a thousand years before we had warfare, violence, torture and human sacrifice.

The cosy picture painted by the Horizon program of unbiased scientists looking for the truth and finally finding it in the excavation of Caral is basically false. The archaeologists who strongly believed in the warfare theory and then were willing to admit they where wrong in the face of the evidence, or lack of evidence, in Caral, need to be congratulated. Yet this has not been the case for most archaeologists in the past. The truth is that the whole archaeological world for a period of 50 years has had to be dragged kicking and screaming into accepting the evidence, that the first civilisations live in a world where warfare was unknown. It was not just the evidence from Caral that made them ditch the warfare theory but evidence coming from Neolithic, Copper and Bronze age sites in Europe, the Middle East and China.

What happened in Caral at the beginning of the 21st century also happen 40 years previously in the 1950s and 60s in a place called Catal Höyük in Turkey. Unfortunately the way Archaeologists reacted to this excavation was very different.. An archaeologist called James Mellaart found in this location, the oldest city ever discovered, going back 9,000 years. Making it far older than the ancient Egyptian and Sumerian civilisations. Again the archaeologists couldn't find any evidence of fortifications or weapons of war. Nor any paintings or carvings showing images of violence, or for that matter any form of centralised government. What were found instead, were feminine images of childbirth, Goddesses and animal life.

This city was unlike anything discovered since. In that it had few streets, and most houses were built so close together that the only access was through the roof. This then means that to many people in the city to gain access to their homes they had to walk over the roofs of other people's houses. This was to greatly puzzle archaeologists.

It is impossible to understand Catal Höyük while we think in terms of a civilisation that had masculine values. Unfortunately what is not being considered is the possibility of civilisations those values were feminine, by mainstream archaeologists. In later civilisations we see the masculine values of war, power and status glorified in images and writings. In Catal Höyük we see images of the feminine values of childbirth, fertility being represented. So clearly women were the dominant sex in this community as it is their values that are represented and strongly influence the nature of the civilisation. As it is women's superior social skills of co-operation and communication that allows the city to function.

So disturbing was these findings that the whole site was closed down for thirty years by the Turkish Government. James Mellaart was criticised by many archaeologists for claiming that the people of Catal Höyük worshipped Goddesses. One of the most vocal critics was another archaeologist Ian Hodder. So it wasn't a surprise to find that when the excavations were reopened in the 1990s, it was the sceptic Ian Hodder who was put in charge. In the thirty years the excavation was closed down, the academic world kept quiet about the discoveries made at Catal Höyük. Though there was one archaeologist Marija Gimbutas who broke ranks and began to tell the world about implication of the findings. Not only have Catal Höyük but other Neolithic sites in Southern and Eastern Europe. She wrote about a peaceful world in ancient

Europe that worshipped the Great Mother that was ended by violent Indo-European tribes that came from the North and invaded these peaceful civilisations.

Marija Gimbutas wrote books about the Neolithic excavations in Malta, Crete, Greece, Bulgaria, Romania, Moldavia and Ukraine, all these finds showed a world without war and violence and where the people worshipped the ancient Great Mother. It seems that when a society worship feminine deities, war and violence were unknown. But when societies worship male gods or both male and female deities then violence becomes commonplace. She was criticised and condemned by her colleges and it was claimed her work unscientific because it when against the fashionable warfare theories of the time. No other archaeologists at the time would support what she claimed, and she was dismissed as just a strident Feminist maverick of no importance.

Then similar finds began to be written about in the in Indus Valley Civilisation in Pakistan. (Although it was first discovered in the 1920s) Recently archaeologist have found its beginning goes back as 7,000 years making it again one of the oldest civilisations discovered. And again archaeologists couldn't find evidence of fortifications, violence and warfare, and it was a civilisation that worshipped horned Mother Goddesses. It was also claimed this civilisation was ended by a violence invasion from Aryan people from the North. Though his is know being disputed, as there is no evidence for this, as it came out of the imagination of 19th century archaeologists.

The first excavations of Neolithic sites started back in the 1940s. So why did it take over 50 years for archaeology to accept the evidence of an age in the past where warfare didn't exist? Controversies like this have happened before in science, new evidence and theories can take a long time to be accepted if they go against existing theories. The problem is that knowledge of a Golden Age of peace ruled by a Mother Goddess doesn't only just come from archaeology. They also come from myths and legends all over the world. What is clear there is a campaign to suppress and destroy all evidence about this Golden Age has been going on for thousands of years. The attack on Marija Gimbutas theories is only latest chapter in this crusade. At Catal Höyük their are now Feminists and Goddess groups who are attempting to keep the archaeologists on the site honest. So when they attempts to dismiss evidence of a Mother Goddess culture out of hand they find passionate and articulate Feminists who are willing to contradict them. An example of this is a posting I found on the Internet in a Yahoo E-Group called Goddesssites.

Dear Diana,

That's great you enjoyed the site, it's so beautiful, and holds so much important history (herstory?) It's good they didn't make negative comments about the Goddess, I wouldn't really expect that. But did they mention the Goddess at all? The problem for me with the visitor's center was the ABSENCE of the Goddess, and the absence of what I would call "Goddess consciousness." Mellaart and other early archaeologists were congruent with the material they dug, in the sense that they were able to use language that explicated what they were looking at (peaceful, fertile, nurturing, egalitarian, spiritual, artistic, and so on) while the more recent archaeologists seem to shy away from anything remotely connected with "matriarchal" theories. By the way, matriarchal actually means "beginning with the mother," which makes it technically quite a good term for describing matrilineal, peaceful, mother-centered agricultural peoples of the Neolithic, although perhaps the term "matristic" used by Marija Gimbutas is more appropriate for our time. At the visitor's center there are two murals displayed—two versions of the same one—which happens to be the only wall painting from the site that was predominantly male. All the others are female-central and mostly Mother Goddesses and Double Goddesses. Interesting choice to represent the site, then, don't you think? In the display case showing the reproduction of the beautiful ivory-handled flint dagger, the artifacts are described as having to do with "hunting and war." This is a travesty, since the piece comes from the Neolithic and there is absolutely no evidence of any kind for war or violence. As I have written in an article recently, the knife is much more likely to fall into the category of knives that belong to midwives—for cutting the umbilical cord at birth. These knives were still used b shaman women in Siberia in the 20th century. Fortunately the museum in Ankara still has integrity and shows the finds from Catal Höyük as belonging to the ancient Mother Goddess cultures that are found all over Anatolia. It's too bad the team at Catal Höyük doesn't feel obliged to keep in step with local Turkish scholars and the way they see Anatolian history (and prehistory). I'm not trying to pick an argument, but I was really very upset when I went there. It was a place I had looked forward to visiting for such a long time—two decades at least—and it seemed criminal to me that no one seems to be monitoring what interpretations these "new archaeology" types come up with. There is a culture war happening right now—a concerted effort to block and erase certain approaches to ancient scholarship—and I believe this is quite political and dangerous for scholars of women's studies.

Thanks for listening—Vicki Noble

(Vicki Noble is also a well known authoress)

Also now there was now a younger group of scientists who wasn't so opposed to the theories of Marija Gimbutas. When Catal Höyük excavation was reopened and it suddenly became respectable to write about it. Richard Rudgley recently wrote two books and made a TV program called "The Secrets Of The Stone Age" that broadly supported Marija Gimbutas theories. So in recent years there are many people in the academic world who are now more accepting of the evidence that the first civilisations live in peace.

Richard Rudgeley comes straight to the point when he says, "The widely accepted view of the human story is wildly inaccurate." He then goes on to point out that because historians have ignored what happen during the Neolithic age it seems that to the general public that civilisations suddenly appeared out of no-where. Because we are taught that the people in the Stone Age were ignorant savages, who then suddenly created sophisticated civilisations like ancient Egypt and Mesopotamia. Then because orthodox archaeology gives no explanation to the public of how this suddenly happened, in this vacuum people outside science have invented their own theories. Like Erich Von Daniken in his book "Chariot Of The Gods", or the many theories of a lost continents like Atlantis, Mu and Lemuria.

The point he is trying to make is that if the general public was aware that Stone-Age people were not ignorant brutes and that civilisation didn't start with the Egyptians, but thousands of years earlier in the Neolithic age. Then we would not need aliens from outer space or lost continents to explain how civilisation got started. He explains that the first large stone structures were not built in the Nile Valley but in the island of Malta. When the first archaeologists first excavated the Temple complex of Malta they assumed it was a crude attempt to copy what was built in ancient Greece, but when it was carbon dated it was found to be built 5,500 years ago. A thousand years older than the Great pyramid in Egypt. He then says that the comment of archaeologists hearing this news was that is was the wrong date in the wrong place. The reason apparently for this attitude for this is that Malta is off the beaten track. Which is strange because Malta is just off the coast of Italy and not that far from Ancient Greece and Egypt. A more plausible explanation is that the archaeologists didn't want to know that Malta had the oldest freestanding stone buildings in the world, because the Temples in Malta are Goddess Temples, with Giant statues of the Great Mother.

Can it be, that the reason we have such a large gap in our history that Richard Rudgley complains about, is because it is an age when people clearly worshipped the Great Mother? As all the "lost Civilisations" that he writes about where all full of feminine images. It strongly suggests that his silence is simply male bias, in men who discovered these sites wanting males to be the ones who created the first civilisations and not women. Or is there more to this than that? Archaeology like most science is very expensive, so most archaeologists are either very rich individuals like they were in the 19th century, or they rely on funding from universities, governments or religious sects like the Roman Catholic Church. As in everything else in life, "he who pays the fiddler calls the tune". Archaeologists finding the "wrong" things or advocating the "wrong" theories, in the eyes of the people who sponsor them, could have there funding cut off.

The First person to do a "scientific" excavation on Malta was a Jesuit priest called Father Emmanuel Magri in 1903. His form of excavation was to rub off paintings on the walls of the largest Goddess temple in Malta. Then to dig up the floor of the Temple and what he discovered there mysteriously disappeared. In other words, his work was to destroy the site for its archaeological value. This is not unusual. In the 19th century European explorers discovered in Zimbabwe an ancient city that was built by African kings between the 12 and 16th century. Europeans at first carelessly destroyed all evidence that it was Africans who built this city searching for gold and wouldn't entertain the idea that Africans built it. Simply because if it was known that Africans were able to create civilisations in the past, it would undermine the right of European countries to colonise Africa. Because the justification of colonialism at the time was they were civilising the people of this continent, whom were called savages.

Not only did archaeologists keep quiet about the first civilisations of the Neolithic and Bronze Age period. They have also kept quiet about the Amazons. Some time ago I accidentally come across information that Western archaeologists have found graves of female warriors all over Europe. Yet they seem to think these finds are an "embarrassment", (where have we found this expression before?), and so they are never published. The only people who have let the cat out of the bag are archaeologists of the old Soviet Union. In the 1950s and 60s they have published finding graves of Female warriors in the Ukraine and Georgia.

Both the ancient Greeks and Romans have reported fighting Amazon warriors on the northeast coast of the Black Sea. This is where the Soviet archaeologists have discovered the graves of women with armour and weapons of war within them. So it seems from the Soviet finds we can say that the Amazons existed in the places the Greek and Roman historians said they did. Unfortunately the silence by Western archaeologists about their discoveries of female warriors is censoring an important chapter in human history. It seems that after the Goddess civilisations were invaded from the North not all women meekly submitted to this. Some it seems fought back and created Amazon armies and communities. Though it has to be said they were all finally defeated.

This process of censorship is being clearly shown in the archaeology of what is called, "the holy land". The Bible gives an impression that the people of Israel worshipped Yahweh from the time of Abraham. It even suggests that the people in the Bible before Abraham like Adam, Cain, Able, Noah and Jonah also worshipped a male God. Yet modern scholars have found a hidden Goddess in the Old Testament. It seems there is 40 coded mentions of a Goddess called Asherah.

In support of this, archaeologists have discovered in Israel over 3000 clay figurines of Large Breasted women, some are pregnant and other are nursing children. There is a possibility that more have been found but when excavations are sponsored by Christian sects or Zionist organisations, then images of Goddesses are strangely not discovered. These statues it seems are of the Goddess Asherah, showing that the Children of Israel were worshipping other deities than Yahweh.

In the 1960s a young archaeologist found a inscription that read, "Blessed by Yahweh and his Asherah." It seems he was too frightened to publish this find until another archaeologist published a similar inscription he had discovered. The reason why he was so reluctant to publish his find is that archaeology has become very political in Israel today. This is because archaeologists are being accused by politicians of undermining the legitimacy of the Jewish people's right to own modern Israel. Because the legitimacy of the Jews owning Israel comes from the truth of the Hebrew Bible. Start proving that the Bible is not accurate and it undermines the Israelite's case.

It seems that Asherah was openly worshipped in Israel up until a series reforms between 721BC and 609BC when by royal command Yahweh became the only God that was allowed to be worshipped. Though in this period some later Kings backtracked on this reform so it seems there was in this period a religious power struggle, that the worshipers of Yahweh finally won. Though the ordinary people were still worshipping Asherah in the privacy of there own homes. As shown in the images archaeologists found in ordinary people's home after this date. Also in this period the Hebrew Bible was written to create the belief that the Jews had always worshipped Yahweh. This rewriting of history was so successful that people even today are shocked to learn that the Jews once worshipped a Goddess.

The success of the Jewish ruling class in rewriting their own history seems to have inspired other rulers of other nations to follow suit including that of the rulers of the Roman Empire.

When the rulers of Rome decided to create a religion to unite the whole of the Roman Empire they chose a Jewish sect called Christianity. They followed up this by destroying all knowledge of ancient history burning down libraries throughout the Roman Empire and attacking educated men and women. The Moslems also done the same thing in adopting their own version of Judaism called Islam and also tried to destroy all ancient knowledge. Yet it seems some ancient knowledge did survive like the legends of a Golden Age of the past.

The Golden age is written about by Hesiod the 8th century BC Greek poet, in which he says.-

"they lived like gods, free from worry and fatigue, old age did not afflict them, they rejoiced in continual festivity." " All the blessing of the world were theirs: the fruitful earth gave forth its treasures unbidden."

The Golden age would probably be before humans began to use agriculture. Now there is some evidence that people then lived better lives. Modern nutritionists are coming to the conclusion that human beings are healthier on what is called, "the Stone-Age diet". This is because this is what our bodies have been used to over millions of years of evolution.

Then came agriculture, which gave us a far greater supply of food, but it also brought about a change in our diet that also brought about diseases caused by dietary deficiencies. The same is true with the modern Western diet today in that we are now eating foods like margarine, refined flour and sugar that are completely new to our bodies. Also it seems we didn't really benefit from agriculture in the way we should. Because with the increasing food supply the human population became larger and larger, which was all right while they had good harvests. Then suddenly when where there was famine, the population was too large to find food for everyone to eat and there was mass starvation.

Hesiod goes on to talk about the Silver age.

"After the Golden Age came the Silver Age, during which lived a race of feeble and inept men who obeyed their mothers all their lives."

Clearly he is talking about the Neolithic age confirms this age was ruled by women. Clearly Hesiod had contempt for these men who were dominated by women.

Then there was the Bronze age which he says.-

"The men of the Bronze Age were robust as ash trees and delighted only in oaths and warlike exploits. 'Their pitiless hearts were as hard as steel, their might was untameable, their arms invincible."

We now see the rise of the warrior who ruthlessly conquered the peaceful matriarchal world.

After the Bronze Age Hesiod talks about a Heroic age which declines to the Iron Age which is the age that Hesiod lived which he says is a period of misery and crime. "When men respect neither their vows, nor justice, nor virtue"..

Yet the myth of the Golden Age doesn't only come from Ancient Greece. Probably the most ancient religion that survives today is Taoism in China. Again in the Tao-Te-Ching it talks about a Golden age in the past, and the slow deterioration to our present world.

We even have a Golden Age Legend in the Bible in the story of the Garden Of Eden that probably came from Mesopotamia. Though the story was rewritten to blame women for the fall from grace and claim it happened as a punishment from God for disobeying him.

Hinduism also has a Golden Age myth similar to the Greeks where they write about an eternal cycle of Golden, Silver, Copper and Iron ages. They claim that when our present Iron age finishes, then a new Golden Age will dawn.

Now that archaeologists are unwittingly proving that the ancient Golden Age legends are not myth but historical fact. This could bring about world wide political revolution. For the last five thousand years we have lived in a world of violence that has resulted in wars, conquest and genocide.

We also live in a very unfair and uncaring world where the majority of the world's wealth are in the hands of only 3% of the world's population. Today in spite of all the advances in modern technology we still live in a world where billions of people live in poverty.

Yet world wide the common people are forced to accept this because we are told there is no alternative. We have always lived in an unfair and uncaring world of violence and war and so nothing can change. Yet what archaeologists have been finding over the last 50 years in the earliest civilisations shows us there is an alternative view of our past. Which means that these finds are becoming highly political.

6

Why the Hand that Rocks the Cradle, is not Ruling the World

When Dr Ruth Shady began to make know her findings at Caral the local people were proud that the earliest civilisation found in America was in Peru, but they were also very puzzled. The question that she is frequently asked is: "Why did our ancestors have the capacity to build such an important city, and we live so poorly and don't have the ability to do similar things?". The only answer she is able to give is: "the society was organised with a population that worked to do things collectively for the collective good." (http://www.csmonitor.com/2002/0103/p11s1-woam.html Though she didn't go on to point out that whereas today everyone works for the benefit of the ruling elite who keep the wealth of the country in their own hands.

The Peruvian government is now feeling the political ramifications of these finds. Already they have cut her funding making it very difficult to continue her excavation or preserve what she has already discovered. Universities in USA have offered to fund the site, but their condition is that they themselves will take over the excavation. So it seems there are political moves to sack Dr Ruth Shady and put someone in charge who will toe the political line. Which could mean censorship of what is being discovered.

So it seems ancient discoveries are very political. If it became common knowledge that thousands of years ago people lived in peace and equality, then people world wide will begin to ask the same questions that the Peruvian peasants are asking today. This is turn could create new political and religious movements that will challenge our present ruling elite. Because if in the past we lived in a world of peace and equality then why can't we do the same today? This is why archaeology today is becoming increasingly political, as it is questioning the way our world has been ruled for the last five thousand years.

The stability of any ruling elite is a belief that life is better now than any time in the past, because if the people are to believe that life in the past was better. It would create great unrest as they will want to recreate the better conditions of the past. So the leaders need to be able to tell the people, "you never had it so good." This is what the ruling elite have successfully convinced the people over the last couple of thousand years through censorship and destruction of all knowledge of early civilisations. Now this is changing, there is evidence that people in the past where able to live in peace and equality that is unmatched by any country today. Then if this knowledge was to become common knowledge, people will ask why can't we do the same today? Which could cause a worldwide revolution that could undermine all governments all over the world. It is no wonder there is a attempt to censor all the archaeological finds from the Neolithic age.

As I have pointed out before many Feminist are uncomfortable about the findings of the Neolithic age to the degree that some are as critical of the concept of pre-historic matriarchy as many male chauvinists. Even women like Riane Eisler and Marija Gimbutas have claimed that the people in the Neolithic age lived in a age of sexually equality. Which is a very politically correct Feminist line.

The problem is that we have no writings from the Neolithic age has been satisfactory translated. So we know nothing about the social system of that era. This means there is not real proof that people then lived in a matriarchy, patriarchy or an equal society. (Though the fact they worshipped Goddesses and lived in a non-violent society is more likely to suggest matriarchy or equality.)

The suggestion of sexual equality in the Neolithic age does present a few problems for men. It means that when women had power they used it to create a equal society. Yet when men later had power they used violence to dominate society and women. This then makes men out to be the "bad-guy", while women come out of it being paradigms of virtue. So many men would be very resistant to ideas of pre-historic equality, as it puts them into a very bad light. It seems to prove the children's saying, "What are little boys made of? Snakes and snails and puppy dog tails. What are little girls made off? Sugar and spice and All things NICE." For this reason, many men would prefer the opposite extreme where women did rule men harshly in those days and preferably walked around in black leather and carrying whips in which to beat men.

Another problem with a equal or matriarchal society is how did women prevent men from competing with each other and with women? A clue to this is what I mentioned in the last chapter. If men live in a society without violence and competition then their testosterone levels greatly decrease. So men in these societies would be more amiable then than in the later very brutal patriarchal societies. Problem solved then. Just keep men away from violence and competition and everything will be all right. Except how did it happen that these peaceful non-violent men of the Neolithic age suddenly became the brutal savages of the Bronze and Iron ages?

Marija Gimbutas suggests this happened through invasion. In that violent patriarchal tribes from the North conquered the peaceful matriarchal communities. That doesn't solve the problem because how did these Northern tribes become violent and patriarchal? A possible explanation is that life in the North was so harsh, it brutalised the men. Raising their testosterone levels and they became violent and competitive with women. Resulting in them dominating women through violence. That explanation sounds reasonable enough but there is another explanation that comes from the myths of Pandora and the story of Adam and Eve.

Pandora was the Ancient Greek's Eve, in that she was the first women and lived in a Golden Age like that of the Garden of Eden.

She was given a jar or box and one day she opened it to find out what was inside. Then from it out come all the plagues of illness, envy, spite and revenge that have been with us ever since. This at first sight seems to be a absurd and fanciful tale and a attempt to blame women for all this ills of the world. Yet if we look at modern research on the Stone and Neolithic ages we find it is a metaphor of what could have happened.

When palaeontologists and archaeologists began to discover the remains of humans during the Stone Age they were surprised to discovered in carved statues and wall paintings there was far more images of women than men. At first they didn't take the feminine images seriously and female statuettes were routinely discarded as just fertility images or Stone Age pornography. It was only because some people in the art world got interested in these statuettes that we know about them today. As palaeontologists found they had a profitable sideline in selling female statuettes to art dealers.

Yet the surprise of scientists that Stone-Age people seemed to be more interested in making images of women rather than men has a lot to do with the Judeo-Christian attitudes. For the last two thousand years it has been accepted by the main religions of Christianity, Islam, Buddhism and to some degree Hinduism that god is a male. We have then been so brainwashed into believing this, that it is hard for us to think of a Creator that is not a male. Including it seems scientists whom many profess to being unbiased and logical atheists.

Yet it was not always like this and from the evidence coming from the Stone and Neolithic Ages, it seems people then naturally assume our Creatix was a women.

When humans first became self aware they began to ask themselves, "what created the world?" It then would be natural for them to assume that the intelligence that created our world would be feminine. Because if we look at animal and human life we find that life is created within the bodies of females. In fact it must have seem to our ancestors that women had great magical powers to create life like this. So it would be logical for them to assume that the whole of creation was born from the body of what they called, "The Great Mother". This belief it seems gave women great power and status in human societies, because if the Creatrix was female then all women were created in the image of the Great Mother. This then made women very sacred and holy because it was only women who could create in the same way the Great Mother had done. This is seen clearly in the many images found in Stone Age and Neolithic sites that show images of the sex-act, the genitalia of women represented as V or slit symbols and the very many naked images of women themselves. The picture that comes from these ancient times is that people then regarded the sex-act, menstruation, childbirth and breast-feeding as all being very sacred, because they were all part of the process of creating life.

Some palaeontologists have speculated that people in the Stone Age were unaware that the sex act produced childbirth. So women suddenly producing children would be seen as a wondrous miracle where men had no input. They also went on to imagine that when men realised this role in conception, he no longer worshipped women as magical beings and took over the role of Creator himself. To support this theory we do find in Ancient Egypt that the God Atum created the world in a act of masturbation. The problem is that we do find the sexual act portrayed in Stone-Age art.

So the people then, may not be as daft as we assume they might be. Also the input of men in the act of creation can be over in two seconds, (wham, bam, thank you ma'am). Which is not anywhere equal to women carrying a foetus for nine months, the pain and drama of childbirth itself, then the ability of the women to feed the newborn baby from her breasts. Not to mention all the mysteries of menstrual, which was seen as something very holy and sacred in matriarchal societies, and something as unclean and taboo in later patriarchal societies.

So we can see from this that the ancient religion of the Great Mother would be a very feminine religion and empathise the feminine virtues of compassion, caring, nurturing, loving and creativity. This is supported by the fact that in the first civilisations of the Neolithic age, warfare and violence against other people was completely unknown. We only begin to find weapons of war, fortifications and images of violence in the later bronze and iron ages. Where it seems people began to worship male warrior gods.

It seems that men started to began to dominate our world about five thousand years ago through violence and conquest. They then also created male dominated religions that made the Creator a male and claimed that the sexual act; menstruation, childbirth and breast-feeding were all unclean, sinful and taboo. Even today few women dare to breast feed in public. While back in the 1950s and 60s male doctors all but banned breast-feeding claiming that cow's milk was better for the child! It was only later scientific research showed the obvious fact that that human milk was best for human babies. As it had been discovered that mothers pass on their immunity through the breast milk. Unfortunately there is still resistance because mothers are not encouraged to keep breast-feeding too long, and to switch to cow's milk as soon as possible. In spite of the fact that the research shows that mothers keep on feeding their immunity to disease to the baby right up to time the baby is weaned.

Some Christian women, even now will after birth still go to priests for a cleansing ritual to clean them of the "sin" of childbirth. Children also go through the cleansing ritual of baptism, which originally was to clean them of the sin of being, "born of women". So we can see through patriarchal attitudes an attack on the importance of women's roles. As Feminists have pointed out so often, child rearing is the most devalued work in our society. When some Feminist in the 1960s and 70s suggested that women should be paid to bring up children they were laughed at and ridiculed. After all bringing children and caring for them is clearly not as important as the work of a general who make plans to wipe out whole cities with nuclear weapons, or politicians who tell the public lies, to get votes.

So this is the difference between matriarchal and patriarchal religions. The feminine Goddess religions were about the celebration of whole act of creation from the sexual act to giving birth and breast-feeding. So it empathised the maternal instincts of women of compassion, caring and love. The masculine religions on the other hand have throughout history have been about the glorification of violence. Where religious wars have been commonplace and still go on even today. The irony of this is that in Christianity, Jesus preached love and compassion yet Christianity has been one of the world's most violence religions, throughout it's history.

This has been the great tragedy of the last five thousand years. While humans believed that the world was created by the Great Mother, the feminine maternal instincts of compassion, nurturing and love became the ideal for everyone. Then people began to question this belief and accept that our Creator could be male and female. This allowed people to accept masculine principles and instincts of competition and aggression. In time this was allowed to grow until it turned into violence, and conquest. Creating the world we know throughout recorded history of war, oppression, poverty and suffering.

So we see a similar story to that of Pandora's Box. Some Feminists have commented that because Pandora and Eve are blamed for bringing all the ills into the world these are anti women stories. Yet blame also implies power. Suggesting that in the past women did have power and gave it away.

In societies that worshipped the Great Mother, women would be the superior sex because only women had the magical power to create life. This would then make men the inferior sex who would have no real power or status except to serve women. It then must have occurred to many women that perhaps this was a bit unfair. So we find that the Great Mother then has a son, this son soon becomes the lover or brother of the Great Mother and they became co-creators. This probably reflected on the growing status of men in society as women allowed men to have equal rights.

The anthropologist Eva Meyerowitz discovered the way one African tribe change over from matriarchy to patriarchy. Living in Ghana she got friendly with the Akan people and learnt their history, which she wrote in four books. It seems in the past they were once a matriarchal tribe ruled by a Queen. Then over time some Queens allowed their sons more power to rule men's affairs. Slowly over time if the son was more assertive than his mother then the son would take more power to himself. While on the other hand if the Queen was more assertive then things stayed as they were. So in this way the power of women in the tribe was slowly eroded over many generations. Then when the British came they only dealt with the men and ignore the Queen and the power of the women. Which confirmed to the men they didn't need a powerful Queen and she was overthrown in colonial times and all the power given to the King.

In some ways this research confirms the ideas of Steven Goldberg that women are not assertive enough to allow men to slowly take over. Yet women did rule in the past suggesting in this tribe women were once far more assertive in the past than they are now. Suggesting that the patriarchal age came into being not only because of men's aggression but also of women's apathy in allowing it to happen. This apathy could only come about through women not realising that men would create a world of conflict and suffering if they ruled the world.

So it is probably true that equal rights between men and women is possible, in the change over from matriarchy to patriarchy. Anthologists have studied Stone-Age culture who have practised this in modern times. Perhaps in a hunter/gather community this wasn't a problem but in an age of agriculture, it sowed the seeds for its own destruction. People who have become dependants on their crops to feed themselves become very dependant on having a good harvest most years. One bad harvest is not a real problem if grain is saved from previous years. Three or more bad harvests in a row is a real problem and can destroy a civilisation.

In situations of starvation people can become very selfish and violent. Archaeologists have even found cases of cannibalism being practised in very bad drought conditions. Starvation created a true situation of the survival of the fittest. This means that men being bigger, stronger and more aggressive will have a big advantage over women in taking what small amount of food that is left. So men will gain dominance over women through violence. Then once the drought is over it is doubtful if men will give up their dominant position and continue to dominate women.

Now this wouldn't of happened if women still retained a strong sisterhood. They could of stuck together and ganged up on the men in starvation conditions. Ensuring it was them and their children that was fed first, an example of this was written by Paul Vallely a Christian aid worker.

In visiting many refugee camps he was used to them being taken over by the local alpha males who run them like a Mafia, where food was used to as a weapon to give the alpha males greater power over the population, and if the food aid charities objected, they were threatened with violence. Yet in a place called Tendelti in the Sahara desert he found something different. This was a refugee camp of ten thousand people most of whom were women. (The men had either died in wars or were still fighting wars). The women organised the food aid in a very different way, in that they gave the small amount they received equally to the children. While the adults lived on mokheit and the other scant famine foods in which the desert people turned to at times of desperation. It seems that without alpha men in the camp it greatly increased the survival chances of all the people within it.

The above shows what women can do if they organise themselves into a strong sisterhood. They will put the welfare of the children first and try to share what food they have fairly. Unfortunately if the sisterhood is broken down through patriarchy or equality, women then become very vulnerable to the violence and dominance of men.

The story of Pandora's box and Adam and Eve suggest that once women were the dominant sex and people then lived in a non-violent Golden age and later Silver age. Then women decided that making men the inferior sex was unfair. This is represented by Pandora opening the box or Eve tempting Adam to eat from the tree of knowledge. The very act of doing this suggests that Eve was in charge.

Unfortunately in giving men equality resulted in him eventually becoming competitive with women and dominating society through violence. This resulted in our present world of violence, injustice and poverty. As the Bible points out this was a tragedy for both men and women as Adam found that outside the Garden of Eden were he had to, "work by the sweat of this brow". In other words in a masculine world of winners and losers there are few winners and many losers. So the losers in a patriarchal society which includes both men and women found themselves having to work, not only to support themselves, but the ruling and warrior classes and the patriarchal priesthood.

The problem is that whatever theory you subscribe to does seem that women will always have problems in the long run in trying to tame men. If women are able to create a society where violence and competition is unknown and it brings down the testosterone levels of men. Or they convince men that the Creatrix is a woman and so all are Goddesses in the same mould. It doesn't always mean that men will always be like this. There is always a chance that a natural disaster may happen and in the fight for survival, men's testosterone levels may rise again.

While men are naturally aggressive and competitive there is always the chance that this aggression will break out into violence and brutality. So is that it? Does it mean that although women can tame men, in the end men's instinctive competitiveness will break through and we will be back to the violent world we have seen over the last five thousand years.

The question is, is it natural and normal for men to be violent and brutal? The evidence from the whole of recorded history, with its countless wars, genocide and torture and would be a resounding "Yes". Yet five thousand years is a very small period in the four million years humans have lived on the Earth. Were men always very brutal and violent during that period? Most palaeontologists would probably say, "yes" to this as well. Unfortunately most palaeontologists are men and seem to be very chauvinistic men at that. So we will have to accept some bias in this assumption. There is another way to look at our early ancestors that shows us in a completely different light.

Recently I learnt of surprising statistic. It seem that of all the British soldiers that experienced military action during the Falklands War, more of them have since committed suicide, than died during the conflict. There is an even more shocking statistic about the Vietnam War. Where THREE TIMES as many ex-soldiers that saw action, have since committed suicide, than died in the war.

Though this figure is hotly disputed there is still an agreement that it is still a very large number. So if men do get very traumatised by war where many kill themselves afterwards. It begs the question, if war and violence is normal and natural for men? It is true some individual men enjoy war and enjoy killing as we see in the case of serial killers. Though there is still a high suicide rate in men who have committed multiple murders. So it seems that men can be made into killers through brutalisation, but do they really want to be like this?

If killing traumatises men, it also begs the question whether all the wars and massacres we see in history is also normal and natural for men. As previously pointed out the Japanese military had to brutalise their troops in the Second World War to turn them into trained killers. The German army also brutalised their young men in the same war, to again make it possible for them to kill without mercy.

So we are back to the nature verse nurture debate. Is violence and male dominance over women only possible by the brutalisation of men? Or is it "all in the jeans" and men are naturally programmed by their genes to be violent and dominant over women? I would personally think it was the third option and that it is a bit of both. We can see clearly that if you brutalise men that will become violent and will dominate others less violent then themselves, like women. So men do have this potential, which is probably programmed in his genes, but without this brutalisation it seem that men are not naturally violent. Nor do they naturally dominate women. As we can see today in Western societies where men are less brutalised then they were in the past, and seem far less inclined to commit violence on women.

So was this true in the Stone Age, which makes up 95% of human existence? Were men violent brutes then, or were they able to live lives of peace and harmony in those days. We cannot know because we have no written record of those times, but their is evidence coming from the behaviour of one ape that throw a very different light on the behaviour of early humans.

Since Darwin, it has been accepted that humans have evolved from apes. The general public know about four different species of ape, Orang-utan, Gorilla, chimpanzee and Gibbon. You will see all these apes featured on wild life programmes on TV. Yet there is one other ape that doesn't get the same coverage, and that is the bonobo. Along with the chimpanzee this ape, the closest species to us. So we can learn a lot about our ancestors by examining the behaviour of both apes. Interestingly people are comfortable with the behaviour of chimpanzee because the males are very violent and brutal. (Just ordinary, good o' macho males) Yet they are not so comfortable about the behaviour of bonobos and this is because they are the, "the make love not war, ape."

7

Make Love not War

The bonobo was first discovered by Europeans in 1929 and was considered then to be only a subspecies of the chimpanzees. More recent research has shown it to be very different from the chimpanzee. Being more lightly built and having longer legs, it has the body structure more like a human than any other ape. But the main difference is in the way it behaves, which is very human.

Back in the 1960s professor Leakey in trying to understand how early humans behaved decided that a insight in this could be gained by observing different species of apes in the wild. He decided that women were better observers than men, so he used women like Jane Goodall observing chimpanzees Diane Fossey studying Gorillas.

The result of this brought about a revolution in the study of apes, and many new things were discovered. Like chimpanzees were able to make tools, as up until then scientists believed that only humans could do this. Also it was discovered that gorillas were gentle and peaceful creatures, as it was formerly believed that gorillas were dangerous and aggressive animals. All the other apes were observed in the same way, with the bonobo being only intensely observed in very recent times.

One of the first surprises about this ape is that it is very sexual in its behaviour. Like the human female the bonobo female can still have sex even when her body is not ready for fertilization. It also indulges in homosexual sexual behaviour with both sexes doing this and can copulate face to face. (Though the orangutan has also been observed to do this as well).

In many other animals and apes aggression between males and against females is quite common. Most animals overcome this aggression by having a strict hierarchical system where everyone knows its place. With the animals with lesser social status giving way to those with higher status. The animal's place in the system is controlled by its strength and aggression. So fights only break out when a animal of lesser status wants to achieve higher status in the pecking order.

The bonobo does have a similar system but aggressive behaviour between them is far less than other animals because of the way they use sex. In a article by Frans B. M. de Waal, it compares the different behaviour of chimpanzees and bonobos when two females and a male come across some food. In the case of the chimpanzees the food was bananas. Their behaviour was very straight forward the male chimpanzee fed first until he had enough and he then took away as many bananas as he could carry. Then the dominant female fed herself, and the subordinate female it seems got nothing. In the case of the bonobos it was sugar cane, and their behaviour was more complex. The two female started by indulging in sex by rubbing their genitals together. While the male bonobo displays his erect penis to them, but they ignore him. Then the two female fed together equally and only when they had finish was the male allowed to feed.

This is it seems is normal bonobo behaviour where there is a possibility of a dispute, the first thing they do is to have sex together which seems to defuse the situation. In this situation the natural aggression of the male seems to work against the male bonobo in contrast to the way it helps the male chimpanzees. As the female bonobos are less aggressive it is easier for them to bond with each other, which they reinforce through sexual play. It then makes it easier for them to gang up on males, who although do also bond together through sex, are still more aggressive towards each other. This makes them less able to co-operate and work together in the way the females can. Which suggests that the bonobo could also be called, "The Sisterhood Is Powerful" ape.

As the bonobo males are bigger than the females they stand a better chance in a one to one situation but even here they can lose out. In a conflict say over food, the female will immediately have sex with the male, the sexual bonding defuses the natural aggression of the male and they will share the food equally. It also has been observed of a male who had found a large fruit and a female immediately had sex with him and he afterwards gave her his fruit. Which seems to be the first case observed in the animal world of prostitution. Female bonobos will also encourage males to help in looking after their children in return for sexual favours. Which also sounds very much like human behaviour.

So this it seems is how the slogan "make love not war" can work in practice, by having disputes settled by sexual bonding. Comparing the bonobo's behaviour with that of the chimpanzees' can assess how effective this is. Both animals share 98% of the genetic makeup of a human and we were all the same animal as little as eight million years ago. In fact of the body structure of the bonobo looks very similar to that of a australopithecine, a early pre-human with similar length arms and legs. From this it is speculated that the bonobo is more similar to our common ancestor than either the chimpanzee or the human. With the human later growing longer legs and a more upright stance while the chimpanzee growing longer and stronger arms to climb trees. As our body is shaped by our behaviour over evolutionary time, it is reasonable to suggest that how the bonobo behaves today is more like how our common ancestor behaved in the past.

The behaviour of the chimpanzees is of the traditional patriarchal society. Chimpanzees only have sex to fertilise the females when they are on heat. This is the ideal of the patriarchal Christian Church who has tried to enforce this type of behaviour for hundreds of years. Claiming that sex only for the sake of pleasure is "sinful" and should only be used for conception. So it is strange that the Christian Church has never held up the chimpanzee as a ideal of moral virtue!

Chimpanzees tend to bond through fear and mutual protection, with a group of males holding on to a territory against other groups of males. There seems to be sometimes war between these different groups over land, resulting in males getting badly injured or even killed. The effect of this is there is always more females in a community than males as so many males get killed through violence. As the males have to stick together to fight off the territorial ambitions of other groups of male, they bond closer together than the females. Males not only show aggression to other groups of males but to each other, as they will charge each other or show off their strength to try and intimidate each other to gain more status in the pecking order. Aggression is also shown towards females who being smaller than males have to give way to them in all disputes.

In contrast the bonobo society nearly all aggression is defused through sexual bonding. It has been observed in zoos that if say a cardboard box is thrown into the enclosure and more than one bonobo shows interest in it. They will then briefly mount each other before playing with the box together. Or if one jealous male chases away another male near a female. The two males will then reconcile with each other by engaging in scrotal rubbing together. The same will be true if two adult females have a dispute over the behaviour of one of their children. They will reconcile by rubbing their genitals together. Male bonobos rarely fight each other over status. A male bonobo stays attached to his mother all his life and his status in society depends on the status of his mother, whom he will look to for protection from any aggression from other bonobos. Even though she may be smaller than him in size.

In human behavioural studies it has been noted that people who live in very stressful situations like extreme poverty, war, prison, an aggressive family or neighbourhood, tend to become very desensitised and so they are far less affected by fear and pain. In Hellabrun, Germany, in the World War Two there was a zoo, which housed both chimpanzees and bonobos. One night the city was bombed and the bonobos died of fright from the noise while the chimpanzees were completely unaffected. Demonstrating how desensitised chimpanzees have become living in their brutal patriarchal society, and how sensitive bonobos are, living in a more peaceful matriarchal world.

Apart from the fact that chimpanzees do not get married or "pair-bond". Its society is very much like a normal human patriarchal society. And until bonobo behaviour was studied properly, chimpanzee behaviour justified the patriarchal society as being "natural" for humans. So it is of interest that when primatologists first started to study bonobos in zoos during the 1950s the first findings were completely ignored by the scientific establishment until the 1970s. Even today most people are unaware of the behaviour of the bonobo or even that such a creature exists. The reason for this silence is because the bonobo's behaviour undermined all our patriarchal beliefs about human and pre-human behaviour.

If the bonobo is a very sexual ape than it has to be said that so is the human. Though chimpanzees only partake in basic reproductive sex, bonobos share all kinds of sexual pleasures, including cunnilingus, fellatio, masturbation, massage, bisexuality, incest, body-licking, sex in different positions, group sex, and French kissing. Also like humans in love, copulating bonobos often look deeply into each other's eyes.

Although patriarchal societies have attempted to enforce sexual relations in the confines of marriage, many human have always had urges to want more than this. So in all patriarchal societies none have been able to prevent prostitution. While in secret and sometimes quite openly both men and women have had relationships outside of marriage. In very recent times with the decline of the patriarchal society, marriage is breaking down in Western countries. Which has resulted in many people frequently changing sexual partners, having "one night stands", joining sex-clubs, going to sex-parties, advertising for sex in contact magazines or having "open" relationships. So why do many people have the urge to have sex with many different partners? To the degree that the patriarchal society with all its laws, religious and social censure fail to stamp this behaviour out. The only reason could be is that before the patriarchal society took control with all it laws to restricting people's behaviour. People's behaviour must of been very similar to that of the bonobo.

Bonobos like humans also tend to eat food in the company of other bonobos in big dinner parties. It seems that when fruit is in abundance bonobos will collect the fruit for a large community feast. Then will eat it together, in a big banquet after the high status females have eaten first. This is very unlike the chimpanzees that will generally hide food from others and eat alone. Another interesting point is that human couples have romantic evenings together. This involves sharing a meal together, either at a restaurant or sometimes at home, then having sex together. Which is also what bonobos couples do, though they tend to have sex before the meal and not afterwards.

It is well know that many couples when they have a "flaming row", they will afterwards "make up" by having sex together. To the degree that some couples claim that they enjoy a turbulent relationship because they greatly enjoy the making up afterwards. This then is similar to bonobo behaviour of using sex to defuse a conflict.

So like the bonobos, humans do associate conflict and food with sex. In times of war it used to be that when a conquering army takes a town or city, all the women and even sometimes the men are raped. This behaviour is generally seen as an expression of power over conquered people. Which is probably true but looking at bonobo behaviour their could be another reason for this. Perhaps it is a form of unconscious reconciliation by rape. Soldiers in warfare can become through extreme fear, very aggressive in battle. Even disciplined troops have been known to slaughter defenceless civilian populations after a battle, because of this fear induced aggression. So rape may defuse this situation, making possible for the soldiers to calm down and prevent a killing spree.

In the past when people used to worship Goddesses which is a indication of a matriarchal religion. The later patriarchal priests condemned the priestess of Goddess temples as being prostitutes. When the Romans first conquered Britain many of the Celtic tribes were still ruled by Queens. Their behaviour was seen as being very scandalous by later writers, as some of these Queens would openly have sex with large numbers of different men. So it does suggest that the old matriarchal societies were far more sexual than the later patriarchal societies. Which does suggest that a matriarchal society could perhaps be as sexual as a bonobo society. With people bonding together through sexual behaviour, allowing people to be more intimate with each other. Which will in turn will create a more intimate, caring and loving community.

War has been "normal" throughout recorded history, where there has never been a time when there hasn't been a war going on in some part of the world. Many people have written about the senseless suffering of war, and have looked unsuccessfully for ways to prevent future wars. The study of both the chimpanzee and bonobo societies shows there is a alternative to war. In the non-sexual chimpanzee society, conflict and war is normal. In the very sexual bonobo society conflict is rare. So because of the study of these different ape societies we find that the slogan "make love not war" is not a joke but does in fact work.

It is of interest that Frans de Waal who has written books and articles about the bonobo was criticised by Dawkins for "bad science". Which is understandable because observations on the bonobo undermine completely his belief that we are all basically selfish. Perhaps it would be "good science" to ignore the bonobo completely and only concentrate on the chimpanzee. It is of interest that Dawkins also criticises the anthropologist Margaret Mead. Her crime being that she observed human nature in a positive light. Also the fact that she was both a famous scientist and a feminist at the same time upset many of her male colleges.

It then means we humans have a choice. As pointed out previously both the chimpanzee and bonobo are the closest species to us, and we can clearly see similarities in their behaviour to ours. The behaviour of the chimpanzee is very similar to a patriarchal society in that it is very violence and relatively non-sexual.

In contrast the bonobo live in a very sexual world where both males and females bond together through many different forms of sexual play. So it means we all get to be laid and with multiple partners and can experiment with heterosexual and homosexual sex play. We even would get to try things that are considered to be kinky.

The bonus is that by bonding through sex we won't have to fight wars any more. Is it that easy? Well probably not, as human society is far more complex than that of the bonobo.

Yet we can see many similarities with bonobo society.

1. Over the last hundred years in the West women have gained equal opportunity, and guess what? As women have gain more status, power and freedom, our society has become more sexually liberated at the same time. Is that a coincidence?
2. Patriarchal societies create oppressive laws and customs not only to restrict women's freedoms but also women's sexuality. In fact patriarchal Christians have declared that sex is dirty and sinful and can only be used for reproduction. Which is what chimpanzee do.
3. Goddess religions in the past were called an abomination by patriarchal priests because they openly used sexual rituals. Goddess priestesses were condemned by patriarchal priests as temple prostitutes. Was this just sour grapes by patriarchal priests because they weren't getting laid? Or had they worked out the connection between sex and intimacy versus war and sexual frustration. It is of interest that even today many sportsmen will not have sex before an important sporting event because they believe sex will weaken them. Doctors claim that this is a myth because sex only weakens a person temporary. So having sex the night before is not going to affect any sportsman physically. Yet coaches ignore this advice, so perhaps sex will lessen men's aggression and this is why it will weaken men. Some coaches have even banned wives and girlfriends when going to sporting events in other countries. Does this suggest that even the presents of girlfriends and wives undermine the sportsmen's aggression?
4. In the Neolithic age we find many images of sexual expression as we find the presents of Goddess worship and non-violence. Is this just another coincidence?
5. The famous psychiatrist Sigmaund Freud discovered at the beginning of the 20th century that most of his patients were suffering from mental illness because of sexual repression. So it seems that suppression of sexual desire can not only make men violent but also it can cause female hysteria.

This concept was taken even further by the controversial psychiatrist Wilhelm Reich, who has been dubbed, "A scientist with attitude" He was originally a disciple of Freud but Reich took Freud's theories to the extreme, claiming that our whole society was insane because of sexual repression. This was a step too far for Freud whom was very aware that his theories were controversial enough already. He wanted social acceptance and scientific respectability for them and didn't want to alienate everyone by taking it too far. This wasn't a consideration for Reich who was willing to, "rush in where angels fear to tread".

He created a storm in Austria in the 1930s by trying to encourage young girls to have sex before marriage and teach them about contraception. This in a society that then rigidly believed that it was a sin and a social disgrace for a woman to have sex before of marriage. He was forced to leave Austria and went to Germany in 1933, where he wrote a book called *The Mass Psychology Of Fascism,* which linked fascism with sexual repression and insanity. Which didn't exactly go down a storm with the Nazi party and he had to flee Germany in disguise. He then went to Copenhagen and managed to upset the Danish Communist Party and other left wing intellectuals. (They claimed that his book *The Mass Psychology Of Fascism* was counter-revolutionary). The Danish government had him thrown out of the country and about the same time, the Congress of Psycho-analysis, also expelled him for his views and opinions. He ended up in USA where he continued to make waves and upset people. Then after the Second World War he was sent to prison where he died and the FBI destroyed his papers and laboratories. To make enemies of the Nazis, the Communists and USA authorities, is quite a feat, and he probably died in prison wondering, "was it something I said?"

The irony is that he was put into prison by a country that proclaimed freedom of speech. All right, he clearly didn't read the book, *How To Win Friends And Influence People,* and some of his theories and research was very wild and controversial.. Yet why did the authorities need to destroy all his research papers and try to burn all the books he had published? After all he had lost all scientific credibility by chasing UFOs in the Arizona desert, and trying to shoot them down with something called a cloudbuster. All right, perhaps he did go potty towards the end of this life. Yet his earlier work was just a logical extension of Freud's work. Saying what Freud dare not say, for fear of upsetting too many people. What probably upset the authorities so much was the fact that Reich was brave or foolhardy enough to claim that the whole of our society was insane because of sexual repression. Which although sounds like a extreme position, is valid when we realise that the whole of human kind became very close to committing global suicide during the Cold War. We must remember that USA was gripped by the McCarthyism at the time Reich was put into jail. So the last thing the authorities at the time would want is a psychiatrist claiming that they were paranoia in wanting to persecute communists. More so if he was to comparing them to Nazis in the way they persecuted people.

Oppression, genocide, war and male violence in general is justified through the concept of good and evil. The concept is one of the biggest con tricks ever invented. This can be illustrated by a story about an encounter between Lady Astor and Joseph Stalin. Before the Second World War Lady Astor was a member of a party of British MPs who visited the Soviet Union and were made guests Stalin. Lady Astor being a very out spoken woman verbally attacked Stalin for the millions of peasants that had died, because of his policies of the collectivisation of agriculture and forced industrialisation. He listened to her patiently and then explained that it was very unfortunately that all these people died, but it was needed if the Soviet Union was to become an industrial country and was able to efficiently feed itself in the future. He clearly didn't see anything wrong with what he was doing, and believed it was necessary to make the Soviet Union a modern prosperous country.

The point is that to many people Joseph Stalin was one of the most evil men in history. Yet he didn't see himself like this. He honestly saw himself as a good man who was attempting to do the best for his country. Likewise the same can be said of even worse tyrants like Hitler and Po-Pot the Cambodia dictator. Hitler felt justified in the genocide of the Jews and Slavs because in his mind they were a evil and inferior race. This means that in his mind he was a good person, fighting what HE had decided was evil. The same is true of Po-Pot who slaughtered millions of his own countrymen and women who didn't share his ideal of a perfect society. What is clear is that all these men believed very strongly that, "the ends justified the means". So in their minds war, violence, torture and genocide were all acceptable in creating, what they believed was a better future for their countries.

I remembered once reading about a prison governor who relating his long experiences dealing with prisoners explained the surprising fact, that most criminals see themselves as good people. It seems that criminals tend to blame society, the police or the system for their crimes. To be fair, there is some justification for this, as the majority of criminals come from the poorest and least educated sections of society.

This then means that if we divide the world up into good guys and bad guys. We find it is very much a matter of opinion who is who. For instance in the conflict in Northern Ireland the Roman Catholic assume it is the Protestant para-militaries and the police who are the bad guys. While the Protestants assume it is the IRA. With both sides claiming that the other side are the evil and they off coarse are the good guys. It makes peace talks between the two sides very difficult, if not impossible.

The IRA and the Protestant terrorist groups are also in a strange collusion, because they are justified in their existence and actions by the behaviour of the other side. As both sides can point to the atrocities done by the other side to give credence to their violent behaviour. This keeps a cycle of violence going in perpetually.

This is true for every war ever fought. With both sides claiming that they are the good guys while the other side is off coarse evil. This was brought out in the open in the Xmas of 1914 during the First World War. The British and Germans in the trenches began singing Christmas carols with each other, and then calling out to each other over no-mans-land. In the end some soldiers came out trenches and began to talk with each other and organising football matches against each other. When they began to talk British and German soldiers ask each other.-

"What are you fighting for?"

"For freedom and my country," came the replied, "what are you fighting for?"

"The same."

Exchanges like this caused many of the soldiers to ask the obvious question,

"Why are we fighting each other?"

Unfortunately no one came up with a sensible answer to this question. The incident greatly worried the politicians and military leaders on both sides as it threatened to turn the whole war into a farce. (Which is what war is, although it is a very tragic farce). In the end "normality" was restored and both sides went back to murdering each other. The problem this highlights is that war is easy if you believe the people you are fighting are bad or evil. Once you realise they are just human being like yourself, then this greatly undermines the moral justification for wanting to kill them.

The result of condemning someone as evil is that it de-humanises them. Once it has been agreed that someone is evil then it becomes acceptable to hurt, torture and kill them. For instance the justification of Europeans to massacre and steal the land of the native people in the Americas and Australia was that they were "savages". Which is just another de-humanising word like bad and evil.

In many action and adventure films, books and TV programmes the concept of good and evil comes across very strongly. A villain is established; who behaves in an appalling manner and this gives the hero the justification to commit violence and murder on the villain. Some commentators claim that these stories are just harmless fun. Yet as any advertising executive knows, people are greatly influenced by what entertains them. So in the end it becomes just another way to indoctrinate people, that hate and violence is perfectly justified.

Even intelligent and academic people can be seduced by the concept of good and evil as in the case of the Christian author and academic C.S Lewis. He wrote a trilogy of Science Fiction books to explore religious themes. I read the first one, *Out of the Silent*

Planet and I thought it was very good book but the second one *Journey To Venus* shocked and horrified me. In it, he had a hero and a villain travel to Venus, where they find a Garden of Eden complete with a Venusian Adam and Eve. (This was written before and spacecraft flew to Vesus, to show what a inhospitable planet it is.)

Both men then set about influencing this couple's beliefs. Initially, the villain was successful; the Venusians listened to him more than they did the hero. Eventually the hero became desperate, believing there was nothing but misery for the Venusians if they followed the villain's ideas. His solution was to beat the villain to death with a rock. The logic being that his actions were justified because the man was evil. Yet it was an appalling message to give to the Venusians, if you can't win an argument, kill your opponent! C. S. Lewis was a respected academic. He wrote children's books, which are still hugely popular, and a number of books on religion, as well as his novels. Yet it's clear that illusions about good and evil were able to blind even an intelligent man like him.

The concept of good and evil also prevents us from solving problems like crime. The "macho" solution to crime is that when you catch a criminal you then punish him. (it is far more likely to be a him than a her). Yet prisons are known and the "university of crime", in that they are more likely to confirm a man into a life of crime than cure him. This happens for four reasons.

1. In going to prison a criminal gets to mix with other criminals where he learns better ways to rob and steal from other prisoners. He also gets to make criminal contacts, which he will probably use once he is released.
2. In mixing with other criminals he gets to believe that crime is a 'normal' way of life for him.
3. Once a man has a criminal record it is much harder for him to get a legal job. So he is more likely to drift back to a life of crime even if he has intentions of going straight.
4. Although in theory criminals are not longer punished. Being put into a over crowed prison can be hell, which results in criminals becoming brutalised. So they learn to hate the society that put him into prison. Teaching a man

to hate society and then releasing him back into the community, is not a good idea.

Prison should be about rehabilitation. This has been put forward as early as the 19th century but even now in the 20th century many politicians and prison governors still only pay lip service to this concept. In many Western countries today prisoners are still not properly educated and get no support or help to become productive members of the community.

Although it is natural for people to want to punish criminals more so if you are personally a victim of crime. Revenge is certainly not the answer and it only makes a bad situation even worse. This is clearly illustrated by happened in Tihar jail in India.

In the 1980s Kiran Bedi was a very successful female tennis star, but she then abandoned her jet-set life to become the first female officer in the Indian police force. She rose swiftly through the ranks and her success made her enemies of some of her superiors, who firmly believed that a women's place was in the home. So to bring her down a peg or two they gave her the poison chalice, of one of the toughest jobs imaginable. They made her the governor of Tihar jail.

To quote, -

Tihar Jail in New Delhi is the size of a small town. It was designed to hold three thousand people. Instead, it holds ten thousand men, women and children. The desolation of the surroundings reflects the dire poverty of the inmates. There are no means of occupation, education or recreation, and the prison is a breeding ground for the very crimes it was designed to punish.

Drugs are endemic, prostitution flourishes, corruption breeds and violence and fear lurk in every corner. Remand prisoners, including women with their children, can languish here for up to ten years before their cases come to trial, sharing overcrowded cells with petty thieves, murders and addicts. Under a succession of male governors, mob management barely maintains the status quo, and the problems are more than the staff can handle. Inmates are sometimes shot at random by prison officers out of control.

So in July 1993 this small Indian woman stepped into the hell of Tihar prison. Yet she had the self-confidence to adopt a very feminine strategy to govern the prison and quickly changed everything.

She fired the worst prison officers, then began a radical restructure of the prisoners day. She introduced a complaint box for inmates to air their grievances. She initiated drug rehabilitation, health care, yoga therapy, prayer meetings, music, arts and crafts sessions, adult literacy and physical fitness programmes. Idleness was banished, every hour of the day was positively accounted for, and she achieved this by motivation and encouragement, not by the 'compelling force of law'...To men and women used to the rule of the stick and the gun, the arrival of Kiran Bedi was like a gift from the Gods.

She even called in a famous guru S.N. Goenka to teach the prisoners meditation. The authorities who appointed Kiran Bedi in the expectation of destroying her saw her turn every obstacle to her advantage, winning the trust, respect - and love - of both prisoners and officers. She was given the Magsaysay award for public service, and although her time at Tiher was short-lived, the changes she instituted had a lasting effect. Prisoners who leave the jail do not usually return.

Punishing prisoners is the masculine solution to crime while rehabilitation is the feminine way. In the West both methods are used. With politicians and newspaper owners trying to whip up hatred by the general public against prisoners. So they can once again use the masculine methods to brutalise prisoners. Although in theory politicians claim that prison is for rehabilitation, they tend to starve the prison service of money so prisons are vastly overcrowd and don't have the staff or resources to rehabilitate the prisoners properly. This has resulted in Britain in recent years of some prisoners being locked up 23 hours of 24 hours in a day.

Yet the ideas of reforming prisoners instead of punishing them goes back to the early 19th century.

Elizabeth Fry (1780-1845) came from a wealthy Quaker family, and enjoyed the benefits of a very academic education, which was unusual for women of those days. In 1812 she began to take a interest in the plight of prisoners and visited London's Newgate prison for women and was appalled at what she saw there. Prisoners were crowded into single cells where they had to eat, sleep and defecate. Typically a woman's children would accompany her to prison, where they lived in destitute poverty, obtained clothes, alcohol, even food by begging or stealing. To tolerate this hell many prisoners only begged for alcohol and sat around in a drunken stupor stark naked.

Other prisoners who were unable to beg or cared for by families or charities simply starved to death. Children often remained in the prison until their mothers died or were executed. They clung to their mothers and watched as they were led to the gallows and hung.

The attitude at the time that prisons were places of punishment and that the inmates were evil, so this perfectly justified this appalling treatment. Elizabeth Fry didn't see it like this and set about using all the influence of her position of wealth and privilege gave her.

She started by providing basic food, clothing and medicine for the prisoners. She then turned to education, ministering to the prisoners and establishing a small school. Recognising that occupation was essential to self-esteem and dignity, she convinced the wardens that the school should be run by the prisoners themselves. She also provided materials allowing the women to sew, knit and make goods for sale, in order to buy food, clothing and fresh straw for bedding. In 1817 she enlisted the help of ten friends to form the Ladies' Association for the Reformation of the Female Prisoners in Newgate.

Somehow her work did prick the conscience of the nation. She soon found herself in the role of a prisoner adviser and was invited to other prisons to advice on measures for improvements. She was also asked to give evidence on prison reform before a Committee of the House of Commons in which she advocated compassionate treatment of prisoners. It says something for her personality that in a age when women were suppose to keep quiet, her views and opinions were listened to and some of them became in time encoded in the laws of England.

She was even invited to Ireland, France, Belgium, the Netherlands and Prussia to give advice to prison officials and reformers in these countries. Her work planted the seeds that prisons are place for reforming and not punishment.

Her ideas were tried out by a prisoner governor called Alexander Maconochie on Norfolk island in 1840-44. Norfolk island, which was halfway between Australia and New Zealand, was in many ways the British version of the more infamous French, Devil's Island. Where the prisoners were kept in harsh and degrading conditions to punish them for their crimes. Maconochie instead bravely tried reforming prisoners instead of punishing them.

After receiving contradictory stories about his reforms the authorities sent out a commission. His report was very favourable but Maconochie was still dismissed by a new Colonial Secretary. Yet his success can be measured by the fact that of 920 prisoners he released only 20 were re-convicted.

Back in Britain he was to obtain support from many people including Charles Dickens and became a very controversial figure. Because then people believe in a evil criminal class, the idea that criminals can be reformed undermines the concept of evil and the justification of punishment. Also it makes people also ask questions like, "why are people criminals". If we ask questions like this, then we have to look at the unfair hierarchical system that gives some people great wealth, power and privilege and others only poverty and brutality, because the overwhelming numbers of criminals come for the poor and unprivileged sections of society. So it is not surprising that most, "good" people come from the upper and middle classes and most "bad" people come from the working classes. (The word villain come from the middle ages and originally meant villager. So this word gives an insight about what the upper classes then felt about the common people).

This then is adding insult to injury. Not only do he rich and powerful keep the vast majority of wealth and power in their own hands. On top of this, they condemn the poor as being bad and evil, while they of coarse are good people. Punishment and vengeance are the masculine solutions to problems. That is to say you overcome violence with violence. In other words, "two wrongs make a right". In this situation the person with the biggest stick wins. Yet violence has another side to it in that it ensures that men have dominance over women.

Aggression, competition and violence are the ways that men can always get the upper hand over women, whereas a non-violence and non-competitive community gives all the advantages to women. This has been clearly shown in primate studies.

In many species of primates like chimpanzees, orang-utans and hamadryas baboons male violence against females is commonplace. A female can expect an assault from the larger males on average once a week and can be seriously injured about once a year from these assaults. Observations of these assaults suggest that males do this to gain sexual access. This behaviour is very similar to that observed of men in badly run prisons. If a naïve and attractive looking young man is put into prison he will find himself being assaulted by older prisoners, who want to have sex with him. If caught on his own in a group he may find himself being raped. He quickly learns from this he has two choices. He can continue to be assaulted and raped, or if he wants to stop this he has to align himself with a protector. This would be a bullyboy or alpha man in the prison who will give the young man protection in return for sexual access. It was from this form of relationship the contemptuous expression "sucker" or "bum" come from, in referring to people at the bottom of the pecking order. It is also the origins of the sayings like, "get your arse (ass) over here", or "get your arse into gear", which are very dominant assertions to man about to be buggered. There is nothing about consent or consideration of other people's feelings in any of these sayings. The passive male's response about this form of relationship is the statement, "your just a pain in the arse"(to me).

This expression is similar to, "your a right pain in the neck" in reference to someone who is too demanding. A way a person can get a neck ache is through giving cunnilingus. (This happens because to lick a women's clitoris while she is lying on her back, the man is forced to hold his head back. If this goes on for too long he can get a neck ache). So a man could say that about a women who is too demanding in wanting him to give her long sessions of oral sex. Now this is unlikely to become a common saying in patriarchal times. So it must be a very ancient, going back to a time when women were the dominant sex.

In primate behaviour we can see a strong connection between sex and power. In many primate species, when two male confront each other and one back down he turn his back and allows the winner to demonstrate his superiority by mounting him. Which is also the behaviour of homosexual men in that the man who "takes it up the arse" is seen as the submissive member of the relationship. In Japanese macaque monkeys females have been observed to mount males and rub themselves against the male. As the female is the dominant sex in this species it is a demonstration of the dominance of the female. Again we can see similar behaviour in human beings. In the dominatrix scene some of them wear strap-on dildos and bugger their clients. Who are willing to pay for this privilege.

Male violence takes away the female's right to choose who which males she wants to mate with, in any species where males fight among themselves for the right to mate. The strongest male also uses violence against females to keep them under his control. So violence becomes a way of keeping women, "in their place".

We can see this pattern in human traditional patriarchal societies where husbands are encouraged to assault their wives. In many Islam countries they claim that a man has no "honour" if he doesn't exercise his right to beat his wife. This custom also give him the right to have sex or rape his wife whenever he wants to without contraception, and so taking away the women's right to refuse to have children.

Also in these societies boys are also beaten, the idea being to "toughen them up". Child abuse is needed to make "real men" out of boys. The way it works is that if a child is abuse enough then they only way he can cope with it is to learn not to feel anything. This then makes him not only unaware of his own pain but the pain of others. In fact more than that it teaches him to hate, so he can become a "good" soldier and kill without pity, and become a "good" father and husband and in turn beat his wife and children without mercy. Yet not all primates are like this. Many species are female dominated like the bonobo ape, Vervet monkeys, macaques, olive baboons, patas, rhesus monkeys, grey langus, capuchins, prosimians and Lemus. In all these species the females form a powerful sisterhood, where if one female is assaulted or intimidated by a larger male, then all the females in the area will be quick to defend their sisters and drive the male away. The exception is the Lemus were female dominance seemed to be bred within the species.

So these studies show that in all primates including humans male dominance over females is only possible through male violence. While female dominance came about through a powerful sisterhood. So it seems from primate studies we have we have two choices.

1. We can behave like chimpanzees, and live in a violent; male dominated, and sexually repressed society.
2. We can behave like bonobos and live in a non-violent, female dominated and sexually liberated societies were anything goes.

So which type of society is natural for human beings? It could be that both types of societies are natural for us as we can partly see in the work of Desmond Morris. Whom has attempted to examine human behaviour from the point of view of a zoologist.

8

The Nude Ape, (Or What Turned On, Our Stone Age Ancestors)

Desmond Morris wrote his famous book "The Naked Ape" at the time of the sexual revolution of the 1960s, and reading through it today in the 21st century, we can see how, in many ways, this book is dated. Yet some of the ideas in the book are still revolutionary as he attempts to explain human behaviour through the eyes of a zoologist. Unfortunately his book is greatly influenced by the conventions of the patriarchal society. So although in some parts of the book he gave very invaluable insights, his patriarchal biases limits the conclusions he comes to. Like most academics of the time he mostly ignores the role of women in evolution.

We can see this in the chapter on sex as he tries to put forward the reasons why human beings "pair-bond". Which is a way to explain in zoological terms why people get married and men go to work, because in the "man the hunter" theory it is men who "brings home the bacon" or the Mammoth. He also rationalises that because humans have a far longer childhood than other animals, it needed women to stay at home to look after children. This was because human culture is far more complex than any other animal so children need longer time to learn. So it needed a man to provide food for the mother and children.

Hunting of course provided this food. As men had a poor hunting bodies, that is to say they didn't have great strength, canine teeth or large claws, they needed their intelligence and ability to co-operate with men to be successful. He notes in other primates and animals that the males do not co-operate very well as they are competing for food, sex and status. This is because the male are competing with each other for the right to mate with the females. So for men to co-operate to the degree that they can hunt successfully this competition had to be broken down. Resulting in each man having his own woman who he looked after and therefore didn't have to compete with others over who could penetrate her. He ignored the fact that many non-Christian cultures don't have pair bonding, where men could have more than one wife.

In recent times the "man the hunter" theory has come under attack. In the excavations of very early humans the bones of animals can still be found, giving the impression to palaeontologists that early humans were carnivores. Then critics of this theory have pointed out that in Africa where humans first evolve, in the Stone-Age communities that still exist there, the vast majority of the food produced comes from the women's gathering. Rather than the man's hunting. Women also do not stay at home but are quite happy to carry their young children with them as they gather food.

The problem with excavations is that the bones of animals tend to be preserved while the remains of vegetable matter soon rot away. Giving the false impression that early humans only existed on a diet of meat. So there is now doubt about the "man the hunter" theory. It is true that in colder climates where the growing season is far smaller or non-existent, hunting became essential for survival, but humans don't really need to hunt in tropical climates, where humans first evolved.

Today in the 21st century there is some doubt whether humans are natural "pair-bonders". In the 1960s when "The Naked Ape" was written marriage was still the normal behaviour of most people. Now with the majority of marriages failing there in some doubt today whether marriage is normal for us all. Marriage has been enforced in the past through laws, religious taboos and social customs. Without these social restrictions today people are now questioning why they should get married. With the result is the increase of single mothers, who are not interested in living with a man, and prefer to bring up their children on there own. Which is the more the normal primate behaviour of the chimpanzee and the bonobo our nearest genetic relations.

Feminists have also pointed out that marriage is a patriarchal institution enforced because it allows men to know who their children are. So they are able to pass on their inheritance through the male line. Without marriages that restrict women to one man, a woman would be able to have sex relations with many men and would herself be unsure who is the father of her children. In other words it is an artificial restriction imposed on women by men, and not natural human behaviour as suggested by Desmond Morris.

It is true that the gibbons "pair-bond" to the exclusion of other gibbons, but are more distant relations to us than the chimpanzee, bonobo and gorilla. Every type of ape (including the human) has a very different social organisation and why they are different no-one really knows.

Where Desmond Morris does break new ground is in his attempt to explain why women have breasts and why unlike other primates we have large exposed lips on our mouths. He points out that other female primates have their genitals on show to give the males "visual stimulus" when she is on heat. Which would of been also true of our ancestors when we still walked on all fours. Then when we began to walk upright, this caused a problem in that the female genital region is no longer easily seen.

What the male used to see when we were on all fours was her bottom and the red lips of the vagina region. So when we started to walk upright because men would be still looking for this visual stimulus, the only thing he would see would be her bottom, and he would be stimulated by this. So women with larger bottoms would have the advantage, as it would be a larger sexual stimulant. This would put evolutionary pressure for women to have far larger buttocks than men. Unfortunately, the problem would still remain that the man wouldn't see the women's vagina from behind when standing upright. Yet can see it from the front. This would encourage face to face copulation, (which more modern research has shown is something both the Orang-utan and the bonobo are able to do). He points out that when female primates are on heat the vagina area colours up to give a strong visual signal. Without these visual signs men would be looking for similar signs on women. So women with larger than usual red lips on her mouth would become attractive to men, as men will see this as being similar to the red lips of the vagina when they used to see when humans were on all fours. (Which might be one reason why we have oral sex, and many men have the desire to put their penises in women's mouths). Likewise women with fleshy chests would also became attractive to men from the front as it reminds them of women's buttocks. So it suggests that women have end up with breasts, large buttocks and red lips because of sexual selection. As women who have these attributes, are more likely to mate with men

.Even today this is still true where women paint their lips red and know if they have large breasts they have a better chance of attracting men. Desmond Morris backs up his claim by pointing out that the mandrill and gelada baboons mimic the colours of their sexual area on their faces and chests. Which makes sense for these primates, because they spend a large part of their time sitting upright

In the same chapter he points out that compared with other primates the penis of a man is very much larger then any other primate. (The average size of a penis of the largest ape, the gorilla, is smaller than a human's little finger). In his attempt to explain this he is on more shaky ground. He also points out that in other primates, female don't seem to have orgasms and after the sex-act walk away as if nothing had happened. He explains this that if women were to do the same, then because she walks in an upright position the seminal fluid would, under the weight of gravity, flow back out of her vagina. So she needed a reason in which to lie down for a while to allow time for the fluid to fertilise her. So an orgasm that leaves her exhausted for a while would have this effect. So far makes sense and he goes on to point out that it is the stimulation of the women's clitoris that allows the women to have an orgasm.

Desmond Morris reasoning then breaks down because he claims that it requires a large penis in a man to stimulate a women's clitoris. Unfortunately more modern sexual research has shown that a man with a small penis is as just as able to bring a woman to orgasm as a man with a far larger one.

What he seems to have missed, and it was probably his patriarchal bias that caused this, was that when humans were on all fours to some degree the penis is concealed. When men started to stand upright his penis is very much on display. Now if large breasts, buttocks and red lips on a woman, are a great sexual stimulation to a man. Then it would mean that a penis would also be a strong visual sexual stimulation to a woman. So like men being stimulated by very large breasts, the larger the penis the stronger the visual affects it will have on women.

This is confirmed by the mating behaviour of birds like peacocks and birds of paradise. The male bird in these two species has developed extraordinary, very large and colourful feathers. It seems that the evolutionary pressure for male birds to develop these feathers come from the female bird who picks which male she wants to mate with. It seems that the female bird picks her mate on the basis of who has the most colourful feathers and so over evolutionary time the most successful male birds in mating has been those who have the largest feathers.

For Demond Morris in the 1960s such a theory would have been unacceptable. Because even though women's liberation did get started then, it still wasn't acceptable that women could enjoy the sight of completely naked men. Also the patriarchal bias dictated that it was men who always ruled society and took the initiative in all things. So for women to pick men, only with large penises, with this resulting in men evolving even larger penises because of this. Means that there was a time in the past when women could choose their sexual partners.

Now clearly this doesn't happen in patriarchal societies and it is noticeable that in most of these societies the genitals are concealed. Even in very hot climates where people wear very little. It is of interest that in some tribes in New Guinea where men openly display their penises, it is the men with the largest ones that have the highest status in the tribe. This suggests that the women are the dominant sex in the tribe or were in the recent past. Because it strongly suggests that it is women who have the final say in which partner she has sex with. This is such a concern for men in these tribes, that they will tie weights to their penises in an attempt to stretch them or to push hollow tubes of wood over them to make them look longer. Which gives a clue as to why in patriarchal societies the genitals are covered. The more ambitious and aggressive men in a society would have problems if his status were only governed by the size of his penis. So these men had to bring in laws and taboos for a cover-up to ensure that more well endowed men couldn't challenge them for status and power.

So it means for men to grow large penises it needed a society in the past where men had their genitals on display, and for women chose their sexual partners, to the degree that it is mostly well-endowed men who have sexual intercourse with women. In our patriarchal society we have men who expose themselves who are called "flashers". Many women find this behaviour offensive and threatening and can be frightened by it. The reason for this is because women fear these men will come after them and try and rape them. So to have a situation where women are not afraid of "flashers" and are even willing to choose her sexual partners on the size of his penis. Means a woman has to be very confident that she is in control of the situation and the man. Also women in a patriarchal situation can be frightened by men with extra large penises because they fear it could hurt or damage them. So for a woman to approach a well endowed man for sex means she is confident she can dictate to him if she wants it inside her, and can order him to withdraw it if it physically hurts her. In other words she has to be in control of the situation, unlike the situation in strict patriarchal society where a wife was unable to refuse her husband sex.

In the patriarchal society women have always dressed to attract the man with red lipstick or low-cut dresses. Even when dress codes dictated that women cover-up, as in the Victorian times, women then started to wear bustles, which greatly exaggerated the size of their buttocks. Even today women wear tight jeans, to show off the shape of their bottom and vagina, or skimpy and high-cut swim wear to show themselves off to men. It is true some men have done the same as we can see with codpieces in the past or the padded tights of male ballet-dancers. (So it is of interest that male ballet-dancers have the reputation of being feminine or "wimps"). But it is mostly the women who have attempted to dress in a sexual way rather than men. In recent times this is starting to change some men are now attempting to look sexy in the same way. As they also wear tight jeans and tee shirts or wear skimpy bathing suits when swimming. Which shows that they are putting out a signal to women that they want to attract them and even for them to take the initiative.

Many of the ancient Gods in the past like Pan did have very large penises, and in many pagan religions and even in Hinduism today the penis was, and is still, worshipped. Societies where the penis is worshipped and openly displayed by men is going to create large problems for men who are not well-endowed. In a strictly patriarchal society where it is covered up and women are only suppose to have knowledge of the penis of her husband this is no problem. Today when there is more sexual-freedom, men are having relationships with women who will openly talk about having had sexual relationships with many other men before. This creates a problem for men in how they "measure up" whether his girl friend or wife had sex with men who were bigger than him. Even though sex therapists and agony aunts have tried to reassure men that "size doesn't matter", no one is really persuaded by this. Because although technically size doesn't matter, as a visual stimuli it matters a lot.

In recent times because of the advances in plastic surgery many women who can afford it, are having their breast sizes increased. Likewise some surgeons are also claiming to be able to do the same for men's penises, and this is also becoming popular for men who can afford it. (Though there are still worries about the safety of these operations). Also for a number of years sex-catalogues have been selling vacuum pumps to increase the size of the penis. Which men still buy although there is some doubt as to whether these devices really work. So like the New Guinea tribesmen who tie weights to their penises, men in Western societies are starting to become obsessed with the size of their penises.

Many men today with small penises can feel inadequate and even depressed about it. Women who want to humiliate men know that one of the best ways is to suggest their too small to satisfy them. Men have an instinctive feeling that penis size is important to women. In the Stone Age it probably was, and as women become more sexually liberated, it might turn out to be just as significant in the future. Just imagine how interested men would be if doctors found a safe, cheap and reliable way to enlarge their penises? Most men would be very tempted. In the recent past penis size wouldn't of mattered too much if a man's wife had to be faithful to just her husband. In that she is not in a position to compare her husband's penis with other men. Today with sexual liberation most women get to compare the penis sizes of many men. The very fact that men do worry about the size of their equipment to the point of getting very depressed about it, points to a time in the past when this was very important to men's status and importance. Suggesting a matriarchal society where women choose their sexual partners, so the hang-ups about size must be instinctive feelings coming from this time.

If this were a problem today then it would have been one in the past when people worshipped "well-endowed" Gods and walked around completely naked as the early ancient Greeks did. As this would only be a problem for men and not for women, it points to such a society being either equal or dominated by women.

So what this seems to suggest is that thousands of years of patriarchal rule will through sexual selection cause women to have larger breasts and buttocks. While matriarchal rule will again through sexual selection cause men to have larger penises.

So what does this tell us about our early ancestors? The large breasts of women strongly suggest a patriarchal age, while the large penises of men strongly suggest a matriarchal age. Or does it suggest both and men a women were equal then? This will mean an equal society where both men and women choose their sexual partners and the result would be a free-for-all. You may have an elite group of large-breasted females mating with males who have big penises, but what will the rest of the population do? They'll be mating with each other as well. So there would be no survival advantage in having either large breasts or a large penis. The reason why a peacock has such enormous tail feathers is because the peahen finds them sexually attractive, and it is she who chooses. If the peacock had a say in the matter then there wouldn't be such a strong evolutionary pressure to develop such ridiculously large feathers. This means that this kind of evolution can only happen to the male if the female alone does the choosing. The same goes for male-dominated societies where the alpha males only select women with large breasts. The offspring of these women will be more likely to survive, protected by the alpha males. So it needs one sex doing the choosing to exaggerate the sexual characteristics of the other sex. If both sexes are doing it, then survival remains dependent on other factors.

This could suggest that a sexually equal society has never happened in human history. Where the only time we had equality is when we were changing from a patriarchy to a matriarchy, as is happening now, or vice-versa, at the end of the Neolithic age. Which I admit is not what Feminists would like to hear. Though even Feminists admit that equality is very difficult because we live in a masculine society, designed by men exclusively for men. There's little provision even today for women who have both a career and children. If a woman has children she has two stark choices. Pursue a career while simultaneously caring for her family, which is enormously stressful, or leave work for a number of years, thus reducing her promotion prospects. The alternative is, the woman has a househusband, but that can't be called equality, because the male then has to sacrifice his own career, for her. We also live in a highly competitive society that favours aggressive men rather than co-operative women. If we change our society so that the feminine virtues of co-operation and caring are rewarded, this would help women, but it would severely disadvantage the average man. Because as shown in the war between Capitalism and Communism, men respond best under the very competitive environment of Capitalism and didn't do so well in a Communist system. Where competition is not encouraged. Equality between the sexes becomes very difficult to sustain over many generations. What helps men, disadvantages women and vice-versa.

9

Sexual Evolution. (Or, How did Men and Women Get to be Sexually Incompatible?)

Back in the 19th century and early 20th century it was commonly believed that respectable women didn't enjoy sex. Then with the rise of women's Liberation in the 1960s women came out and claimed that they were capable for enjoying sex as much as men. Since then women's sexuality has been openly discussed to the degree that men are becoming aware that women probably can enjoy sex, as much, if not more than what men can.

The 19th century belief was that women do not enjoy sex, fitted in nicely with the belief that men had always been the dominant sex. This is because in evolutionary terms if this is true, then there was no need for women to enjoy sex because it was assumed that men initiated all sexual encounters. Men being the dominant sex were at liberty to have sex with women or their wives whenever they felt like it. (Women up until very recently were not legally able to refuse their husband sex). This means in evolutionary terms there was no need for women to enjoy sex, as she didn't have a say in the matter. So even if women had no sexual desire, women can still have children, because she plays the passive role.

The acceptance today that women do enjoy sex, shows that in the past women must of had a choice about whether they wanted to have sex or not. Because having sexual desires means that women have a drive to initiate sex. Certainly today with far fewer patriarchal restrictions on women they are showing they are capable of being assertive and even dominant in wanting sex. These desires don't come out of nowhere and suggests that they come from behaviour that was once commonplace. Before women were controlled by patriarchal laws, customs and taboos.

This then presents a very different picture of our Stone Age past than what palaeontologists have led us to believe. We now can go back four million years, to the first humans, compared with the four or five thousand years of recorded history. This means that 99.9% of human existence is unknown. So we can see that what happened in the Stone Age is far more important in making us what we are, than recorded history.

It always has been assumed that men have been the dominant sex, so all images we have of the Stone-Age is of man being the dominant and brutal hunter while women have been the submissive and brutalised slave. Millions of years of brutal men and brutalised women would make it unlikely for women to enjoy sex because it would have no evolutionary advantage, if men were at liberty to rape women. So the fact that women have a clitoris and sexual desires and can have an orgasm suggests that in the Stone Age women were not as submissive as portrayed, because in evolutionary terms something that is not used ends up disappearing. So it means that women's sexual desires and pleasure must of been an important aspect of the mating between women and men during the Stone Age. Which suggests that the development of women's sexual desires means that in the past women were capable of initiating sex as much as men are.

This could suggest the relationships between women and men were equal during the Stone Age. Because if both sexes had an equal desire for sex then it suggests that sex only came about when both partners wanted it. Unfortunately it is not that simple, as women's sexuality is more complicated than this. What has become very clear in recent years is that not all women can enjoy sex through penetration. This is because the clitoris is located near the outside of the vagina and with many women the clitoris is not stimulated by a male penis inside them. To make matters even more complex, it seems that the timing of sex seems to be different for most men and women as well. Most young men it seems can become aroused and ejaculate far quicker than most women. This has caused real problems in the sexual relationships in recent times.

Back in the 19th century sex was easy for men. No wife was able to legally refuse sex from her husband. So he could have sex whenever and however he wanted to. As it was believe that women didn't enjoy sex he didn't have to worry about her feelings, as foreplay then was unknown, as was the female orgasm. He was a liberty to put his penis in his wife and not worry if she was aroused and lubricated. As it was his wife's duty to lie back and endure any pain she might have from having his penis in her dry vagina. Anyway it usually didn't last too long, as most men can come within a few minutes.

In the 20th century sex has become far more difficult for men. Women demanded that men give them foreplay so their arousal will lubricate their vagina. So the man in a aroused state had to wait, until she was ready, then when he was inside her he then was told to delay his ejection until she reached orgasm before he was allowed to come. Unfortunately many men have been unable to manage all this and as we can see with the popularity of the drug Viagra, impotency has become commonplace among men in modern times. This is because in foreplay, some men loose their erections while their wives or girlfriends are slowly aroused. If a man gets past this hurdle he then has to control when he ejects. Not all men are able to do this, if he ejects too early he is accused of being a selfish and if he has to hang on for too long he again can lose his erection. While other men they find they can keep on pumping away as long as they like they will never bring their partner to orgasm, because her clitoris is not stimulated by the movement of this penis. All this has undermined the confidence of many men sexually whom today are considered to be failures if they cannot give their wives an orgasm with their penises. Resulting in many men buckling under the pressure, and becoming impotent.

So to protect their partners some women have to fake orgasm. The irony is that in the 19th century a good Christian woman if she has a orgasm had to suppress this feeling and pretend she didn't have it, because "respectable" women didn't enjoy sex. While in the 20th century when social customs change, women who didn't have orgasms with their husband had to "fake it" for the sake of his ego, or because she could be accused of being frigid.

What many women have discovered is that to enjoy sex it is far easier for them to masturbate themselves than to have a man's penis inside them. This is also true if a man wants to give a woman sexual pleasure, for many women he is far more likely to do a better job with his finger or tongue than with his penis. This then means for many couples if a man wants to give a woman sexual enjoyment it would be far better if he forgets about his penis and his own sexual pleasure and gives his partner oral or manual sex.

Does this mean that nature has played a cruel trick on the human race? In that women and men do not seem to be sexually compatible. Human beings seem to be set up sexually to make it difficult for men and women to mutually enjoy sex together. It is far easier for the man to enjoy sex if either he or his partner is worried about her sexual enjoyment. The same is true if a woman wants to enjoy sex it is far easier if the man gives her what she wants and not worry about his physical enjoyment.

Certainly sex between homosexual couples seems to be far easier than between heterosexual couples. This is because two men or two women together have very much the same attitude and feelings about sex as each other. While women and men seem to live on different planets not only are they physically incompatible, for reasons I have mentioned, but are incompatible emotionally as well. Men think about sex in terms of power, pleasure, a quick ejaculation and little emotional involvement, while women think about sex in terms of love, romance, unhurried sensual pleasure and personal feelings.

This then could point to men and women having homosexual relations in the Stone Age, like that of the bonobo. In that women formed a strong Lesbian sisterhood. The position of the clitoris does make it very easy for lesbian women to enjoy sex with each other. Also if Stone-Age lesbians did began to fashion dildos and use them on each other, (Dildos have been found in Stone-Age excavations,) this would mean in evolutionary terms women's vaginas would become used to having long sex sessions as she wouldn't be in a hurry to orgasm. The same is true for men. It is a strange fact that men's anus can lubricate in the same way as a women's vagina lubricates when sexually aroused. So in evolutionary terms homosexual sex play must of been very commonplace in the four million years of human history. To make these physical changes in our sexual make up.

Homosexuality was prominent in some civilisations in historical time like in Ancient Greece where it seems that as one time homosexuality was more commonplace than heterosexuality. Because of this in Sparta the women formed a strong lesbian sisterhood that allowed them far more freedoms and power than in any other part of Greece. Unfortunately this freedom and power in the end worked against them.

Although Sparta was a military State where the young boys were trained to be soldiers from a very early age. The freedom given to it's women, was in complete contrast to its neighbour Athens. Which although was the birthplace of Democracy, the men completely subjugated their women. Although Sparta was a very successful military state and defeated Athens in 404 BC, it seems its military downfall was caused by the freedom it gave to its women. In Athens and other Ancient Greek states women didn't have control over their own bodies. So they couldn't refuse sex from their husbands and were forced to have large numbers of children. In Sparta on the other hand women had complete control over their own bodies and could refuse her husband or any other man sex, (it seems the Spartan women even had the freedom to openly have sex with other men). This then means they were free to decide how many children she wanted to have. As the result over many years as the population of the surrounding Greek states grew, the population and in Sparta declined. Resulting in Sparta being heavily outnumbered when other Greek states, finally ganged up on her.

In modern times we still have the same problem. Western counties where women have greater freedom, have stable populations while inhabitants in countries where women are still subjugated keeping on growing at a alarming rate. Fortunately the Western countries are very powerful both economically and militarily and so are not likely to be conquered by a much larger military force in the foreseeable future. Like what happened to the Spartans.

Though this could be the problem for female freedom in the future. In any Feminist or matriarchal country the population will be stable and even decline. While in patriarchal counties the population will keep on growing. This then makes it very difficult for patriarchal and matriarchal countries to live together, because matriarchal countries will be under increasing pressure of immigration or conquest from patriarchal countries. Because patriarchal counties will need somewhere for its surplus population to go, and they will want live in the less crowed matriarchal countries.

So in the long term the concept of female freedom is a worldwide issue. Because while there are countries where women do not have control over their own bodies, the population of these countries will continue to grow. Which means in time they will import their culture and beliefs into countries where women have greater freedom through immigration or conquest. It is true at present immigrates that go to Europe and North America tend to be converted to a more Western lifestyle after a generation or two. Yet the pressure is still there, and we have the possible danger of the whole world going back to a extreme form of patriarchy through the population explosion in patriarchal countries. In other words what happened to the Spartans could also happen to Western countries if their population rate declines too fast.

All this seems to show that the Feminist ideal of sexual equality is very difficult on both the personal and global levels. If this strange state of affairs is brought about through evolution then what is this telling us about our ancestors in the Stone-Age? If Stone-Age men and women were equal in status with each other, then the sexual timing of women and men's orgasm would be very similar. They would take about the same time to get aroused, in that it would take the same amount of time for a man to get an erection, as it does for a woman to be lubricated. While the clitoris would be in a position to be stimulated by the penis when a man penetrates a woman. The fact that these things don't often happen, suggests that equality between the sexes wasn't very common during the Stone Age.

For women's sexual organs to evolve through millions of years where many women today can only enjoy sex, with a partner stimulating their clitoris with their finger or tongue. Means that women had to be able to control men. To the degree that men were willing to give up any idea of sexual enjoyment with women and only concentrate on her enjoyment, for thousands of generations. Or women had other women as sexual partners instead of men.

What we don't know about the people of the Stone Age is whether they linked the sexual-act with childbirth. Some academics claim that human being have only discovered this in the last few thousand years in civilised times. Yet recent research has discovered that human beings in the Stone Age were as far more intelligent than was previously thought. In fact some skeletons of Stone Age people has shown they had larger brains that the average person today. The more scientists find about Stone-Age people the more sophisticated and intelligent they become, so there is the possibility that human beings worked out the connection between sex and childbirth a half-a-million or a million years ago or more. It has to be remembered that in Western countries a birth control pill was only discovered only in the 1960s. Yet the Aborigines of Australia who had a Stone-Age culture before Europeans settled there, had knowledge of herbs that would also prevent women from having children. This means we know of one Stone-Age people who were far in advance of Western knowledge about birth control until the 1960s. Thus suggests that if in the Stone Age women knew about the connection between sex and childbirth it would make sense of why women then and now have evolved to a state where they have separated sexual pleasure from conception.

If there were matriarchal societies in the Stone Age and women also had worked out how to have sex with a man without having a child. What women could do is to order their male sexual partner to stimulate their clitoris and not to penetrate them. Or alternatively they would order the man to hold back their ejection and withdraw after she has an orgasm or if he cannot hold back any longer, if this practice continued over many thousands of generations. It would increase the length of time it would take women to orgasm because having men under control it wouldn't matter how long she took. Also if women regularly practised having men stimulate their clitoris with either a finger or tongue. They again wouldn't be in a hurry to orgasm and may even try to delay it so they can enjoy the pleasure for a longer period of time.

So we can see that having matriarchal sex with women in control with over many thousands of years can physically change women. As many women will start to get all their sexual pleasure from clitoris stimulation rather than penetration. So they will evolve to a degree where it doesn't matter if their clitoris is not stimulated if there is a penis inside them. Because they only time they will want penetration is when they want children. Or if women did prefer penetrative sex then they would train men to withhold ejaculation. This has been practised by men in historic times in Chinese and Indian through the religions of Taoism and Tantra. Where men learn to have sexual intercourse without ejaculation. The reason they give is that they claim ejaculation weakens a man's spiritual energy. Yet it also has to be admitted that it gives women a great advantage during sex. In that she can take as long as she likes in coming to orgasm. Suggesting that if was probably a woman who invented this concept. It is of interest that Tantra worships the Goddess Kali, while Taoism worships the Tao, which in the Tao-Te-Ching is called, "the mother" or "the mysterious female". So Taoism and Tantra practices that give women all the advantages in sex also worshipped Goddesses. Strongly suggesting that both these religions originated in a ancient matriarchal society.

It is of interest that scientists have found that in Neolithic times and even back in the times of the old Stone Age people then were obsessed with creating calendars, the most famous being Stonehenge and the many stone circles found in Britain, Ireland,

and France. Yet scientists have discovered markings on bone that clearly show Stone-Age people keeping track of the phases of the moon 30 thousand years ago. So why was Stone-Age people so obsessed with time and the phases of the moon? A obvious reason would be that Stone-Age women probably worked out that their menstruation period roughly fitted in with the phases of the moon. They also may have worked out from this when they were fertile and when they weren't. This would mean that they might have worked out the best time when they would allow men to ejaculate inside them to have children. This suggest that men having been trained to withhold ejection, when given the chance to ejaculate inside a woman would probably come very quickly. This is because the women would be more interested in conceiving than sexual pleasure, when she wanted to conceive. So the man would want to come quickly in case she might change her mind. This certainly would be a consideration in a society where there is no marriage, as the women may have other sex partners lined up if he didn't perform quickly enough.

In many patriarchal cultures even today the clitorises of young women are removed. Perhaps the original reason for this is the knowledge that sexually active women are dominant woman. So men attempted to make women more submissive by removing their clitorises. This suggests that when this practice was first started off in the ancient past, men were aware that very sexually active women were also dominant.

If this is true then were the patriarchal and matriarchal ages equal? With both women and men ruling at about the same length of time. It is of interest that women are far more sensual than men in sex play. For thousands of years men have dominated women and used them as sex-slaves. Yet if a man goes to a very submissive prostitute even though he can use her however he likes for his own pleasure, in the end most men seem to be more concerned in ejaculating quickly, than any sensual pleasure she can give him.

Yet it has been shown in recent times when the roles are reverse and a woman can buy sex from men they have a very different attitude. A woman can enjoy hours of sensual and sexual play and massage. While although men can enjoy sex play and being massaged they soon get tired of this. This has been discovered in massage parlours where men soon get aroused when being massaged by a young woman and he quickly wants to ejaculate. This might be because women have in the past have enjoyed men giving them sexual and sensual pleasure far more than women doing the same for men. So men are not used to receiving sensual and sexual pleasure from women and only want a quick orgasm, while women in the past through many thousands of years of matriarchal rule are used to men giving them unhurried sexual and sensual pleasure.

This then suggests that patriarchal rule by men are in evolutionary terms were fairly brief. After a patriarchal age women would know the reason why they must keep men under firm control. Because if all patriarchal ages are the same then both women and men will know how much conflict, fear, hatred and violence is caused when men rule society. So a warning would be passed down from mother to daughter never to allow men to get into a position of power again. Yet over many thousands of years this warning would become weaker and may even be forgotten, or just dismissed as an exaggerated myth. So some women will take pity on men and decide that it is unfair to treat men like slaves and give them equal rights. This then allows the competitive nature of men to be reawakened and soon men are ruling society through fear and violence. Until all people, including men, get fed up with the patriarchal world of suffering and go back to matriarchy again.

So there is probably a matriarchal/patriarchal cycle, but as women have a greater capacity to enjoy themselves sexually when they are in the dominant position then men, it suggests the patriarchal ages are far shorter than the matriarchal ages. As it seems from their behaviour women have had far more experience of dominating men sexually.

10

She Who Must be Obeyed

Now there is a big mystery about the 20th century that no one seems to comment on. Throughout the last five thousand years of history it has been accepted that men are the dominant sex. This was true up until the end of the 19th century when women all over the world had less rights than a slave. Yet a hundred years later at the end of the 20th century women in the West have equal opportunity? What suddenly happened in the 20th century than women have gain more rights and power than they had over the last four thousand years?

In answer to this question people look to the work of the Suffragettes, women's Liberation Movement and Feminists. Yet to be frank women have had it easy. If we say compared the Feminist struggle with say with the civil rights struggle of black people in USA, there is no comparison. The savage violence that black people have had to endure is incredible, with white lynch mobs being able to hang black people without fear of the law, and even today the vast majority of the prison population in USA are black people, as they are the poorest sections of the community.

It is true some Suffragettes and Feminists have been victims of violence but it has not been in the same league as endured by black people, or even trade unionist fighting for workers rights. So why has it been the case that men have successfully kept women in virtual slavery for thousands of years have suddenly caved in to Feminists demands, and gone belly up, without hardly a fight? Though I have to say this is not true in many Moslem countries where Feminists have been beaten up and murdered.

If you take a cork and hold it underwater it is very easy to hold it down but it will only stay there while you keep holding it in that position. If at any time you arm gets tired or you get fed up with keeping the cork underwater, and then let go, the cork will automatically rise to the top. This concept gives a good metaphor of what is happening today in the politics of female power.

For anyone who has read the history of patriarchy over the last five thousand years what it very striking is the great efforts needed to keep women powerless. Up until the end of the 19th century, there were laws to ensure that women couldn't own any property or wealth. As the law stated that her father or husband owned everything a woman had. The law also make it very difficult for any woman to inherit property. Women were also barred from all jobs and professions except being a housewife, servant or prostitute. So women were unable to acquire any wealth of power in her own right. Husbands were also encouraged to dominate their wives, and women had to swear to obey their husbands when they were married. The law even gave husbands the right to beat their wives with either a stick or whip.

In other cultures the laws oppressing women were even stricter than in the Western world. It was traditional for the Somalis people of Somalia, Kenya, Ethiopia and Djibouti for a bride to start married life with a flogging from their husbands. It seems the newly wedded husband would wait for her in the bridal chamber with a whip in his hand. This was also true with the Sifon people of Tibet, who traditionally would again start of married life with the husband whipping his bride. In many places like Sicily, Ethiopia and Eastern Europe where it was commonplace for men to choose their bride through kidnap and rape. A young man would pick out which girl he wanted to marry and then with a few friends kidnap and rape her. The girl was then force by social custom to marry her rapist. This went on in Sicily up until the 1960s and it still goes on in Ethiopia.

In India there is the custom of "Suttee". This is where when a husband dies his wife is put on the funeral pile to be burnt alive. So what are the origins of this very barbaric custom? It seems that in the past women would frequently poison their husbands, so to discourage this all women were made to die with their husbands. So the Suttee tradition was created by a brutal sex war between men and women in India, which men finally won by simply being more violent than women.

In China there was the tradition of foot binding. Again this is a very strange custom, but the end result is that women were left crippled. So this tradition suggest that at one time men were so frighten of they women that they had to cripple them to be able to dominate them.

Yet we are taught at school and in our history books that men have always been the dominant sex going back to early Stone Age. The irony is that if it is natural for men to be the dominant sex why do then men had to create very oppressive laws and customs against women? If it is natural for men to be the dominant sex then they shouldn't need any laws, custom or propaganda to keep their place as the dominant sex. For instance they only reason way we have laws against stealing is because many people do steal. If people didn't steal there would be no reason to have laws against this behaviour. The same is true of all customs and traditions. The custom of marriage with people swearing to be true to each other is only needed because people do tend to have sex outside of marriage. If pair bonding was completely natural for human beings then we wouldn't need customs like marriage, enforced by laws and social censure.

This then means that oppressive laws and customs to keep women in a subservient position suggests that it is not natural for women to be the submissive sex. If it was natural for men to be the dominant sex then there would be no reason for men to have oppressive laws and customs to keep women in bondage.

If you think about it, from the time the original Aryan invaders conquered Matriarchal communities in southern Europe to the start of Christianity and Islam was about 3,000 years. This means the Patriarchs needed 3,000 years of brainwashing all men and women into believing that our Creator was a male, that sex, childbirth, and menstruation was sinful or dirty and that women was inferior to men. This suggests that women were held in such high regard in ancient times that the original patriarchal invaders with all the advantages of violence and intimidation still took thousands of years to overcome the power of women.

If we compared this with what is happening today, where women in a position of complete powerlessness in the 19th century, has in just over a 100 years gained near equality with men. Through the undermining of the patriarchal religion Christianity we can now see women rapidly rise to power once again. So it is like a holding a cork underwater. It is easy to hold the cork down, but once you let go the cork rises to the surface. Patriarchy could only keep women down while it was actively suppressing them, and when the pressure was release we know find women are naturally moving back to ruling society once again. This suggests to me, that it is probably natural for human beings to be ruled by women.

Not only has women gain political power over the last hundred years but the relationship between men and women are also changing rapidly. With the undermining of the many customs, beliefs and social conventions that men are the dominant sex, the personal relationships between men and women are rapidly changing. It is now more commonplace for women to openly claim they are the head of the household and we even now have househusbands. While sexually attitudes are also changing, from very tiny beginnings during the early 1970s the FemDom sex industry has grown strongly and steadily.

It has been patriarchal religions like Christianity and Islam that has been in the forefront oppressing women. Even today extreme Islam countries try to force women to wear facial screens and discourage female education. Restrictions like this wouldn't be needed if men didn't fear the power of women. In the past Christianity used extreme violence against women. In the infamous Witch hunts of the medieval age the vast majority of millions of people who were tortured and burnt alive were women. Suggesting again a real fear of women becoming too powerful.

It was only the decline of the power of Christianity in the Western world through the rise of science that took away the oppression of women. With the ending of oppressive laws and customs throughout the 20th century women have quickly gained near equality with men. I know to us a hundred years might seem a long time but in historical terms it is very quick, for such a far-reaching social change. If this rate of progress for women was to continue during the 21st century then clearly women will be ruling the world within a hundred years.

It has been claimed that, "the hand that rocks the cradle rules the world". Now at first sight this seems to be a stupid saying because it a woman's hand that rocks the cradle and women are clearly not ruling the world, and never have done in recorded history. Yet it is still quoted because within it is a kernel of truth. Patriarchal religions and oppressive dictatorships like Nazism and Communism know that it is very important to brainwash children from a very early age. The Roman Catholic Jesuits boasted that, "give us a child for the first seven years and we have him for life".

Children up until the 20th century were basically brutalised in the Western world. It was normal for parents and schoolteachers to cane, birch and whip children. Favourite saying then were, "spare the rod and spoil the child", "children should be seen but not heard" and "if you see a child look guilty. Hit him. You may not know what it is for, but he does". Children were brutalise even as babies. Male "experts" wrote, that a crying baby was being wilful, and mothers where encouraged not to pick up crying baby. They were also told a baby that cried too much was to be put in a room and lock the door to let it cry itself to sleep. Then infants the moment they began to walk and talk they were subjected to physical punishment. (Boys in general were punished more severely than girls.) This was done not only to teach children discipline from a very early age. It was also done to make, "real men" out of boys. In other words by being brought up in a environment of violence, the children naturally became violent themselves. They then make good soldiers and they are able to kill without pity and they are more likely to, "keep women in their place".

Then as the 20th century progressed, women not only gained power over their own bodies but their children as well. Female child experts and more moderate child male experts like Dr Spock began to write books on child care. The development continued to the point that today what was normal for children in the 19th century, would be seen today as child abuse.

Children in the past were subjected to sexual abuse as well. That man who the "whistle blower" was surprisingly a young Sigmund Freud. In the past men have got away with child sex abuse scot-free. Then in 1896 a young Sigmund Freud presented a paper entitled "The Aetiology of Hysteria". In this paper he said he had discovered that the neuroses suffered by his patients stemmed from sexual assaults and violence they had suffered as young children, with most of these assaults coming from their own fathers, brothers or other male relations in "respectable middle class" homes. This paper went down like a lead balloon and his colleges put great pressure was put on him to suppress his paper. Which was singled out from all the other papers presented in Vienna in 1896 to not be published in psychoanalysis's Journal "Wiener Klinische Wochenschrift". Moreover no discussion of his work was allowed. In the end Freud caved in. (he wasn't a Wilhelm Reich). To save his career Freud did suppress his paper and then came up later with other theories like "Penis envy" and the "Oedipus complex" to explain neuroses. Which hinted at child sex abuse but never openly said it. These theories explained how the abused child felt and how it will affect them later. Unfortunately because these children were in reality were abused, but this fact was censored, this meant that the blame of the neuroses was put on the abused and not the abuser.

Now child sexual abuse is out in the open and not even Roman Catholic priests find they can get away with it. The result is that now children are being far less sexually and physically abused in the Western world. This lack of childhood abuse is causing men to be far less assertive, while women are becoming far more confident in themselves. So what is happening today was predicted back in the 19th century. When it was claimed that if you didn't "harden" (brutalise) boys they will become wimps.

The degree Western men have become wimps can be seen, as previously mentioned, in the number of suicides of soldier after both the Vietnam and Falklands wars. There are probably similar figures for the first Gulf war but the "Gulf War Syndrome" obscures these. (This is going on in spite of the extremely violent film; TV programmes and video games young people are encouraged to watch.) To some people today, it is terrible that our young men are losing their, "manhood", but if we want to live in a world of non-violence and peace, this is a very good thing. It is of interest that the most violent group of men in USA and UK are those of African decent. Black people seem to have been left behind in the reform of child rearing as many young black children are still routinely beaten by their parents. So it is not surprisingly that young black men still tend to be very violent. Though it also doesn't help that more black people are unemployed or work for low wages, than any other ethnic group in Western societies.

If you watch sport or action adventure movies you might be forgiven for thinking that men are really strong creatures. Well I'm afraid to tell all you "macho" guys out there, but compared but for its size and weight the human animal is just about the weakest animal in the world. Arnold Schwarzenegger is a weakling compared with an average adult chimpanzee.

In most animals it seems that the males fight over the right to mate with the females. We see this clearly animals like cattle and deer where the males head butt each other until the weakest male backs down and the strongest mate with the females. We also see the same behaviour among cats and dogs and other carnivorous animals where it is the strongest and most aggressive male is more likely to mate.

Now the advantage of this according to Darwin's theory of evolution is that the strongest and fittest males will mate and past down their genes to the next generation. So this means that the weaker males are eliminated from the gene pool of any species. This seems to work very well with many species of animal but there are exceptions like us Human beings and bonobos.

What is remarkable about us as a species of animal is how weak we are. An average male chimpanzee is about three times as strong as the average man, even though he is smaller in statue, while the gorilla is about four times the strength of humans. This is also true of any other animal of about our size. A deer, dog or big cat of about the same weight as a human can run 3 to 5 times faster than the average human. While one blow from a big cat or large ape will kill even a very strong man.

So why has the Human become so weak compared with other animals of a equal size? Does this suggest that some time during Human evolution the need for males to compete with each other to mate with females no longer became a important for the survival of the species? This can be seen clearly in the relationship between the Neanderthal man and the first modern Humans over 40 thousand years ago in Europe. The skeletons of the Neanderthals showed they were far stronger and more heavily built than modern Humans living at that time. Both species had about the same size brains and both used tools. Yet it was the Neanderthals that became extinct and not the physically weaker modern Humans. So it seems that the increased intelligence and tool making ability of Humans made the need for physical strength no longer an important aspect of survival.

The relationship between the Neanderthal and the first modern humans we can see in two species of chimpanzees today. The Congo River in Africa is one of the largest rivers in the World and is in some places it is over 10 miles wide. The result of this is that the chimpanzee living on different sides of the Congo River have evolved into two different species. Living on one bank is the normal chimpanzee you see in other parts of Africa but on the other bank is the bonobo. In spite of its name it is not really smaller but is more lightly built than the heavier and stronger Common chimpanzee.

Bonobos males like humans do not compete with each other through fighting for the right to mate with females. This is what makes both species physically weaker than chimpanzees and other animals of a similar size.

It is a curious fact that in all the Lemur species of Lemur on the island of Madagascar the female is the dominant sex. It has be observed many times by biologists, That if a male lemur approaches a female before she has finished feeding, he is swiftly put in his place. Female lemurs drive males away from food until they and their young have eaten and will even jump at them, bite them or cuff them. Then the male will retreat and give a submissive call.

Unlike with bonobos this behaviour is not re-enforced by a powerful lesbian sisterhood. It seems to be a part of male Lemur's genetic behaviour. It has also been observed that when adult males begin issuing submissive signals to adolescent females, the young females are taken by surprise. After a while they figure out what's going on and enjoy it, demanding that the adult males play with them. It also seems that young females also play more than males, a behaviour commonly linked to dominance in young male mammals.

The theory put forward by the biologists observing this behaviour is that it is caused by the extreme weather conditions on Madagascar, which makes it very tough for the wild life living there. During four months of the year, the island experiences torrential downpours that nourish the lemurs' food supplies of leaves and fruits. The other eight months of the year tend to be cold and dry. During these dry spells, lemurs rely on low quality foods like bamboo pith. Overall, survival is very difficult, more so for the female, than the male. Pregnancy and providing milk for infants require energy. So Lemurs cannot afford the luxury of males assaulting females, pinching female's food or even feeding before the female and her young. This means having males who are very submissive towards female is a very important consideration for the survival of the species. Lemur groups with alpha males would quickly die out because only the males would survive. This is because they would hog the short supply of food in the dry months, and the female and young would be first to die. While in female dominated groups even if only one male survives a bad year he is still able to fertilise all the females in the group. So survival pressures have made Lemurs on Madagascar matriarchal.

Scientist now believe that the Neanderthals died out because of the changing climate of Europe at the time of their extinction. But the mystery is why it was the Neanderthals that died out and not the first modern humans. As the bones of Neanderthals show they were physically far stronger than humans. This suggests this was brought about in evolutionary time by Neanderthals males fighting each other in a test of strength for the right to mate, with only the strongest males reproducing. This makes the species far stronger than humans. Who because of their weaker body strength it shows that the male humans were not fighting each other for dominance and right to mate. If we assume that the physically powerful Neanderthal had a similar society to present day chimpanzees, then females being at the bottom of the pecking order would have to always give way to males in disputes over food. Now this wouldn't be a problem when they had food in abundance. Yet we know during the ice age because of times of rapidly changing climates, food became very difficult to obtain at certain times. So it would only be the alpha males who were allowed to feed and survive. The females and their children being at the bottom of the pecking order would be the first to die, and even if some survived they would be so undernourished that they would be unlikely to be able to give birth and feed their young. This means that in times of scarcity the evolutionary strategy of only allowing the most strongest and most aggressive males to breed would work against the Neanderthals, because although the alpha males would survive they would be incapable of breeding a new generation.

On the other hand the weaker modern humans that no longer had this evolutionary strategy. Their weak and slight bodies suggest they would be more like the bobobos with female at the top of the pecking order. It would then be more likely the alpha females that would survive in times of scarcity. The deaths of the lower order males wouldn't be such a problem because it would only require a few males to survive to continue the breeding of the species. In that one male can father hundreds children of different mothers. It wouldn't even matter if the male dies after he has done his job, of fertilising the females, as the caring of the children he fathered would be in the hands of the mothers.

This then means that in the changing climate conditions which brought about the extinction of the Neanderthals, it would be humans a matriarchal society that would be more likely to survive.

It is true that in recorded history we have lived in a patriarchal society and this may of come about because of agriculture and the abundance of food that this created. While humans lived conditions where survival was difficult. It would mean that matriarchal tribes would be the one who would survive and continue to breed. Certainly in the time of the Ice Age and the changing weather conditions made survival for all animals difficult. Then once the Ice Age had ended and the climate settled down into a stable pattern and human intelligence found ways to acquire an abundance of food. Like when humans began to grow crops and herd animals. Then the advantages of living in a matriarchal society for survival declined. This would allow patriarchal tribes ruled by alpha males to be created. They in turn make war on their more peaceful matriarchal neighbours who would be defenceless against organised male violence. In these conditions of abundance of food put females on the lower end of the pecking order as patriarchy would no longer be a threat to the survival of the tribe. This allowed men to indulge in their favourite pastime of war with other tribes, and so over a few thousand years the whole world would become patriarchal through this violence and warfare

So the study of bobobos gives support to the work of Mariji Gimbutas. It also gives a reason why Neanderthals became extinct and not our ancestors.

What is clear is that men can only become the dominant sex by enforcing through violence and propaganda oppressive laws and customs against women. This means that it is not natural for men to be the dominant sex if men have to brutalise each other to become violent and dominant. If we get rid of all these artificial laws and customs created by patriarchal men and follow our natural instincts then we may end up with a equal society. Or we might end up with a female dominated world.

11

The Aquatic Ape

Scientists have for a long time puzzled over why humans are so different from other animals. In the early 20th century it was simple, it was because humans developed larger brains than any other animal. So because men had bigger brains, they could figure out how to walk on two legs, how to speak and make tools. The problem with this theory is that the elephant, and most species of dolphins and whales have larger brains than us. So a theory was developed that intelligence relied on a brain v body weight ratio. There was no scientific proof that this theory was correct, but then you can't have another allow another animal to be more intelligent than man, can you? More so, if you are the one making up the rules.

It was the same when I.Q. tests were invented, also in the early 20th century. The first time they tried it out they discovered according to the tests, women were smarter than men. So of course the tests must be wrong. They had to fiddle about with I.Q. tests until they came up with the "correct" results that made men smarter then women. After all women had smaller brains than men and were too emotionally unstable to vote. So they couldn't possibly be smarter than men.

These men also decided that it was hunting skills that made man so intelligent. It must be this, because hunting is very much a "macho" pursuit. It couldn't possibly be anything to do with gathering because that is a female thing. As in the Stone-Age communities that have survived into modern times it was observed that men do the hunting and women gathered food. So it must be hunting skills that made men so intelligent. It also made man number one on the food chain. (In no way does man what to be number two, that is to say a plant eater and have carnivores feed off him). And it confirmed he was always ruthless and aggressive as well as the superior sex. So from this, the Great White Hunter theory was created.

Then in the 1960s a scientist called Alistair Hardy noticed that the blubber around a seal was very similar the fat around a human. Now fat is commonplace in all aquatic animals but rare in land mammals. This is because fat is a better protector against the cold in water than fur, while fur is a far better insulator for a land animal than fat. From this Hardy began to wonder if we were once an aquatic creature. (Hardy as it turns out wasn't the first scientist to make this observation, but he was the first scientist to publicise it). He also wondered if it would make sense of why we are also the only primate that is hairless. He notes that other hairless creatures like dolphins, hippos, pigs and manatees are aquatic or semi-aquatic animals. Being hairless only makes sense if you spend a large amount of time in water or swamps, where hair can get wet and drag you down.

This theory immediately received the thumbs down by the scientific community. A typical reaction came from Prof. Emeritus Phillip Tobias FRS, -

"Ever since Sir Alister Hardy put it forward in 1960, it has been scorned, derided, made fun of. Nobody has really taken it seriously. You either burst into guffaws of uncontrollable laughter or you tap your head in respect of the person speaking it."

With reactions like this, Hardy dropped it like a hot potato. (He was street wise enough to know that to advocate an unpopular theory would ruin his scientific career). Fortunately it was taken up by the Feminist, Elaine Morgan, who has since developed it further. As she is a journalist and screenplay writer, she had to intellectual freedom to write about the theory without fear of jeopardising her career. If she had an academic career it would of been ruined by the hostility of other academics to this theory.

The beauty of the Aquatic Ape theory is that it explains so much about how humans evolved from being so much different than any other ape. For instance bipedalism, the great white hunter theory claims that man walked on two legs to see above the high African grass on the savannah. The problem with this theory is that you also have large numbers of grazing animals eating this grass. So these conditions don't last for very long and would only be a temporary situation every year.

Yet in the past there was another ape, which was biped like us. This was the long-extinct Oreopithecus, known as the swamp ape, which means it was also probably a aquatic ape. Scientists have found it had a pelvis like ours, making suitable for bipedalism. In modern times the two primates that are able to walk upright are the proboscis monkey who lives in the mangrove swamps of Borneo. (This is a real swimming primate and some have been found by fishermen swimming in the ocean.) Also the bonobo who lives in forests that are seasonally flooded every year. Both species wade through the water in a similar way to human beings, so this suggests that bipedalism in primates come from living in flooded or swampy areas.

Although there is another primate that stands on two legs and that is the sifaka or leaping lemur of Madagascar. Unlike some species of ape like gibbons or chimpanzees who use long powerful arms to swing among the trees. These lemurs are leapers and will use long powerful legs to leap from branch to branch or even from tree to tree. Some have been observed to leap as far as 30 feet from one tree to another. The problem for these Lemurs is that when they come to the ground their legs are so long that they are unable to walk on four legs. This means they are forced to stand upright and jump or skip along the ground, so why couldn't of this happened to humans? Because like Sifakas our legs are too long of us to comfortably walk on all fours.

The bonobo like many primates have almost the same length of arms and legs. The chimpanzee developed from a bonobo like ancestor to become a swinger, resulting in long powerful arms, to swing through the trees. So it would be logical that humans evolved from the same ancestor to become a leaper. To leap through the trees which resulted in the development of long powerful legs. Which would force humans to walk upright when they had to walk on the ground. This could happen simply because of the types of trees these apes lived in. Some found themselves in trees where it was easier to swing through them, developing the chimpanzee. Others found themselves in trees where it was easier to leap from tree to tree, developing the hominid type ape. While others were living in trees where there was no advantage in becoming a specialist leaper or swinger, resulting in the bonobo. This would then give a great advantage to the hominid ape when they came to ground. Because walking on two legs it would have its hands free to pick up things it might need to carry, or develop tool-making skills. Bonobos and chimpanzees have been observed to use tools but are restricted by the fact they also use their hands for locomotion either on the ground or in trees.

This occurred to me years ago when I saw a picture of a sifaka and read why it could only stand upright on the ground. Being young and very naïve I couldn't understand why scientists had overlooked a obvious reason why humans had become bipeds. It is only now being much older and wiser, I realise that scientists are not going to be interested in such a explanation, because it doesn't in any way support the Great White Hunter theory. Anyway lemurs are highly suspect because the males as so wimpy that they give way to female in all disputes. Clearly male lemurs lack moral fibre, and so not "real men", so the least said about these creatures the better. We wouldn't want yellow belly male lemurs contaminating the "macho" Great White Hunter theory, would we? So hopefully they will go away, if we forget about them. Which is what they might do, as some species of lemurs in Madagascar are considered the most endangered of all species of primates.

The Aquatic ape camp also wouldn't be interested in the leaper idea because again it doesn't in any way help their theory. So anyway, to continue to explain this theory. Human being have voluntary breath control, which is unusual for land animals but commonplace for aquatic mammals. Voluntary breathing is need for aquatic mammals because they need to hold their breath to stay underwater for long lengths of time. The adaptations resulting in this has also allowed humans to speak.

At one time scientist believed that only humans had language. (Because man is so much smarter than any other animal, right?) Then a maverick scientist Dr John C. Lilly put forward the research that showed that both dolphins and whale also can communicate through sound. Not something that egoist male scientists wanted to hear, so he was either ignored or savagely criticised. Then up popped a husband a wife scientific team, the Gardners. Who also wasn't a team player either and badly let the side down by training a chimpanzee to speak using deaf and dumb sign language. Again they were savagely criticised by other scientists who had to redefined speech to "prove" that this chimpanzee wasn't really using language. Perhaps the Gardners were a bit naïve in choosing a female chimpanzee. Had they of trained a male chimpanzee instead, mentioning just how violent and "macho" he was, they may of got more acceptance. It is true that working with adult male chimpanzees is dangerous because of their great strength and aggression. Yet if you want scientific acceptance you have got to do things like this. If they had paired a male with a female chimp this would of established pair bonding, which would of gone down well. Then mention the violence that the male chimpanzee dishes out to the female. Perhaps even have the male chimp sign, "I like bashing females". Now this would of been very popular, as it establishes he is an O.K. guy. There would be no talk about him not really using language if he said intelligent and sensible things like that.

So it seems that language is not exclusive to humans. Apes don't speak, simply because they don't have the vocal ability to do so, not because they are stupid. This is not true of dolphins and whales whom like humans have a large brain and the ability to take conscious control of our breathing. So it seems our ability to take conscious control of our breathing has also resulted in a far greater variety of the sounds we can make, compared with other apes. It is this greater variety of noises we can make, which has resulted in the formation of speech.

Other human characteristics that support the Aquatic Ape theory is that we sweat salt and water from our skin glands. Which for a land animal is a waste, more so in a hot country like Africa, as water is very scarce at certain times of the years. So sweating water is a very inefficient method of keeping cool for a tropical animal. Salt, is also scarce for land animals who will travel a long way to find salt licks. Yet sweating salt makes a lot of sense to aquatic animals that need a way to get rid of an excess of salt in their bodies when swimming in the ocean. Humans can also get rid of excess salt through their tear glands, again something common to aquatic animals but not land animals.

Also being naked is not a good idea in the hot African sun. (Even black people can get sun burnt, or skin cancer from too much sun). Fur protects the skin from the deadly effects of the sun and is also a far better insulator than fat for land animals. This is because a land animal can shed fur in the summer and grow it again in the winter. It can also fluff up fur in the heat, to allow the air to get to its skin to cool down. Or bring the hairs closer to the body, trapping the air in the fur to allow better insulation, in the cold. Fur also makes it far easier for animals to adapt to very cold conditions. In the 19th century when the first zoos were created in Europe they attempted to house tropical animals in heated rooms, but the animals quickly died. So they tried leaving the tropical animals outside and they quickly adapted to the cold by growing thicker fur. It was found that even Russian zoos have no problems in caging tropical animals out in the open, as they grow fur thick enough to adapt to the Russian weather.

It is true that some animals like bears, grow a layers of fat around them for the winter when they hibernate. The trouble is that humans don't hibernate, not even the Eskimos, who for thousands of years endured dark arctic winters living in Igloos.

So it begs the question: what is a tropical animal like human beings walking around using a layer of fat as insulation? Because another disadvantage is that it is unnecessary weight for us to carry around. If you want to stay alive either as a predator or a plant eater on the African plains, speed is a big advantage. So lightness and strength is very important for most animals the size of humans. It seems the only advantage of the fat we have around our bodies is that fat is a better insulator in water and it gives us buoyancy. This then makes it easier for us to float and swim in the water.

We also have large oil glands in our skin. Again this is of little use to a land animal in that they only need enough oil in their skin to keep out the rain. Aquatic animals on the other hand have very large oil glands to make their fur or skin, waterproof. Our oil glands are as large as that of a aquatic animal, rather than a land animal.

There is an old saying that oysters make you brainy. There is some truth in this as brain tissue needs an adequate supply of Omega-3 fatty acids. Which is found in abundance in fish oil but is very scarce in the food found on land. So living on food from the sea would be a big advantage in helping humans to develop a large brain. Some people also have vestigial webbing between their fingers and toes. Which suggests that at one time the webbing was more pronounced giving us an advantage in swimming.

Just how aquatic humans are, can be seen in the very modern sport of "free-diving", that is to say diving without the use of oxygen tanks. When scientist observed people doing very deep free-diving they found that there heart beats would go right down until is was barely beating. The lungs were crushed until they had little more space than a drink can. While what little oxygen left in the body is used to just keep the heart and brain going. In other words human body behaves in exactly the same way in a deep dive without diving gear as a whale or dolphin. Free divers now go deeper than the rescue divers that tried to save the crew of the doomed Russian Kursk submarine. The Norwegian divers in this rescue bid had to spent five days recovering in a decompression chamber. While a free diver do not suffer from bends at all. It seems that the first moment cold water hits the face of a human diving in the water the human body starts to behave like a aquatic animal.

Which makes it more than capable of dealing with the problems of deep diving. On August 17, 2002- a new Freediving World Record has been set by Tanya Streeter, at a depth of 160m/525ft in a total dive time of 3 minutes and 26 seconds. This dive shatters the previous women's No Limits World Record held by Canadian, Mandy-Rae Cruickshank (136m/446ft) and even surpasses the men's No Limits World Record of 154m/505ft held by Frenchman, Loic LeFerme.

There is a lot of other points that have been put forward by Elaine Morgan like the fact that human legs are very similar in shape and mechanic function to that of a frog. Which is adapted to make it easier for both frogs and humans to swim better. Some mothers today have, water births where the mother gives birth in a tub of water. Apparently birth like this is made a lot easier for mothers suggesting that at one time in our evolution this was commonplace. Also it has been found that newborn babies can float and swim straight away after birth. Whereas with other apes, like a new born chimpanzee or gorilla, it will quickly sink and drown, if not rescued. Water births are not just some new-age fad. There is a tribe in Indonesian called the Suku laut, or the "Sea People", who live a semi-aquatic existence. The Sea People spend up to 10 hours every day in the water, they give birth in the water, and the children dive before they walk and the people harvest all their food from the sea.

So how did our ape ancestors become aquatic? It seems that for a ape that can use it's hands to pick up things from the ground and wade through water, shell fish and edible seaweed would be a very easy way to obtain food. Unfortunately if too many apes take advantage of this, the shallows will quickly become over fished. Forcing them either to mover further along the coast, or to start to dive under water further out. Clearly at first it they would just quickly duck their heads under the water, to collect shellfish deeper than a arms length. Then in time becoming specialist feeders their bodies would adapt to going further and further out to sea.

So you can see there is a very strong arguments for the Aquatic Ape theory. Yet most male scientists still resist this theory. To quote the Anthropologist Prof. Leslie Aiello

"Until there is actual evidence to support a serious aquatic involvement, I don't think that we're going to be able to say that that's at all a contender for a theory for human evolution."

There is no actual evidence of the man the hunter theory, but this hasn't stop scientists presenting it to the public as fact. In recent times they are backtracking they now call it the savannah theory and acceptance that early humans might of scavenged for food instead of hunting. There is even a acceptance nowadays, that the mighty hunter might be black! Elaine Morgan now has the confidence to declare that the Man The Hunter theory is defunct. Yet she is clearly puzzled that with all the weight of evidence she can present for her theory, it is still not widely accepted in the scientific community. As we can see from the quotes from two other scientists.

"It is difficult to see how all the points assembled to back the Aquatic Theory can be explained away." - Dr. Desmond Morris, author of 'The Naked Ape'

"The aquatic hypothesis... cannot be eliminated yet." - Prof. Glyn Isaac

Now this begs the question: Why does this theory need to be, explained away or eliminated? Or for that matter why is the Aquatic Ape theory so popular among Feminists but extremely unpopular among male scientists? Is it because of a very strong gender bias in comparing the Man The Hunter theory with the Aquatic Ape theory?

Apart from the fact that the Aquatic Ape theory doesn't in any way support the ideal of man the mighty hunter, another big problem with this theory is that women are more adaptable to water than men. Because women have less body hair than men, and have more body fat. So what is the problem with that? The trouble is that when we look at modern day communities that still dive for shellfish we find that women have a distinct advantage.

There is a group of islands between southern Japan and southern Korea where before the tourist trade got going, the main source of food and income on these islands was shellfish and edible seaweed. Which is harvested by female divers.

To quote, a Korean travel guide:

Women have dominated this profession because they are physically better suited for it than men, women possess a higher percentage of subcutaneous fat, which insulates them from cold, allowing a longer stay in the water. Thus, it has long been customary for Cheju-do's men to mind the children at home while the women work, culling shellfish, seaweed, and sea urchins from the seabed, on which many of the island's inhabitants depend for subsistence and livelihood. Ranging in age from 10 to 60, these women divers can plunge as deep as 45 to 60 feet and stay underwater for as long as three to five minutes without the aid of breathing equipment. The average dive, however, lasts about 30 seconds at a depth of 15 or 20 feet."

The Cheju-do women are referred to by some Korean commentators as Amazons, because they are far more assertive than ordinary Korean women. In the extremely "macho" society of Korea, these women and their "weak" husbands are an embarrassment, and for this reason knowledge about Cheju-do customs were once kept quiet.

The Japanese islands have a similar story to quote, the late Jacques Cousteau.

For 1500 years in ancient Japan, as well as neighbouring Korea, these women have traditionally dived for pearls. At least 30,000 of their kind remain. Today they mostly dive for food. Wearing only a loincloth, they have begun to wear masks and snorkels within the 20th century. They dive both during the warm summers and the cooler winter months when temperatures can reach 50° F. They plunge to depths of 20 to 80 feet – sometimes 100 – to gather food, in the form of shellfish and seaweed, which they place in a net around their waists. They learn to dive around puberty and do not stop till they are about 60 years old. They are known to dive right up to the point of childbirth and having given birth, resume shortly after, nursing their infants between dives! A similar group of women once dived in the wave tossed waters off Tierra del Fuego. (Islands at the most southern point of South America). *They descended completely naked, through waters averaging 42° F to collect clams and crabs for food.*

The Japanese and Korean women divers did experiment with modern equipment like scuba gear, but it was soon found that using such equipment would quickly over fish the area, so scuba equipment was banned by the authorities.

There is also some reports of women divers in other parts of the world. In Barents Sea, palaeontologists and archaeologists have for a long time been puzzled why such large amounts of shellfish shells have been found in Palaeolithic sites without any evidence of fishing gear and boats. This would only be a puzzle for male scientists who are blind to the role women play in ancient communities. Before the 1920s when the Russian authorities began to use modern diving gear and motorboats equipped with dredges, there was still a local tradition of using professional women-divers similar to that in Japan and Korea. Even in these cold waters on the coast of Siberia these divers would continue diving in the cold autumn months. (Needless to say when they adopted modern equipment the area was soon over fished and fishing in the area was banned in 1960).

If male divers had been doing this job these scientists wouldn't of had no problems in putting two and two together. They would of praised the male divers about how tough and macho they were, given it wide coverage, but because they were women, the fact was ignored.

It is perfectly possible for women to swim in these waters without a wet suit. In the sporting world we are used to men outperforming women, yet there is one sport where women are now outperforming men, which is the sport of marathon open water swimming. In the 21 miles across the English Channel, the first women to do this was Gertrude Caroline Ederle of USA. In 1926 she broke the record of the fastest man by one hour and fifty-nine minutes. In spite of having to battle through heavy seas in the second half of her swim. Since then the record for the fast channel swim has been held at different times by both men and women. In 1987 Lynne Cox of USA, (who also held the fastest time for swimming the English Channel for awhile), swam the across the Bering Strait, from the U.S. to Soviet Union with water temperatures at 38-42 degrees Fahrenheit, without wearing a wet suit. She done it wearing only a normal swim suit, cap and goggles. At this temperature most normal men will freeze to death in the water within 20 minutes.

The censorship by patriarchal authorities of women divers many be responsible for the mermaid legend. Once a Dutch ship was wrecked on Cheju island's coast. Subsequently, its crew was detained for 13 years. One of the seamen, Hamel, published a record of their experiences upon his return to Europe, describing the 'haenyo' (women divers) as mermaids. Which is interesting because being on the island for 13 years he must of known they were ordinary women. So why did he write that they were mermaids? In may be because in those days a story of mermaids was more acceptable to people than female divers. After all, the Korean authorities at one time forbade and written record of these divers.

The official version of the mermaid story is the sailors have mistaken animals like seals and dugongs as mermaids. Which is a typical patronising attitude from academics towards uneducated working class people, in assuming they are stupid. I personally find it hard to believe that experienced sailors couldn't tell the difference between a seal and a women swimming in the sea or sitting on rocks. Korea and Japan the authorities have tended to keep quiet about women divers up until recent times. Because it undermines patriarchal beliefs, to have assertive women doing a physical job better than men. So the same was probably true in other parts of the world. The patriarchal Jews went as far as to ban shellfish as a taboo food. Was this because in those days women divers were still collecting them from the sea? Had not female divers in Japan and Korea survived up until modern time we today wouldn't know nothing about them. There is other evidence that women divers were still commonplace all over the world in the recent past. For instance in the 19th century peal industry, some of the European traders were horrified to find the locals using women peal diving. To the degree that in the Torres Strait islands they banned women divers.

Because of the patriarchal conspiracy of silence, sailors would be shocked suddenly coming across women divers. To these very patriarchal sailors used to their own women being very submissive, shy, retiring and modest. To suddenly see naked, (They probably were naked as the bathing suit was only invented at the end of the 19th century and clothing is a hindrance in the water), athletic and confident women going about their work would be something completely outside of their personal experience. As we can see from this following sighting in Britain.

"A SCHOOL MASTER OF THURSO IN CAITHNESS, William Munro, wrote in a report in THE TIMES on September 8, 1809 that twelve years earlier he had been walking along Sandside Bay shore when he saw what he first thought was a naked woman, sitting on a rock and combing her light brown hair. The face was plump, with ruddy cheeks and blue eyes. If the rock where the woman sat had not been so dangerous for swimmers, Munro would have assumed it was human. After a few minutes it dropped into the sea and swam away. Others had seen it too. ."

He clearly states is that he saw a naked woman, sitting on a rock. Yet it is reported as a mermaid sighting. Probably in isolated fishing villages all over the world women divers may of been used up to fairly recent times. Because people living on the edge of survival couldn't afford to ignore a important food resource like shell fish and edible seaweed. In traditional mermaid stories from Europe there is stories of fishermen marrying mermaids. Now, if it was to a women with a fishes tail this would virtually impossible, so in some of the stories the mermaid obtains legs by magical means. Yet if we take a more sensible view, that mermaids are women divers then there is no problem with this. Most women divers were probably married to fishermen anyway.

They would also have to keep this tradition secret because of patriarchal condemnation of women doing men's work. There would be a even more deadly reason to do this, churchmen in the past have condemned mermaids as pagan. Now this is a real threat, because the Church in the middle ages had murder millions of women as Witches. It seems that country people in the times still had many pre-Christian beliefs, which was stamped out as pagan during the witch-hunts. (The word pagan comes from the word peasant). This includes women healers who practised the ancient art of herbal medicine. (There was no problem about educated men giving out herbal medicine, they were called doctors, so that was all right, but a women doing this was condemned as a witch). To protect themselves, one of the ways of keeping the tradition of women divers secret, would be to invent stories of mermaids. Then to tell strangers who did see them, that it was a mermaid that they saw.

So why was it that women become more aquatic than men? A possible explanation is that wading in the water was also a protection from predators, who are unlikely to try and swim out to catch a ape who can stand upright in the water and can walk out as far as it's neck. To this ape the water will come a safe haven in much the same way a tree is, so instead of climbing a tree to escape from a predator it can run into the ocean instead. In fact a beach is a difficult hunting ground for predators as there is not much cover a large cat can hide behind to stalk their prey. This then would make shell hunting more popular among females if she is pregnant or breast feeding a child as she is protected by the water she is wading through. Even when the child is too big to carry, the mother can leave the child on the water's edge and then quickly snatch it and take it out to deeper water if she sees a predator coming down the beach. So there is a lot of advantages of female apes becoming marine food gathers. Though not so much for male apes, who would be bigger and stronger anyway and don't have the burden of trying to save a helpless baby from a predator as well. So it would cause a division of labour of men gathering on land while women gathered in the sea.

So the Aquatic Ape theory seems to be very much appeal to women, and this also may be why many male scientists don't like it. Instead of having a great white hunter, coming home from a hard day of hunting to be greeted by his adoring wife, who will submissively wait on her lord and master hand and foot. We now have women who are the breadwinners and it is the men who have to look after the home and children! Well, we can't possibly have that can we? More so if you realise that it is claimed by Elaine Morgan that it took a 6.5 million year for humans to evolve into a semi-aquatic animal. Does this mean that men were under the women's thumb all this time? It couldn't be possible be that our male ancestors were a bunch of yellow belly wimps, can it?

Large deposits of shellfish shells have been found in South Africa in early human sites. Proving that shellfish was being eaten by early humans. Also very early hominids like Homo erectus had very thick tooth enamel and powerful jaws. Which it is speculated that they were needed, to break open nuts and shellfish with their teeth. Later on they would of used stones or clubs to do this, which may of been the first use of tools for hominids. Yet most male scientists still do not accept the Aquatic

Ape theory and still cling desperately to very watered down versions of the Great Hunter theory, or prefer to have no theory at all. This then means that it is possible to make out a case that human society was dominated by women from the time when we were still a ape to the end of the Neolithic Age. We can briefly summarise this in the following points.

1. The skeleton of the bonobo ape is very similar to the australopithecines oldest discovered is 3 million year old and the australopithecus ramidus which dates back to 4,4 million years old. The teeth of these primates show that they were vegetarians, which is another blow to the man the hunter theory. So as the bonobo ape lives in female dominated communities can we also assume that the australopithecines was the same? Now I am sure that male chauvinists scientists will correctly claim that you cannot make such a assumption on such slender evidence. Yet we know that if these skeletons were more like that of a chimpanzee than a bonobo. These same scientists would be very quick to claim that humans then had exactly the same social structure as male dominated chimpanzee communities.
2. Then we have the Aquatic Ape theory that shows that humans went through a Aquatic period in their evolution. The bones of the australopithecines were found at the edge of ancient sea, which means the this ancient human could of used this sea as a means of obtaining food. It is true that many bones of ancient humans have also been found inland, but what we don't really know is whether any of these hominids were our direct ancestors. There has been many species of hominids in the past yet only one species, the modern human, has survived into modern times. It seems that because of the aquatic adaptations to our bodies it was only the aquatic species that survived. If we accept that Aquatic Ape theory then we also have to accept that "macho" hunting had little to do with our evolution. Also that because women's bodies are more adaptable to aquatic life it was women and not men who became the main, "bread winners".

3. As we move forward in time to the more modern humans that came into existence about 200,000 years ago. What we find compared with other animals of a similar size is that we are incredibility weak. In fact far weaker that apes like chimpanzees and gorillas and other hominids like the Neanderthals. As evolutionist point out one of the main reasons why a animal becomes very powerful and strong is the competition between males who have a test of strength and aggression for the right to mate. The fact that the modern human is so weak compared with its nearest species except the bonobo, is probably because there was very little male competition for the right to mate with females, among our ancestors. This points to women selecting which males she wants to mate with instead of men. Suggesting a situation where women were either equal to men in status or the dominant sex.
4. Of the many species of hominids it was only the modern human that has survived. This was because of periods of rapid changing weather conditions during the last ice age. When many large species of animals became extinct. Even we were probably nearly wiped out because genetically it seems that all humans today had only one female ancestor about 200,000 years ago. In the survival of any species, women are far more important than men. This is because one man can father hundreds of children, while a women is very limited on how many children she can have. More so in the state of stress and starvation, it is important that a women is reasonably well fed to nourish a baby. So like the lemurs in the island of Madagascar, communities that give preference to alpha males are less likely to survive than communities that give preference to females.
5. Then in the Neolithic age we find evidence of people worshipping Goddesses and no evidence of war or violence. Which changed dramatically when in the bronze and iron ages where the use of weapons of war, fortifications and the worship of male warrior gods became commonplace.

Taking all the evidence from above it would seem that women have always dominated human society up until five thousand years ago. I have to say that is unlikely. The point is that what you read in this book readdress the balance of sexual bias scholarship, archaeology, zoology, biology, anthropology and palaeontology, which claims that man was always the dominant sex.

Ever since I went to school in the 1950s to now all I have ever read in mainstream science is that we have always lived in male dominated societies. It was only by reading a book called, "The First Sex", by Elizabeth Gould Davis in the 1970s that opened my eyes to different possibility. Since then I have taken a interest in this subject and soon found that to get any information on anything that suggests human beings were once dominated by females, very difficult to find. The truth is that the general public is only given one very sexual biased point of view.

This is because of very egocentric academic males who very much want to believe that men have always been the dominant sex. The problem is that the censorship about the possibility of women rule or even sexual equality, gives the general public the illusion they only have one choice and that is patriarchy. Which wouldn't be a problem if men were doing a wonderful job in ruling our world. The trouble is that men do a really terrible job of doing this. I would even go as far as saying that, it would be difficult to do a worse job of ruling our world, than what men do.

If we accept that in the past we didn't always live in brutal and violent patriarchal communities. It means we can if we choose create a more peaceful and caring world ruled by women.

12

Masculine and Feminine Cycles

We live in a sick, sad world, which needs to be healed. The first thing needed in process of healing is an acknowledgement that there is an illness. For instance with alcoholics or drug addicts attempts to cure them are a waste of time until they acknowledges they have a real problem. Then the healer needs to convince them that they have a workable method that will bring genuine healing.

So the first hurdle is the universal admission that we do actually live in a sick world. The problem is that we are taught from childhood that the world we live in is "normal". We have all been brought up from childhood to believe war, crime, violence and hatred is customary for human beings. If we think about it a bit deeper we find that all the major religions of the world has failed to make our world a better place. Communism and Socialism with the ideal of equality also seems to have completely failed. The only thing that seems to have worked is Democracy, which it is clearly a step in the right direction. Yet even Democracy is being undermined by corrupt, two faced politicians who seem to be incapable of telling the truth. So the message that comes to us from history and the media, is that the world of conflict, hatred and violence we live in is simply human nature and there is nothing we can do about it. The reason why we seem to be incapable of making our world a better place is because we are caught in the trap of a masculine cycle of fear and violence.

We stand on the brink of two possible futures, either a masculine or feminine destiny. These two possibilities come through two very different cycles. The masculine cycle began with the end of the Neolithic age. Somehow women lost control of a handful of men who became very violent. The male cycle probably began with men who find they can obtain power over other people through violence and aggression. Probably at first they were simply outcasts who survived by robbing people moving between towns and villages. Then in time some of these men formed groups and become bandits. They would be joined by other men who would be drawn by the attraction of power over others, through violence. In time these groups would become so large that they were able to take over towns and villages and impose on the people a protection racket. "you give us what we want and we leave you alone". This would be in effect the first taxation. Then different bandit gangs would then start to fight each other for territory. Until one bandit leader got on top and conquered other bandit gang and he would become a king.

The bandits would exploit their power over the people and probably would steal whatever they wanted. As well as rape and kidnap women and use them as sex slaves. Understandably the people would get angry with this behaviour and perhaps rise up and against the bandits. Some of these revolutions would fail and the people would find themselves receiving even worse treatment than before. Other revolutions would succeed but the people will find that even getting rid of the bandits, will not allow them to return to their previous life of peace. If the revolution is led by men they will become as violent as the bandits and will end up behaving the same, once in power. If the revolution is led by women they will become Amazons and still have to learn warfare to defend themselves from attack from other bandits. In the end the Amazons died away probably because violence is not as natural for women as it is for men. So in the end women will be subdued by male violence.

This violence is very similar to what we observe in apes like chimpanzees and the male hamadryas baboons.

As female chimps come into season males start to become attractive to them, but many females can be choosy and only prefer certain males. Males who are not chosen by females counter the females right to choose by aggression and violence, by repetitively attacking the females he wants to mate with. Jane Goodall who has observed this behaviour claims that alpha males train the females he wants to mate with through intimidation and fear. So she will be too frighten to refuse him when he wants to mate with her.

A graphic account of this was observed by the Japanese primatologist Mariko Hiraiwa-Hasegawa. She was observing two chimp communities she called M and K group. One day she discovered the alpha male of M group called Ntologi with four of his side kicks attacking a lone female from K group and her three year old child. With the help of a companion Hiraiwa-Hasegawa attempted to beat the male chimps off by beating them with canes, but the powerful males ignored them. Then her companion threw a rock at the males and this had the effect of making them backing off. (Had the male chimps had instead attacked the two humans they wouldn't of stood a chance against the powerful chimpanzees). The life of the female was saved although she and her child were covered in blood and badly injured. A year later the same female had another child and was again attacked by the Nitologi and his henchmen. This time her baby was eaten alive by them. After this the female defected to M group and mated with her baby's murder. Probably because she couldn't no longer find safety in F group for herself and her children. A post script to this, was that Ntologi himself was later murdered by his second in command, so he could take over the position of the alpha male. While Hiraiwa Hasegawa herself have given up observing chimpanzees because she was so appalled by their behaviour, that she learnt to hate them.

Male hamadryas baboons are also very aggressive. They kidnap females to become part of their harems from a young age and maintain it through continuous threats and intimidation. Usually by biting the back of the necks of his females. Which is a real threat as hamadryas baboons have large razor-sharp canines. So he is capable of killing or bad injure the female if was to bite hard. The males frighten the females so much that they will not stray too far from them, so that even a stare by the male will so frighten the females they will run back to the male. They are so under the control of the male that they will never refuse sex when they are into estrus.

The behaviour of humans in extremely patriarchal societies is very similar. It use to be that the alpha male, the king or local lord, could have as many wives he wanted. Even when Christianity come into force and man were suppose to have only one wife. Many lords still had conjugal rights to all the peasant women working on his land. In places like Sicily, Ethiopia and Eastern Europe it was commonplace up until recently that if a young man wants to marry a girl, with some of his friends he would kidnap her and then raped her. After that there would be social pressure put on the girl to marry her rapist. This was only stopped in Sicily, when one young women in the 1960s was brave enough to take her rapist to court and have him charged with rape. In doing so she had to not only resist social traditions but also the Mafia. So we can see that this behaviour is not far removed from that of the hamadryas baboon.

We can see a contrast in the behaviour of the bonobo. Milwaukee County Zoo had a group of bonobos and they attempted to train them in the same way they train chimpanzees and other animals. The bonobos reacted by becoming extremely non co-operative. They would scream loudly at the zoo keepers and urinate on them if they come into the pen. Then a female keeper took over and she adopted a system of kindness and positive reward. The behaviour of the bonobos changed and they became very co-operative and easy to work with. So it seems that bonobo females will not accept force and intimidation. Yet this is not the attitude of the male bonobos.

In zoos it was found that bonobo males were frequently assaulted by females who would gang up on a single male. To the degree of having fingers and toes bitten off and in one case a female bit off male's penis! It seems that this is normal behaviour in the wild but the differences is that the male can run away, but in a zoo he has no form of escape. So it seems to be normal behaviour for female bonobos gang up and assault lone males to show them, who is the boss. (They also assault male zoo keepers who come into their pen).

Scientists have not been slow to compare primate behaviour with human behaviour. Where domestic violence between men and women is commonplace. In the past in the Western world it was once "normal" for a husband to beat his wife with a stick. In the Islamic world even today a man is "dishonoured" if he cannot dominate his wife by beating her up. In China as late as the 20th century was the tradition of foot binding which left women nearly crippled. Which is very similar to the behaviour of some male chimps who will not only beat up the female he wants to mate with, but cripple her as well, so she is unable to run away.

So sadomasochism is part of the primate sex war between males and females. Males dominate through violence and the female have to become masochistic to be able to stay sane in a life of brutal beatings and rape. Patriarchal societies also enforce the custom of marriage that forces a women stay with a man and breaks up any chance of women creating a powerful sisterhood. Bonobos and other female dominated primates re-enforce the sisterhood through lesbian sex. Which even today is discouraged by patriarchal custom. Female macaque and rhesus monkeys also mount males and rub themselves against them as a sign of dominance over the male. Which is again similar to human behaviour, it seems some men will go to a dominatrix to pay them to bugger them with strap on dildos. Is this a unconscious desire by these men to want women to dominate them once more?

One of the reasons why male chimpanzees and humans continue to use violence and intimidation against females and other males, is because it works. If people and female chimps adopted the attitude of, "Give Me Liberty Or Give Me Death" (Patrick Henry, 1775). Then this behaviour wouldn't be able to continue. Though admittedly his is a lot to ask of any person or creature. Yet again some women have done this. In certain parts of Pakistan and India some mothers will murder their female babies. Some feminists have seen this as a sign of extreme patriarchal brainwashing on women. But other feminists have pointed out that another reason for this could be that these mothers do not want to bring up daughters in the very brutal patriarchal world they live in. Feminists have point out that a women to gives in to a violent husband and cares for him and has his children is betraying the next generation of women. This is because her sons will think it "normal" to beat up their girlfriends or wives while her daughters will think it "normal" to beaten up by men. Also she is allowing his violent genes to be passed on as well. This then allows this behaviour to continue generation after generation. So like the female chimpanzee or hamadryas baboon if she gives into male violence it encourages males to continue to use it. Though it has to be admitted that very few women are able to stand up to male violence on their own. It was only by Feminists setting up Women's Refuses where women subjected to violence could go to, that allowed women to tackle male violence in recent times. This then is the advantage human females have over female chimpanzees, they are better able to communicate with each other and organise resistance to this behaviour.

In extremely patriarchal countries male dominance is enforced by male violence. Not only against women but men also fight each other for supremacy with violence as well. It seems to be the more violent a society becomes the more men dominate it. A example of this is Afghanistan. Up until the 1970s it was a country that had lived in peace for nearly a hundred years. In that time it began to become slowly Westernised, in that the women were allowed education and all the Islamic restrictions against women were slowly eroding away. Then it was invaded by the Soviet Union. Even after the Soviet Union left in the 1980s war still continued between various warlords. The result of over 20 years of war has been that women's rights have been taken away and Afghanistan has now one of the most harshest laws and customs against women. Even the recent invasion by USA hasn't changed the attitudes of brutalised men towards women, and is still a country mostly ruled by violent warlords.

So the masculine cycle is created by male violence. The effect of male violence is to brutalised men and increasing their testosterone levels. While women become more submissive, to counter male violence by appeasing men. Which undermines women's confidence and self-respect.

The antidote for male violence is peace. Like with capitalism the end result of companies competing with each other is a monopoly where one company comes out on top and competition comes to a end. The end results of competition between warring warlords and states is empire. Where one leader ends up coming out on top and imposes peace, by force. This brings about a time of peace where the testosterone levels of men go down as they become less brutalised by the decreasing violence. Unfortunately peaceful countries then become open to invasion by other states who are still fighting among themselves. This is not a problem while they continue to do this but when they become united under one strong leader, this leader becomes a conqueror. Because finding he has a united army of battle harden fighters he will invade peaceful states on its border. This is what happened to China when it was invaded by the Mongols.

In 1206 Genghis Khan united the warring Mongols under one ruler. These men used to fighting among themselves found it easy to conquer other surrounding countries, who had been at peace for many years. The Mongols invaded not only China, but India and Europe as well and ended up with the largest empire known in recorded history. Then Mongols in turn became less aggressive through years of peace. This resulted in them being driven back to their homeland and finally conquered in turn by the Chinese.

It is noticeable that women began to become liberated in Europe and Northern America during the 19th and 20th century during a time of relative peace and stability, after the Napoleonic wars. It is true in this period we did have the American Civil War, the Franco-Prussian war and the First and Second wars all fought on European and North American soil. Yet between these wars we did have years of peace, with generations of people not knowing what it was like to fight in a war. While Switzerland is one of the safest countries in the world which hasn't had a war on its soil for over a hundred years. In the USA the high rate of crime has been blamed on the freely availability of guns available. Yet in Switzerland shooting is a main national sport encouraged by all men having to do national service. In fact Switzerland has one of the most heavily armed populations in the world. Yet it also has one of the lowest crime rates.

So is it a coincide that Switzerland has also managed not to be involved in any wars for the whole of the 20th century? Also at one time Switzerland boasted that they had eliminated poverty in their country. Recently this has returned through the influx of immigrant workers doing low paid work, but it still remains low. So it means that people in Switzerland have not been brutalised by either war or poverty for a long time, which makes it possible for the male population to be armed with guns without the problem of gun crime.

This means that peace can create a feminine cycle. In times of peace men become less aggressive, their testosterone levels go down and are less likely to commit violence against women. As they are no longer being battered by men, women begin the gain confidence and self respect. This is the danger patriarchal religions understood thousands of years ago. This is why the Christian and Islamic religions made laws and customs to restrict female freedoms and encouraged men to assault women. Christian priests encourage men to dominate their wives by beating them. While in the Islamic world even today, a man is "dishonoured" if fails to beat his wife to make her obedient.

In the 19th century many wealthy women in USA campaigned against slavery. Then as they began to understand the legal position of slaves, they were shocked to find that black slaves had more legal rights than did the average women. This started the women's movement in America. Because men were becoming less aggressive and women more confident, men have little resistance to women's demands for equal rights over the next 150 years. What has been striking in the West is that the Feminist movement has been met with very little male violence. Unlike what happens in Islam countries where women who have been brave enough to fight for equal rights, have been murdered, arrested and assaulted.

As women become more free, so do men. A despotic dictatorship is only possible if the dictator can rely on a army of ruthless young men who will obey him and commit violence, murder and torture against anyone who opposes his rule. A leader who cannot find enough young men to commit violence against the people, then has to rule by consent and not violence. This means that the level of male violence in the general population has to decrease to make democracies and women's liberation possible.

So men and women have two very different strategies to gain dominance over the other sex.

The Masculine method is through violence. men simply using their superior size and strength to batter women into submission. On top of this, patriarchal institutions have created laws and customs to keep women in a condition of slavery. As well as creating competitive masculine societies that favours men and not women.

The Feminine method is through co-operation. We can see this clearly with the female bonobo ape whom have created a powerful sisterhood. This has also been the battle cry of many Feminists that, THE SISTERHOOD IS POWERFUL. Unfortunately up until now, women haven't been able to put this into practise to make a noticeable difference.

Many Feminists have criticised their own sex for not making most of the opportunities that at equal opportunities legalisation gives them. This has also been a similar problem for African Americans. People like Malcolm X have complained bitterly that most black Americans have what he called, "A slave mentality". That is to say although slavery was abolished in 1863 nearly a 150 years later African Americans still find themselves the most poorest and deprived group in USA. Although one of the reasons for this, is discrimination by other ethic groups, like white people. The culture of Black people is not very helpful either. For instance there is a real problem of a anti-academic culture among young black men. Where in schools black men who try to study hard are ridiculed and physically attacked by other black men. It seems that for a black man to get ahead he has to be very secretive or very big, strong and violent, to resist bullying by other black young men.

Women have had the same problem. They also had a "slave mentality" but there are signs that they are now overcoming this. Up until the 1980s, young men were always ahead of young women academically. Girls would be ahead of boys up to about the age of puberty, then girls academic performances would drop away and boys would overtake girls in getting more places in college and universities. Yet in more recent times there has been a slow change where girls are now studying harder than boys at school right through to university. The result is that in school leaving exams in 2002 in Britain there is now a 9% gap in favour of girls and this gap is slowly growing every year.

It also seems that boys are now having problems. The anti academic culture of young black men is spreading to young white boys as well. Where anti-learning laddish culture is being blamed for the poor academic results of all young men.

The result of this is that some commentators are claiming that, "the future is female". The idea is that if more women have better academic qualifications than men, they will have more of the top jobs in the future. This assumes that women will also be able to cope with the very "macho" and aggressive culture of politics and business. For this reason many women who want careers go to assertiveness classes. Which is probably what many women do need, but to go down this road too far can be self defeating for women. This can be seen in the case of the hyena. It seems that females as they develop in their mother's womb they are bathed in male hormones resulting that when they are born the young females have clitorises as large as a male penis and are even more aggressive than males. This aggression allows female hyenas to dominate the males.

The dominance by females benefits their offspring in that Hyena cubs have a far lower starvation rate than other carnivores. So it is a big help in allowing the hyena to survive difficult times.

Some modern sportswomen have taken steroids to boost strength and the side effect has been to become very aggressive as well. So women don't really have to go to assertiveness classes to survive in the patriarchal market place, all they have to do is take steroids. Like female hyenas they can become as aggressive and as assertive as men. The only problem with this, is that do we want to live in a world where everyone is so aggressive? The normal patriarchal society is bad enough with 50% of the population behaving like irresponsible idiots. To have a full 100% would be even worse. Yet this doesn't have to be the only way, there is another choice. In business there is talk about co-operation rather than competition. Business studies have shown that competition within a company can make it very inefficient. This is because if you have staff competing with each other for power and status, they are unlikely to co-operate with each other. This will result in office politics where people with attempt to undermine other members of the staff and even sabotage their efforts. So some businesses want to try to eliminate all this, and get people to co-operate rather than compete. I don't have to tell you that, it has been found that female staffs are far better at this than men.

Another quantum leap could be made in politics as we can see through the leadership of Princess Diana. The genius of Princess Diana was that she was able to portray herself in the media as a genuine caring and loving person. Something any politician or spin-doctor would give their right arm to have. Although she didn't have any political power, in the way she was able to use and manipulate the media made her a very powerful person. Which she used to further her own agenda, to create a more caring and loving world, where possible.

From the very beginning when she became a royal she responded to people in a very caring way. Now this is not unusual with famous people in the media, but she put it across in a way that no one doubted that it was genuine. To the degree not even her critics doubted this. So this made her from the start the most popular royal, and gave her worldwide fame. At first she was just content with this, but then she was to learn a trick from another royal, Princess Ann.

In the early 1980s there was a great famine in the Sudan, but the media ignored this famine so the people in the West were unaware of the millions of people dying of starvation in the Sahara desert region. Princess Ann as president of the Save The Children Fund visited Sudan and of course the media went with her, because they wanted a story on her failing marriage. Then reporters personally saw the great suffering going on in the area, and as the result of this visit the media all over the world began to report on the famine. This in turn got the Band-Aid movement off the ground. Resulting in millions of pounds being donated to try and save these people. So likewise, Princess Diana began use her celebrity status to highlight causes she believed in. One of the most important acts she done was change people's opinions on Aids epidemic. When Aids first started to spread in the West, people greatly feared it and believed that they could catch this disease by touching people with this disease. Also as it was mostly homosexual men who got Aids, this increased homophobia, and some extreme Christians were suggesting that Aids was the way God was punishing deviant acts like homosexuality. The media in Britain encouraged these stories and I can remember reading one scare story in the British newspaper, The Sun, suggesting that people could catch Aids from public toilet seats, if a homosexual man sat there previously.

At the height of the homophobia frenzy whipped up by the British press, Princess Diana fearlessly met this hysteria head on. She visited a hospital with Aids patients inside and talked to and shook hands with patients dying of Aids. Pictures of her doing his was in the newspapers and on the TV and in one stroke she had given homosexual men Royal approval and destroyed the myth that you could catch Aids by touching someone with this disease.

She was later to do the same with leprosy as in many part of the world people still believe it is possible to catch leprosy but touching a leper. She again appeared on TV touching shaking the hand of a leper and helped overcome prejudice against lepers. Charitable organisations were finding that if Princess Diana publicly gave them support of them, she was able to generate large amounts of contributions for their cause. So they became very aware of her power to help the causes she believed in.

She also started to move into politics. In the 1980s in Britain there was high unemployment as well and an increasing number of homeless people living on the streets. The right-wing press in Britain was whipping up a hate campaign against unemployed people, claiming that they were scroungers and work-shy. Princess Diana showed the world clearly where her sympathies laid by again visiting and talking to homeless people. Though by this time the media was now wise to her tactics and wasn't so keen on reporting her doing this. So she didn't get the media coverage in this that she normally expects. The British media also tried to start a hate campaign against Princess Diana but the newspapers that attempted to attack her found that they were unable to dent her popularity with the common people.

She was to move more into politics towards the end of her life. Charitable organisations had for years campaigned again the production and use of land mines, but had never got anywhere with this. In all conflicts all over the world countless land mines were buried indiscriminately, then after the war the land mines would be left in the ground with no one knowing were they were. So the civil population living in the area would continue to be killed and maimed by treading on these mines. Princess Diana then decided to get involved, and simply by visiting a area where land mines had been buried she focused the world's media on this problem and got governments all over the world to take notice.

She was warned by conservative politicians not to get involved in politics. She herself was to claim before she died, that she feared she would be killed, and when it did happen the circumstances of her death was very suspicious, suggested a government cover up.

The great emotional effect of her death on people was immense, which was to surprise everyone. The reason for this is I believe is that in a uncaring world, where selfish and corrupt industrial and political leaders are commonplace. Princess Diana was one of the few people in establishment who showed that she genuinely cared and loved people. So in the very large numbers of people that mourned the death of Princess Diana gave a clear message to the politicians that the people wanted to live in a more caring world. This was picked up by the British Prime Minster who stated that people loved Diana because she genuinely cared. But he didn't learn from this himself and his actions have since shown he is a normal selfish and uncaring politician.

Another women was the have the same effect before Princess Diana and this was Evita Peron. It would be easy to be cynical and say that she was only a the mistress and later wife of a South American dictator. But the emotion effect she was to have on

Argentina, the country where she was the first lady, shows she was more than this.

Like Princess Diana the political influence she had was very limited. Yet unlike any other Argentina politician, before or since, she was able to show to the people that she genuinely cared. The people respond greatly to her and although she was unable to do a lot for the people of Argentina she came across and a person who really believed in what she said. With her early death, people showed clearly how they felt about her at her funeral, and this gave a message to the politicians that people do want to live in a caring society. Something I'm afraid the Argentina politicians ignored.

The story of Evita Peron was given publicity by the stage musical Evita written by Andrew Lloyd Webber and Tim Rice. The genius of this musical was it portrayed clearly the emotion effect Evita had on the people of Argentina.

Unfortunately when it was also make into a film the producers and directors had little understanding of what the story was about. They put a pop star in the title role who didn't have either the singing voice or acting ability to do justice to the music and lyrics.

To a lesser degree the same thing happened with Mary Robertson the first women President of Southern Ireland. Although the Irish Presidency has little political power Mary Robertson was able to present herself as a caring person. She became so popular that when she retired, nearly all the candidates to replace her were women. After Mary Robertson's performance few people were interested in voting for a male.

With the rise of Feminism in the 20th century some female politicians have risen to become leaders of countries like Margaret Thatcher and Indira Gandhi. Both of these politicians have shown clearly to the world that a woman can successfully rule a country. Unfortunately both women more or less behaved like a male ruler and didn't show the caring side of women. Though to be fair to both women, they came leaders of very patriarchal parties and had they behaved like caring women it is unlikely they would of became leaders of their parties and country.

I believe the next step for powerful women is to have a female leader of a country with the political skill of a Margaret Thatcher or Indira Gandhi. Yet also with the ability to express there caring nature in the same way Princess Diana had. So that by becoming very popular through her caring nature she is able to push forward widespread reforms to the patriarchal system.

Once we start to have compassionate and powerful women leaders of countries, very few people will want to vote for male politicians. Male political leaders have had thousands of years to demonstrate they can be compassionate and responsible leaders. Yet very few in all that time can be said to be like this. (Apart from Nelson Mandela I can't think of any genuinely caring male politician). They had their chance and completely blew it.

13

Hostage to Fortune

What is very apparent in a patriarchal society is the lack of love of love and compassion. The prototype of the patriarchal society comes instincts of primates like the chimpanzee or hamadryas baboon where the males threaten and batter females into submission. This is not the action of animals that are capable of loving others. The same is true for men who will rape and assault women to keep them submissive.

This attitude permeates the whole of patriarchal societies. The ruler who decides to conquer neighbouring states clearly has no love for the people in country he wants to conquer, and in fact he probably hates them. He also has no love for this own people, as he must know a war will inflict death and hardship on them as well. Likewise the rich, who exploit the poor and force people to work in sweatshops for poor wages, have no love for the people they employ.

For centuries we have been ruled by uncaring leaders who have shown very little compassion for the people they rule. It is true in the west their has been a improvement where welfare reforms have allowed unemployment pay, state pensions and free hospital care for the poor. Yet these are something the workers have had to fight for and we can see today many politician are looking for ways to do away with these benefits. Because their masters, the rich and wealthy, are complaining they are not getting enough!

Patriarchy is hell for both women and men. We can see this by the number of people who are addicted to alcohol, drugs, (both legal in illegal), gambling and even food and work. Somehow most of us are looking for ways to blot out the reality of our lives. This is because patriarchy only benefits the alpha men and even they have to watch their backs, for fear of others who want their power and wealth. Men have coped with this hell by becoming totally selfish, so he doesn't have to care for anyone but himself. This makes it possible for him to protect himself by being aggressive and even violent towards others. Women on the other hand cannot use this method because they have a maternal instinct, which makes them care for children. So many women to cope with the hell of patriarchy go to the opposite extreme and care for everyone except themselves. By not caring for themselves they are not hurt and can put up with all the physical and mental abuse metered out by men. Which means most women have had to become harden masochists to stay sane in a traditional patriarchal society.

In Jean Liedloff's Book "The Continuum Concept", she describes living among a South American jungle with a tribe where conflict, anger, hatred and violence was unknown. She contrasted this "Garden of Eden" existence with our modern world of stress, where many people need alcohol, nicotine, anti-depression tablets, as well as illegal drugs just to get them through the day. But she didn't explain fully the reason for how this "Garden of Eden" existence came into being.

She said more in a workshop she conducted in London as she explained to us that there were other tribes in the same area who did frequently have wars with other tribes. She implicated that these wars were conducted in the same spirit as we have football games, except that people did get killed. This is also confirmed in studies done on Stone-Age tribes in New Guinea.

In one incident in the 1960s, anthropologists observed a battle between two tribes that was called off because it started to rain! It seems that the warriors were worried that the rain might make their war paint run! Yet this violence was enough to change the nature of the tribe so unlike the non-violent tribes they did have, hierarchical customs, laws and taboos. While the women were made second-class citizens because they weren't warriors.

This then presents a mystery. If we as human beings did once live in a stress free world of non violence that is not only shown in Jean Liedloff's book but also in the archaeology of Neolithic cities and towns. Why did we voluntary move from a stress free world of peace to that of violence and stress?

In our modern world we are unaware that it is possible to create a stress free communities where conflict and violence are unknown. But the same cannot be said of the Indian tribes studied by Jean Liedloff, where non-violence tribes live alongside violent tribes. So the people of these tribes do have a choice of living a free, non-violent and stress free existence or living in a oppressive and violent community. So why would anyone voluntary choose the latter?

The purpose of any competitive game whether it is just a game of football or a tribal war, is to be a winner. It seems that the fleeting ego boost of becoming a winner is enough for men to want to risk their lives in a tribal war. Also in this system there are other ways of gaining an ego gratification. The chief has the ego satisfaction of knowing he has power over all other members of his tribe. While all the members of the tribe align themselves in a hierarchical system where although they know other members of the tribe are above them in the pecking order. They still have the ego satisfaction of knowing others are below them. As women and children are the lowest in this system even the lowest ranking man has the ego satisfaction that he is still above them.

So it seems that the rewards of ego satisfaction is enough for men to want to move from a non-violent, stress free world to that of a stressful and violent patriarchal system. As this system developed, men began to capture other men in war and forced them to become slaves. This became another way of gain ego satisfaction because the victors had the power of life and death over their slaves and so can force them do whatever they want. Sometimes this went to the extreme and developed into sadism where the victors enjoyed the power of being able to inflict fear, pain and suffering onto their captives.

This then becomes a problem for the male slaves because they were now at the very bottom of the pecking order with no obvious way of gaining ego satisfaction. The slave then has a choice of either hating his master and seeks ways to escape. So he looks for ways to get even with those who oppress them. Sometimes this was possible like in the case of Spartacus who led the most successful slave uprising in the history of Rome, (71-73 BC), but this was only a rare success for most slaves. The other option was for the slave to identify themselves with their masters so they could bask in the reflected glory of the success of their owners. Also the identification with their masters also encouraged the slaves to compete with each other to become the master's favourite. (Something a sensible master would encourage). So it is from slavery that masochistic behaviour starts to appear, because it was only from masochism that a slave could gain any ego gratification. This then means that the master had a even greater ego boost in that he has forced men into slavery through violence. Yet in return he receives from many of them great loyalty and devotion. While the men who don't give him this, he has the sadistic pleasure of being able to torture and murder. So the invention of slavery also created sadomasochist desires within people as the only way to stay sane in such a barbaric system.

The path of the women into sadomasochism is different because she has a maternal instinct. Nature has designed women to give unconditional love and devotion to their children, because without the commitment of females, to care and protect their offspring, most animal species would become extinct. This is very true of the human species where the newborn baby is completely helpless and can take up to 20 years before it is fully-grown. This means that the maternal instinct in human mothers has to be very strong for the human race to survive. Because of this, it is commonplace that most women find themselves spending their whole lives caring for their children, grandchildren, their aged parents and their husbands.

When men began to move out of paradise into violent competitive games like war. Women would have resisted this move because they wouldn't want their sons or lovers being injured or killed. So this would of started a battle of the sexes that for a long time women seemed to have won. We can see this in Neolithic sites all over the world. Then this changed about

5,000 years ago when suddenly in the Bronze age archaeologists were finding cities and town full of weapons of war, fortifications and images of violence and conquest.

In the Neolithic sites archaeologists have found a predominance of feminine imagery. To the degree that it is accepted that people then worshipped female deities. Which also suggests that women then were then the dominant sex. They perhaps had to be if they were resisting men's desire for competition and war. To do this they had to find ways to control and dominate men and this was probably done through mothers brainwashing their sons. Yet in the end this failed and men began to compete with each other creating wars and dominating women through violence. Women still continued to resist and even fought back as we can see in the case of the Amazons, but in the end men won and began to dominate the world.

Women then found themselves at the bottom of the hierarchical system in a situation of slavery. So like male slaves, women they had no option but to but to adapt and become masochistic. Though the feminine masochism was different to male masochism in one important factor. Masculine masochism was a way a man could gain ego satisfaction by identifying himself with his oppressor. While feminine masochism was simply an extension of women's maternal instinct. Through her maternal feelings she could love her children unconditionally so she leant to extend this to love all men in the same way, even if men were now taking sadistic pleasure in hurting and humiliating women.

This then meant that men were gaining a even greater ego boost because they now could abuse women as much as they liked and yet only receive unconditional love in return.

This seems to be the case over the last two thousand years where it became commonplace in all relationships between men and women, the husband became the dominant sadistic bully while the woman became the submissive and masochistic wife. While any person that didn't fit this stereotype was considered to be "unnatural". Even up to the 1960s psychologists were claiming that all women were masochists. (Something no psychologist would dare claim today).

Yet if it was hell for both men and women to begin to live in a patriarchal world, it also can be hell to come back out of patriarchy.

There is a story that the great German philosopher, Friedrich Wilhelm Nietzsche became insane when he saw a donkey being beaten by a man. On a superficial level this story sounds silly and is used by Nietzsche's detractors to make him look foolish. Yet on a deeper level it shows a problem that all men have: Most normal men, if suddenly faced with feelings that give him real distress, like seeing a animal suffer, may start to worry that he is going "soft". But someone like Nietzsche being highly intelligent, self-aware and imaginative clearly saw the implication of this. He understood that once a man begins to feel empathy with others, he is at the mercy of a bottomless pit of human suffering.

Another famous philosopher Jean-Paul Sartre had the same problem because he once commented that,

The other is hell.

Indicating that he also had difficulty with his feelings of empathy for others. The problems with empathy is brought out in the poem, *No Man Is An Island* by John Donne,(1571-1631) with his famous line,

And therefore never send to know for whom the bell tolls, It tolls for thee.

The bells were tolling for a man who was about to be executed. Now we can react to a scene of execution in two ways. We can watch it as a spectator sport, which many people have done when we had public executions, and be very glad it is happening to someone else. The understanding of why people like to witness suffering comes from a scientific theory on why people enjoy slapstick humour. It is because watching people who are foolish or have misfortune makes us feel better, to know someone else is more foolish than ourselves, or has had greater misfortune. So these people can feel better about themselves by watching another person being hanged because they know someone else is worse off than themselves. The alternative is to feel empathy with the person who has suffered misfortune and that can be very painful.

Which is what John Donne wrote about in his famous poem. This is supported by a saying on love by Francis Bacon. (1561-1626) Philosophers don't normally talk much about love, but his remark about love goes to the heart of the matter.-

He that hath wife and children hath given hostages to fortune, for they are impediments to great enterprises, either of virtue or mischief.

In other words if you care nothing for others you are free to do as you like, because if you care then that freedom is gone, because you have to think about the needs of others. This is something modern women know a lot about. It they have children, the family takes priority over her career and anything else, she may want to do. The other is not hell for a man who cares only for himself, or for a woman who cares for everyone, except herself. The other can only become hell, when people begin to feel love for both themselves and others at the same time. Because the needs what you want for yourself clashes with the needs of what others want of you. This then will create inner conflict.

A man who is totally selfish and cares nothing for others can be very strong and "macho". This allows great conquerors like Alexander the Great, Napoleon Bonaparte and Hitler to start wars with other countries and be unconcerned and even unaware of the suffering they inflicting on thousands or even millions of other people. In the second world war the Germans had no problem in recruiting young men to be concentration camp guards, while the allies had no problems in recruiting airmen to bomb German cities day and night, killing millions of women and children. This behaviour is only possible by men who are not in contact with the feelings and suffering of others. I remember once reading about a famous pilot in the Battle of Britain. He had shot down many German planes and had been excited whenever he had done this. Yet in one instance he had shot down a German fighter and had got close to it while it was going down in flames and could see clearly the pilot struggling to get out of the burning plane. He was then shocked to realise there were real human beings like himself in the planes he had shot down. It may sound crazy that a man who is fighting a war didn't realise that in the process he was killing other people. Yet the reason for this would be that when men start to be aware of the feelings of others they have to go into denial to continue to enjoy "macho" pursuits like fighting wars. Once a man realises he is killing and hurting other people like himself. Then war and violence become very difficult for him. Men who enjoy watching violent films are doing exactly the same thing. The pleasure of watching say a very violent James Bond film is only possible why you don't connect this in terms of the horrendous suffering going on, if is was played out in real life. In this way the spectators in the Ancient Roman games were more honest than people today who watch violent films. At least the Roman people were not divorced from the violence they saw. Where real people were being killed and maimed. Today we watch fake violent film, yet the enjoyment of violence is still the same.

Women are less protected by the reality of the suffering around her because of her maternal instinct, which teaches her to care for others. This can make it automatic that other people's feelings become her feelings. The masculine on the other hand is individual and in its purest form. So the truly "macho" man is only aware of his own feeling and totally unaware of the feelings of others. This is why it is possible for patriarchal leaders to declare war on other countries and be unaffected by the great suffering that a war will cause.

But many men find they can learn to love and care for others and find this so difficult that they will cut off their feelings for others. Resulting in some caring and loving man suddenly turn into a cold and uncaring monster These men, in learning how to have empathy with others, discovered that empathy was very joyful and easy when they have empathy with someone who was very happy. Their happiness became his happiness. Then when they find that the person they are in love with were also able to be very unhappy then they have a problem. The other person's unhappiness immediately became their unhappiness. So the solution to this problem was is to run away from other until they have got over it.

I know personally of a young woman who became convinced that her father hated her as a child because whenever she cried he would immediately become very angry and sarcastic with her.

Yet in many other ways he did show he was a caring man. Again it was clear to me the father couldn't cope with his daughter when she become distressed.

What many women are discovering today is that they find men who are a real "Dr Jekyll and Mr Hyde". These men seem to be very caring and loving and then suddenly will turn on them and become uncaring monsters. Men who begin to learn how to have empathy with others will naturally only want the joyful part of empathy. Where it becomes a nightmare is when the person he has empathy with becomes unhappy and has no control over the situation because it is another person's unhappiness. Some husbands in this situation then can become very angry with their wives and children. He is telling himself, "why should I have to be unhappy because they are unhappy". This can result in many men physically attacking wives and children simply because they express unhappiness. Certainly there have been many court cases where a man has killed his own baby because the baby was crying too much. While the wife or girlfriend protests that she cannot understand it because he is normally a very kind and caring man.

Women themselves have a similar problem. It was easy in the patriarchal age for a woman to have empathy with everyone else while she didn't care for herself. Now in recent years women are beginning to find they have real problems in empathy with others, when they begin to be aware of their own feelings. It can be wonderful for women when they become aware of their own happiness as well that of others. Before they were always happy when their husbands and children were happy. Now by being aware of their own happiness, they can become even more happy and joyful. Unfortunately when things go wrong they can also be aware of their own misery.

In the past if a woman had a husband who wanted to spend all his money on drink and gambling, she might fight him for enough money to feed and cloth their children. But if she ended up with nothing it wasn't a problem for her, because the needs of her husband and children came first. But women today find that if they end up with nothing it is a real problem for them, because they are aware of their own needs as well. So they find themselves in a "no-win" position if they live with a irresponsible man. They are able to be strong enough to say clearly to their husbands: "No, you cannot spend all our money on drink, gambling, cars and computer games". Yet she can be still be unhappy and feel guilty about denying her husband what he wants. However if she were to give in to these feeling and give him what he wants and deny herself, she would also feel unhappy. It is no wonder that heterosexual women complain today that with men, "you can't live with them and you can't live without them".

It can get even more difficult than this: What women find wonderful about having a caring husband is that she finds she can make him happy by being happy herself. So a virtuous cycle can be created, she can feed off his happiness and he can feed off her happiness. Unfortunately the opposite can be true. Also with a caring man she might find that if she is unhappy it makes him unhappy, so she can feel guilty about being unhappy. This can then create a vicious cycle where both partners feed off each other's unhappiness, making the situation worse and worse.

For this reason many women having had a relationship with a caring man, will leave him to go back to a more selfish man. She knows that with a "strong" "macho" and selfish man he will not be concerned about her unhappiness. So the relationship cannot go into a vicious cycle where the unhappiness of both partners will strongly affect the other. Unfortunately what she will find is that it is impossible to change a very selfish man. If he has a behaviour pattern that makes her unhappy, like spending all the money they have on himself or treating the children badly. She is totally unable to influence him in any way, because he doesn't care if what he wants to do will make others unhappy. But a man, who is able to feel empathy with her, knows full well that if his partner is unhappy he will be unhappy. He then has a powerful reason to do all he can to make his wife or girlfriend happy.

So heterosexual women have two choices: They can have a man who is able to love and empathy with them. But they find he has real problems if they become unhappy. Or women stick to very selfish men, who are able to cope with women becoming unhappy, and will probably be more helpful in this situation. The downside is that there is nothing a woman can do, if he wants to behave in a way that makes her unhappy. She cannot appeal to his better nature because it is unlikely that he has one.

It would be very easy if we could give a quick and easy solution, as you see with many of these "self help" books., but real life is not like this. Even today if a woman gives birth to say a mentally retarded child, it is fairly normal for that woman to devote her whole life to caring for it, even into adulthood. On the other hand it would be very unusual for a man to do this. He might help his wife look after a mentally retarded child, but he would be very unlikely to take full responsibility and back off when the going gets too tough.

So we can see that compared with women men are just beginners at learning how to love and care for others. They haven't been exposed to thousands if not millions of years of a powerful maternal instinct that makes women want to care for children, animals and men. Many men today may have strong desires to love and care for others. But when they have to put these feelings into practice and face the misery, unhappiness and sacrifice these feelings cause, they often back off.

For this reason many men have become very frightened of empathy with others. They do not want to be at the mercy of other people's feelings, so they practice being very hard "macho" men. The same time women are finding it hard to learn to love themselves while loving others. A woman who is learning to love herself finds that she is always betraying herself by putting the needs of children and men before her own. She might then choose to learn to hate men and even learn to hate children, seeing it as a way to prevent her from sacrificing herself for others.

We as a human race are standing at a crossroads. We have before us two choices; one is of a far better future than we could dream is possible for the human race. The other is a far worse future, if that is possible. In the patriarchal age we only had one half of the human race behaving totally selfishly with no regard for the feelings of others. If in the future men continue to resist empathy because they do not wish to feel the suffering of others. While at the same time women continue to learn how to love themselves by hating other people. Then it means that all men and women will be fearing and hating each other. In the patriarchal age men mostly killed each other as well as women and children in wars because they feared and hated each other. But at least it was only 50% of the population doing this. It women were to join in and learn hate and violence from men then the whole of human kind would be behaving in this insane way. In such a situation the human race would quickly become extinct.

The alternative to this is that men stop resisting their desires to give empathy with others, and women do not go down the path of learning to love themselves by hating others. That is to say they stick to learning how to love themselves and love others at the same time. The positive thing about this all is that it gives human kind a far better future. The suffering caused in the patriarchal age was caused by the dominant sex, (men) being unable to care and empathize with others. With men in the future learning how to empathize, and women not suppressing their ability to do this. It means both sexes will be motivated to create a far more loving and caring world.

14

The Denial of Our True Nature

We also learn from primate studies is that the human race has two possible futures.

1. We can behave like the chimpanzee and live in a very violent society dominated by men
2. We can behave like the bonobo and live in a peaceful world dominated by women.

So what are the fors and againsts both types of societies?

I suppose the attraction of our present patriarchal world is that it is exciting and interesting. We can see this from the type of TV programmes, films and book that people read and watch. Many entertaining stories are about conflict and violence. This then suggests that human beings enjoy violence and conflict because this is what they find entertaining. The problem is that many people who do enjoy these things on TV do not necessary want to experience the same thing in real life.

People who enjoy violence have to some degree go into a state of denial to do this. When I was a boy I was very interested in Naval history. One of the most exciting sea battles I read about was the battle of Midway during the Second World War, and I fantasised about being a dive-bomber pilot and destroy an enemy aircraft carrier in a dive bomb attack. Yet I could only do this through ignorance and denial. If I were to think about it deeply then this would ruin the fun and excitement of the fantasy. Denial like this can come in many forms. -

1. Only think in terms of destroying an aircraft carrier as just a ship. I didn't think about the thousands of men they

would die is such an attack, or for that matter the parents who will lose their sons, of the wives who will become widows or the children who will lose their fathers. Nor did I think how some of these men might die. Aircraft carriers carry large amounts of aircraft fuel so many men will die by being burnt alive when this fuel explodes. Other men might have time to jump into the sea, but a fleet under attack cannot stop to pick up survivors, so these men will more than likely be left in the sea, to die a slow death of exposure, thirst and starvation, or to die a quicker death of being eaten by sharks. Some men might even survive and be picked up but will have to live with both the physical and mental scars of such an experience. While other men might become blind or disfigured through being burnt, or loose limbs and spend the rest of their lives as cripples. The trauma of experiencing all your friends and comrades dying terrible death can also leave a man emotionally crippled for the rest of his life.

2. If men do start to think about men dying then you can de-humanise them by saying they are the enemy and deserve to die because they are "evil". This is what happens in ALL wars the justification of war is that the other side is bad or evil. So you then have to deny that that the enemy are simply human beings like yourself.

So denial is needed to make war possible. One of my heroes as a boy was the Duke of Wellington (1769-1852) or Arthur Wellesley as he was known before coming a duke. There as many reason why even now I see him as a great general. In an age when a general would expect to lose more men through disease and exposure than battle, he looked after his men and made sure they were properly fed and sheltered. Also in was common practice then for armies to "live of the land". Which in practice means stealing food from the local population. In the Peninsular wars Wellesley made sure his men were fed by food brought from England, in this way he didn't upset the local population. He also took pride in the fact he done his best to win battles with as few causalities as possible. He was also seen to become visibly upset over the deaths of his men. Yet in spite of the way he cared for his troops he also referred to them as the, "scum of the Earth". At first sight this seems to be a paradox. Of a general through his actions showed that he cared about his men, yet referred to them as scum. Yet a bigger paradox is a general who cared about his men at all! After all this is what war is all about, to order your men to die and to kill the enemy. To have a job of a military leader means you cannot afford to care for your troops because if did you do you wouldn't order them into battle to die.

What made Wellesley a great general was the complexity and paradox of his feelings. The caring side of Wellesley made it possible for him to ensure as few of his men didn't die of disease, exposure or in battle, while his contempt of his men allowed him to order them into battle to die. This meant he led armies, which had high morale, who inflicted greater causalities on the enemy than on themselves. Which is the way you win battles. Because a general who doesn't care about his men at all, will also not care about the causality rate and can lose battles through running out of men. While a man who was a more caring of others than Arthur Wellesley wouldn't of become a soldier in the first place, as they wouldn't of want to order men to die.

In other words it is denial of any feelings for others that makes war possible. The same is true for poverty. Poverty in only a reality in our world while the majority of the people think that the very unequal societies we live in is perfectly acceptable. Or believe that there is no alternative to inequality. Because after all Communism was a total failure in creating an equal society.

Yet as we have seen through Neolithic excavations that war, violence and inequality is not inevitable for human society. It is only inevitable while we keep on allowing very competitive and aggressive men rule our world.

What needs to be questioned is the idea that the "macho" way of doing things is the only way. And for people to be aware there is an alternative to this and that is the feminine way.

When putting forward this proposal people have asked me, "so what would you do with a person like Hitler". In dealing with a dictator who wants to conquer the whole of Europe and perhaps the world, there was no choice but to go to war with him. But the question should be, how extreme political party like the Nazi came to power in a country like Germany? This happened because the Allies try to punish Germany by making it pay for the cost of the First World War. Causing widespread poverty in Germany and fuelling discontent and hatred for the Allies. In the 1930s it was a toss up whether Germany became an extreme left wing Communist country or an extreme right wing country. In the end the extreme right won out. So in was "macho" method of punishment that created an extreme "macho" leader like Hitler.

The "macho" way is to deal with violence with violence and to be fair in the short term this seems to work. In the long term it keeps on fuelling resentment. As we see in case like Northern Ireland, Israel, and the Balkans. Also the "macho" way is to deal with crime is through punishment. You deal with criminals by putting them into prison to punish them, and no one asks the question, what causes a person to become a criminal? The reason this question is not asked is because the vast majority of criminals come from people who live in poverty. This then puts into question our very competitive societies of winners and losers. Where, "the winner takes it all" and the losers get nothing.

The very competitive nature of men is what creates our world of conflict, war, poverty and suffering. And this is what both men are women need to understand.

Women in there own quiet ways are making a difference. For instance as mentioned earlier, back in the early 19th century a wealthy Quaker women Elizabeth Fry visited a women's prison in London. What she saw there horrified her, where prisoners lived in squalor and some even starved to death because they were unable to pay for food. She then used all her wealthy contacts and influence in the Quaker movement to get something done. She started to educate the prisoners and put in the minds of people that prisoners need to be reformed and not punished. This to me is a clear message of the feminine way of doing things.

The problem is that as far as the general public knows the "macho" way is the ONLY way to get things done. This is because the "macho" way is so simple and easy. "If you have a problem, you go in and kick ass", which I have said, in the short term it seems to work. The feminine way of trying to come to grips with the roots of the problem is far more complex. Because we have to see all people as human beings like ourselves and not de-humanise people we fear, by condemning them as bad or evil. In other words you nurture and care for people and not compete against them and punish them for being losers.

The feminine way was once the way human being lived their lives back in the Neolithic age. Then just just a hand full of men created a plague of violence.

These men found you could get your own way through violence and intimidation. In doing so they stole from and traumatised whole communities. In the process they brutalised other men whom in turn also became violent and uncaring of others. This became a plague that swept the whole planet as brutalised men conquered peaceful matriarchal communities and brutalised the people, and taught the men to be macho.

Yet we don't have to continue the make the same mistakes that were made five thousand years ago. The foundation of patriarchy is a whole list of denials.

1. The denial of men having feelings for others.
2. The denial of women respecting and caring for themselves.
3. The denial that war is total insanity.
4. The denial of the widespread poverty and injustice of our world.
5. The denial of the archaeological findings of the Neolithic age.
6. The denial of field studies of the bonobo ape.
7. The denial of the Aquatic ape theory.
8. The denial of the Gaia Hypothesis.
9. The denial of the feminine.
10. The denial of any alternative to patriarchy.
11. The denial that you cannot overcome violence with more violence.
12. The denial that you cannot reform people through punishment.

13. The denial that competition taken to the extreme leads to violence, warfare, poverty and injustice.
14. The denial that aggression leads to fear, hatred, revenge and suffering.
15. The denial that our male leaders do a really terrible job of ruling our world.
16. The denial that if women could do far better jobs, if they don't try to behave like men.
17. The denial that it is possible to live in a caring world of love and compassion.

All these denials and the propaganda that men are doing a wonderful job in ruling our planet, keeps patriarchy going. Not only that, patriarchal denials are a danger to our planet. Back in the 19th century scientists pointed out that if industry keeps on pumping greenhouse gases into the atmosphere it will warm up the Earth. This was totally ignored by businessmen and politicians. Then in the 1950s scientists had the technology to measure the gases in the atmosphere and could prove that industry was increasing the CO2 levels in the biosphere. Again they were ignored and when environmentalist took up this cause, industry employed other scientists to refute this claim. It was only in the 1980s when there was overwhelming evidence that the Earth was warming up that politicians acknowledged there was a problem. Yet this doesn't make a lot of difference because even though they have had "Earth summits" to tackle global warming, very little has been done. Simply because, to do something about this problem would undermine the profit margins of large international corporations like oil companies, but then as capitalists will tell you, "it is the bottom line is all that counts". So it seems that profits are even more important than the future of the human race.

The mass extinction's in the last Ice Age was caused by rapid climate change. Heating up the atmosphere with Greenhouse gases will have exactly the same effect. Signs of this has been already seen with the Sahara desert marching south at a very rapid rate. Charities like Band Aid have tried to help, but nothing has been done about the underlining cause. It is unfortunately that drought caused by global warming has first effected poor and powerless third world countries in the Sahara region where it can be ignored by the rest of the world. Years of famine in the most powerful nations in the world, namely North America or Europe would of made a big difference and you would soon see action being taken over global warming, if it happened there. Though in the near future it is more likely to be flood that will affect these countries.

The fact that the ice around Antarctica is melting at a rapid rate doesn't seem to worry anyone. Even though when the ice on the Antarctic continent itself begins to melt, we will see rapid rises in sea levels, flooding coastal towns and cities.

It seems that in our patriarchal world we have become so adapt at denial, and care so little about the suffering of others like in the Sahara region. We are not going to do anything about it until there is some worldwide catastrophe that affects us all. Then it is going to be too late to do anything.

15

The Sisterhood is Powerful

We are supposed to be an intelligent animal with FREE WILL. As such we are suppose to be masters or mistresses of our own destiny. If this is true, then we are capable collectively of using our intelligence and our ability to choose to create a far better future for us all.

In the past we have not used our intelligence properly and as such have made very bad choices. We have somehow allowed ourselves drift into a world of conflict, hatred, violence and suffering. The sign a intelligence animal is being able to learn from its mistakes and correct them. If we claim we cannot use our intelligence to create a better world for ALL PEOPLE, then we have to revise any idea that we are a intelligence self motivating animal.

Which might be true, after all war must be the most stupidest way to settle differences between countries. Also with all the power of technology we have today, yet we are incapable of using it to prevent millions of our own species die every year from starvation every year. This is not only criminal but shows a real lack of intelligence or our part as well.

If we want to claim we are an intelligent animal then war, crime, poverty and malnutrition cannot possibly exist in our world. As an intelligent animal we are allowed to make mistakes but the sign of intelligence is the ability to learn from them and correct them. To continue to make the same mistakes generation after generation for thousands of years is certainly not a sign of intelligence. It is only very unintelligent animals that are driven by inappropriate instincts which to do things against its own self-interest. We can see this in the case of the Cold War where we nearly went extinct, and it is possible we might still do this through global warming and rapid climate change.

This means that "mankind" cannot have it both ways. Men cannot claim that they are the most intelligent animal on this earth and yet create a world of suffering. It is not an option to say, nothing can be done about war, crime and poverty, if we want to think of ourselves as a intelligent, problem solving, animal.

Clearly war, violence and poverty are caused by man's aggressive and competitive instincts. Now these bellicose instincts may be appropriate in animals like bulls, stags and lions. Where it is essential for the survival of the species that only the physically strongest males get to mate and pass on their genes, but human beings no longer needs to rely on physical strength for its survival. We are an animal that for millions of years has relied on our brains and not our brawn. We know this, because physically we are the most weakest animal for our size in the animal kingdom. Neither do human males fight each other for the right to mate with females. So man's aggressive and competitive instincts are old instincts that are no longer befitting for our survival as a species. What is more, they are certainly very inappropriate for our well-being and happiness.

Five thousand years ago our species was taken over by a plague called violent aggression. Starting off by a few men who found they could dominate others through violence. Men and women on the receiving end of this violent reacted in very different ways. Men receiving violence became violent themselves, while women lost all confidence and self respect. Even though some of them attempted to fight back as in the case of the Amazons.

As the result we now live in a world that is ruled by aggression and competition. In recent years this violence has evolved into capitalism. Now to some degree this is a step forward as it is better that men fight each other for wealth and status through competing businesses rather than on the battlefield. Yet the foundation of capitalism is that, "greed is good". The theory being that men are strongly motivated by greed and competition, which as previously stated has created a world of winners and losers.

Yet is greed the only motivation for human beings, surely it would be better is we were motivated by LOVE. Most women have no problem with this when she has a child. She is motivated by her maternal instincts to want to care and love her children the rest of their lives. Men it seems also have a maternal instinct as well. True it is not as strong that of women. We can see this in many marriage break ups where it is mostly women who are, "left holding the baby". Yet modern experience has shown men are more than capable of looking after children. We even find some men take on the role of househusband and look after the children while the wife goes to work. As well as men who will care for children fathered by another man.

So if both men and women are capable of being motivate by love to care for others. Why do we then need to be motivated by greed, competition, vengeance or hate? We are supposed to be an intelligent animal with free will and because of this, collectively and individually we have a choice. We don't have to live in a world of violence, injustice and suffering if we collectively don't want to. We are surely able to use our brains where we are motivated by love and compassion for others.

From primate studies of apes, monkeys and lemurs, we have a choice. We can behave like the aggressive chimpanzees, orang-utans and hamadryas baboons, where alpha males rule through violence. Or behave like the more placid bonobo ape, vervet monkeys, macaques, olive baboons, patas, rhesus monkeys, grey langus, capuchins, prosimians and Madagascar lemurs. Human beings like other primates have within them instincts, that they can take them in either direction.

For many primates it was just chance that pushed them into the direction of living in either a male or female dominated society. This is clearly seen in the case of baboons. Baboons that live on the open savannah tend to be male dominated. This is because in the open plane there is nowhere for baboons to hide from predators. The only defence a baboons troop has, is for the large males to band together and collectively drive carnivores away.

This means the males have a very important role in baboon society and it is a big advantage for males to be very strong and aggressive. This strength and aggression is also used to dominate the females. On the other hand baboons that live in forests tend to be female dominated. This is because forest baboon males don't attempt to fight off predators as everyone climbs up the nearest tree at the approach of a predator. Because of this the male don't have such an important role, and there is no survival need for male forest baboons to be aggressive. This allows the females to come together in a strong sisterhood to dominate the community.

We can see a similar pattern in human society. Women do look to men for protection, but not protection from predators but from other men! So it is a game men play of both assaulting and "protecting" women. Even today in the 21st century a young women who gets raped because she was walking home in the early hours of the morning are condemned, even by other women for, "asking for it".

The absurdity of this was brought out in the open in India during the 1960s: The Indian parliament then was pushing through a law to place a curfew on women going out at night, because so many Indian women were being assaulted and raped by men at night time. Then Indria Gandhi made a speech pointing out that as it was men who were assaulting and raping women, it would make more sense if a nighttime curfew was place on men! Faced with this logical argument that no one had a answer to, the law was quietly dropped. In Pakistan it is even worse, if a women complain to the police that she was raped it is more likely for her to go to jail. So what men have been running for thousands of years is a type of protection racket against women. In that they assault and rape women and then tell women they have to look to men for protection.

As human beings we have a choice in this, we are not slaves to our instincts like many other animals. Patriarchy is a choice that was made five thousand years ago in encouraging the chimpanzee aspects of our instincts. Which brutalises men who respond by cutting off their feelings for others and becoming very brutal themselves. While women under this reign of terror lose all confidence in themselves and become subservient to men.

In my personal experience as a child of the 1950s, it was still accepted that boys needed to be, "toughened up", by their fathers, teachers and their schoolmates. So it was all right to brutalise sensitive boys because, "in our tough world you need to learn to be a real man". I also remember at that time the police gave women who complained to the police about rape, a really hard time. They would spend hours trying to break down their stories, so only the toughest and most determined women could push forward a rape case. Even if they are strong enough to do this, the judge was still more likely to let the rapist off. It was also commonplace that the police didn't interfere in "domestic disputes" which means husbands were at liberty to beat up their wives whenever that wanted to.

The problem is that we have been taught from childhood is that, the macho way is the only way. We don't hear very much about this alternative to this, namely the feminine way. Throughout the 19th and 20th century the feminine way has slowly and quietly influenced Western society. Not only has it allowed women the vote and equal opportunity laws, as women have gained more confidence in themselves they are quietly changing society.

The result is that human society now has a real choice. We can go back to the chimpanzee model and once again brutalise our children, or we can go forward and learn from the bonobo. The problem with the bonobo model is that we have all been brainwashed by the patriarchy that sex is "dirty". Even though most people in the West today are no longer practising Christians, society is still strongly influenced by Christian attitudes. Though since the 1960s there has been a sexual revolution that is slowly undermining these rigid patriarchal beliefs.

For a powerful Sisterhood based on the bonobo model to be created, women will have to do away with marriage and pair bonding. Women's loyalty to a male partner is one of the biggest blockages to creating a powerful Sisterhood. In the 1960s many hippies attempted to create communes, many of these were failures because the males had real problems with community living. So in the end the ones that survived either done so by having strict rules about community behaviour. Or, all the men left and it ended up with only females in the communes.

For women with children communes are ideal. This is because the children then don't become the sole responsibility of one woman. This allows women to, "have their cake and eat is as well", in that women can easy led a life outside of motherhood in having some of her sisters help in the looking after of her children. Female only communes are not so good for men because they no longer have a exclusive female partner to look after his material, emotional and sexual needs.

Pair bonding gives men a big advantage in the sexual relationship between men and women. In that it allows men to have a wife and family as well as the freedom to live a live outside of the family. Female communes give women the same advantages. In that her sisters can emotionally support her. So what would be that role of men in these communes?

Women have complained that man can change when they get married. A man may be very giving and considerate while he is wooing a woman. Then once a marriage has been established he finds he doesn't have to try so hard to please her and can be selfish and even abusive towards his wife. With the breakdown of marriage in recent times men find they cannot do this anymore, because the women is free to leave the relationship. In a commune it strengths the women's power even more, because she has the immediate support of her sisters, when things go wrong in a relationship with a man.

So it means without pair bonding men cannot take any woman for granted. If he wants to have relationships with women he has to find ways he can please them, all the time. He also finds he cannot afford to upset any women because as women are good communicators and he could find himself with a bad reputation. Which will mean other women won't want to have a relationship with him.

In the few matriarchal societies that have survived up until the present day, like in Minangkabau and Keralal the reason why they have survived is because of a simple custom. In most Eastern countries they have extend families, where brothers, sisters uncles and aunts all live in the same household. In the majority patriarchal communities the wife always lives with her husband's family. So she is at a disadvantage because the family she lives in will mostly take the side of the husband. While in matriarchal communities the custom is that the husband will live with his wife's family. Where he finds himself at a disadvantage for the same reason.

So we can see how a simple change in marriage customs can make such a big differences in the power balance between men and women. What is surprising is that the men in these surviving matriarchal communities do not rise up and demand the same marriage customs as the surrounding patriarchal society. The fact that they don't do this shows us that a matriarchal community has advantages not only for women but for men as well, because any strict patriarchal society only benefits a few alpha males. This is because in a society of winners and losers only a very few males become winners most men and nearly all women end up becoming losers. So even though a matriarchal society is loaded to benefit women, the majority of men are still better off in a matriarchal society as well. Because like women they are not being oppressed by alpha men.

To create matriarchal communities women cannot like men do it through conquest and violence, they will have to do it through persuasion. This is why matriarchy has to be attractive to both men and women. Also both men and women who agree with matriarchy have to resist the type of men who want to use aggression and violence to take over and rule. It means we have to stop making heroes of violent men and stop using aggressive macho methods to solve problems.

From what we know about the bonobo ape, the Neolithic age and modern matriarchal communities that has survived to modern times we know matriarchal does work. There is an old saying that goes, "knowledge is power". People in the past have been powerless against governments of alpha males because they were unaware their was a alternative to patriarchy. Once the common people know there is a viable alternative then the people have a choice of either staying with patriarchy or moving on to a matriarchal future.

16

Women and the New World of Exploitation

Globalization has changed the world. Commodities are bought and sold across national borders and continents with unprecedented frequency. Unfortunately, one of the hottest commodities in this new world order is young women.

The profits gained from trafficking women exceed $8 billion annually. This is comparable to the lucrative trade in guns and drugs. In addition to the considerable financial gains, there are also fewer risks in trafficking women than in trafficking other illegal goods such as arms, drugs, and endangered species of animals and plants. These factors combined draw many people into the business, including well-established crime syndicates such as the Japanese Yakuza and the Hong Kong Triad.

Law enforcement has generally proved inadequate in combating this problem, both nationally and internationally. This is because of a general perception that trafficked women migrate willingly and allow themselves to be sold. According to Lois Chiang, Assistant Dean at U of T's Faculty of Law, "The impediments [to combating trafficking] are first a lack of understanding of what trafficking is--and this in not purely a legal issue. We need a better understanding of this phenomenon, and this gets intimately tied up with issues around women's agency and women's sexuality."

The causes of trafficking are complex and multifaceted. The intensification of international trade and foreign direct investment was intended to improve the economies of developing countries. Unfortunately, it appears that the opposite has occurred and poverty is rising in many developing countries. Large numbers of women are now leaving their home countries in the hope of finding better wages in developed countries.

In addition, the sexual division of labour has also intensified the vulnerability of young women (aged 15-25) to trafficking rings. Girls are often educated to lower levels than boys and have fewer work opportunities in skilled professions. The jobs available to them are often limited to domestic service and factory work.

The merchandizing of women takes a variety of forms including forced labour, mail-order brides, arranged marriages and slavery-like practices in prostitution. As such, trafficking may be defined as the exploitation of women for their labour, with or without pay and with or without their consent.

Surprisingly, many of the manifestations of trafficking can be found in our own backyard. According to Chiang, "There are many instances of trafficking in women in Canada-both as a domestic issue and a cross-border issue. As a domestic issue, we have seen in the press stories of young girls being deceived or coerced and kept forcibly confined and then raped by either the abductors or others and forced into prostitution. We see similar stories about women being brought over to Canada by traffickers and also forced into prostitution."

EQUALITY OF MEN WOMEN: A NEW REALITY

Over a century ago, and for the first time in the history of revealed religion, Bahaullah, Prophet-Founder of the Bahai Faith, proclaimed the equality of man and woman. He did not leave this pronouncement as an ideal or pious hope but wove it, as a basic factor, into the fabric of His social order. He supported it by laws requiring the same standard of education for women as for men, and equality of rights in society.

Equality of the sexes is, for Bahais, a spiritual and moral standard essential for the unification of the planet and the unfoldment of world order. Without the qualities, talents, and skills of both women and men, full economic and social development of the planet becomes impossible. The world of humanity is possessed of two wings the male and the female. So long as these two wings are not equivalent in strength the bird will not fly. Until womankind reaches the same degree as man, until she enjoys the same arena of activity, extraordinary attainment for humanity will not be realized; humanity cannot wing its way to heights of real attainment.

In the present transition of humanity from adolescence to maturity, signs of this evolving equality can be observed everywhere. In the Bahai view this is hardly surprising, for "As long as women are prevented from attaining their highest possibilities, so long will men be unable to achieve the greatness which might be theirs."

The character of this unique age we are entering is further brought into focus in the following statement from the Bahai BIC Document #93-0405 Writings:

The world in the past has been ruled by force and man has dominated over woman by reason of his more forceful and aggressive qualities both of body and mind. But the scales are already shifting, force is losing its weight, and mental alertness, intuition, and the spiritual qualities of love and service, in which woman is strong, are gaining ascendancy. Hence the new age will be an age less masculine and more permeated with the feminine ideals, or, to speak more exactly, will be an age in which the masculine and feminine elements of civilization will be more properly balanced.

UNITY AND EQUALITY IN THE FAMILY

The Bahai world community has, for more than one hundred years, accepted as truth the principle of equality of the sexes and has understood the importance of implementing this standard in individual, family, and community life.

The institution of marriage, the basis of the family in the Bahai community, is part of this process. Before a Bahai marriage can take place the couple, who have freely chosen each other, must obtain the consents of all parents and transmit them to the communitys governing body.

The couple then weds in an atmosphere of loving parental approval and acceptance by the community. With the exchange of vows, in which each partner repeats, "We will all, verily, abide by the Will of God," the newly wedded begin their lives together on a basis of true spiritual unity and equality.

This unity and equality, rooted in the rights and responsibilities of every person before God, unfolds in the family. Here, values and attitudes essential for the development of the individual, the community, the nation, and humanity must be taught from early life. In the Bahai view the family being a human unit must be educated according to the rules of sanctity. All the virtues must be taught the family. The integrity of the family bond must be constantly considered and the rights of the individual members must not be transgressed.... All these rights and prerogatives must be conserved, yet the unity of the family must be sustained. The injury of one shall be considered the injury of all; the comfort of each the comfort of all; the honor of one the honor of all.

Equality in Education and Training

Although both parents share in the overall responsibility of educating the children, the mother is given recognition as the first educator of humanity, and she must be carefully prepared for this task. Her education, in fact, from the Bahai point of view, is more necessary and important than that of man, for woman is the trainer of the child from its infancy. If she be defective and imperfect herself the child will necessarily be deficient; therefore imperfection of woman implies a condition of imperfection in all mankind, for it is the mother who rears, nurtures and guides the growth of the child.

Since Bahais do not separate life into religious and secular compartments, and since faith must be expressed in social action, education for men and women, in all its facts, "holds an important place in the new order of things." For this reason, the education of each child is compulsory. If there is not money enough in a family to educate both the girl and the boy the money must be dedicated to the girls education, for she is the potential mother. If there are no parents the community must educate the child. In addition to this widespread education each child must be taught a profession, art, or trade, so that every member of the community will be enabled to earn his own livelihood. It is also significant that, in the spirit of this new era of human evolution, Bahaullah has "promulgated the adoption of the same course of education for man and woman," making clear that "daughters and sons must follow the same curriculum of study, thereby promoting unity of the sexes."

Contribution of Women to Peace

The Bahai Writings promise that "the entrance of women into all human departments is an irrefutable and incontrovertible question. No soul can retard or prevent it"; that in "no movement" will women "be left behind; that they "will attain in all such a degree as will be considered the very highest station of the world of humanity and will take part in all affairs"; that "when women participate fully and equally in the affairs of the world...war will cease." This contribution-of women to the establishment of world unity and peace will inevitably be recognized and developed.

In past ages humanity has been defective and inefficient because incomplete. War and its ravages have blighted the world. The education of woman will be a mighty step toward its abolition and ending for she will use her whole influence against war.... In truth she will be the greatest factor in establishing Universal Peace and international arbitration. Assuredly woman will abolish warfare among mankind.

An Equal Voice

A great responsibility is, however, placed on woman to develop her potentialities fully.

She must make every effort to attain greater perfection, to be mans equal in every respect, to make progress in all in which she has been backward, so that man will be compelled to acknowledge her equality of capacity and attainment.

Certainly the well-being of mankind depends on the development of the potential virtues and abilities of every individual, regardless of race, nationality, class, religion, or sex. For this reason prejudices, which cause division and oppression, are systematically abolished in Bahai community life. A unique administrative system, rooted in the concept of unity in diversity, both insists on education for all members of the community and allows for the immediate assimilation of all those who in the past have been deprived of their rights. The Bahai electoral system, operating by secret ballot, with no nominations or electioneering, encourages universal participation: every adult Bahai is eligible for election to local and national administrative bodies responsible for decision in the conduct of Bahai affairs. The ease with which women, long deprived of equal opportunities, can now be integrated into the life of society, is vividly evidenced by the participation of women in all areas of Bahai community life.

Today, in the Bahai world community, in over 200 nations and territories, women are joining with men in building a global society. Their full contribution toward the establishment of a world civilization is possible, Bahais believe, because of the all-pervasive spiritual power released in this age by Bahaullah, Who has erased all limitations preventing the fulfillment of human potentialities. For in the Bahai view, since this is the century of light, it is evident that the Sun of Reality, the Word has revealed itself to all humankind. One of the potentialities hidden in the realm of humanity was the capability or capacity of womanhood. Through the effulgent rays of divine illumination, the capacity of woman has become so awakened and manifest in this age that equality of man and woman is an established fact.

17

Rape and Sexual Abuse of Women in International Law

RAPE IN ARMED CONFLICT

This paper will consider the international legal response to rape and other forms of sexual abuse committed against women during the course of an armed conflict: its incidence, impact and consequences. Although both men and women can be and are raped, causing severe injury for both, in terms of numbers rape is essentially a crime committed against women. Further, women suffer from particular after-effects in rape that are not shared by men.

Women are raped in all forms of armed conflict, international and internal, whether the conflict is fought primarily on religious, ethnic, political or nationalist grounds, or a combination of all these. They are raped by men from all sides-both enemy and `friendly' forces. There have been reports of rapes and other forms of sexual abuse committed by members of United Nations peacekeeping forces; women are not free from interference even from those who are in the territory with an international mandate to restore international peace and security. International media attention has been directed towards the widespread rapes, torture and forced pregnancies in the former Yugoslavia. The `mobilization of shame' which has been identified as the primary means of enforcing international humanitarian law has to some extent been activated in this instance. Nevertheless, the international response in itself carries the risk that violent offences against women will be perceived as something exceptional, peculiar to this particular conflict. The reality is that rape and violent sexual abuse of women in armed conflict has a long history.

Numerous incidents of women raped in other international and internal armed conflicts can be cited to illustrate this point. During the August 1990 invasion of Kuwait it is estimated that at least 5,000 Kuwaiti women were raped by Iraqi soldiers. After the liberation large numbers of foreign domestic working women in Kuwait were attacked and subjected to sexual violence from subsequently returning Kuwaitis; women in Rwanda who are caught up in the vicious civil war in that country; women in Kashmir who have suffered rape and death under the administration of the Indian army. The following has been reported concerning a civil conflict in South America.

Throughout Peru's 12 year internal war women have been targets of sustained, frequently brutal violence committed by both parties to the armed conflict... Women have been threatened, raped and murdered by government security forces; and women have been threatened, raped and murdered by the Communist Party of Peru-Shining Path. Often, the same woman is the victim of violence by both sides.

Liberian women have been repeatedly raped in the ethnic violence of that country's civil war and women from East Timor have been raped as well as killed since the occupation by Indonesia commenced in 1975. Another example which occurred longer ago, but which has only recently received serious attention, was the continued sustained rapes of the so-called `comfort women' by the Japanese military during the Second World War.

Numerous other examples could have been cited but this selection illustrates that women are attacked in conflicts across the globe by men of all colours, religions, nationalities and ideologies.

Rape in war is not merely a matter of chance, of women victims being in the wrong place at the wrong time. Nor is it a question of sex. It is rather a question of power and control which is `structured by male soldiers' notions of their masculine privilege, by the strength of the military's lines of command and by class and ethnic inequalities among women'. Radhika Coomaraswamy has identified a number of reasons for sexual violence against women, two of which are especially applicable to rape in armed conflict: violence against women may be directed towards the social group of which she is a member because `to rape a woman is to humiliate her community'.

Complex, combined emotions of hatred, superiority, vengeance for real or imagined past wrongs and national pride are engendered and deliberately manipulated in armed conflict. They are given expression through rape of the other side's women. For the men of the community rape encapsulates the totality of their defeat; they have failed to protect `their' women. Second, studies have indicated the connection between militarization of the nation State and violence against women. Other connections have been drawn between `normal' peacetime attitudes towards women and rape in armed conflict; one that has been controversial in the context of the former Yugoslavia is the direct causal link that has been made by Catharine MacKinnon between pornography in that country and the mass rapes of Muslim women. The connection between pornographic projections of women and the use as war propaganda of these and other media images can be readily accepted; but to identify these as the sole, or even major cause of the abuse of women throughout that area is simplistic and misleading.

Licence to rape has been included as a term of employment for mercenary soldiers. In determining why such a condition is repugnant, Walzer discounts the utilitarian argument that it acts as a spur to military courage. Instead he goes to the heart of the matter:

Rape is a crime, in war as in peace, because it violates the rights of the woman who is attacked. To offer her as bait to a mercenary soldier is to treat her as if she were not a person at all but a mere object, a prize, a trophy of war. It is the recognition of her personality that shapes our judgment.

Rape has also been directed as an instrument of war. In the former Yugoslavia rape has been `massive, organized and systematic'. It was perceived by the Special Rapporteur appointed by the United Nations Commission on Human Rights not only as an instrument of war but as a method of ethnic cleansing `intended to humiliate, shame, degrade and terrify the entire ethnic group.'

THE CONSEQUENCES OF RAPE

The consequences of rape continue beyond the actual attack or attacks, often lasting for the rest of the women's lives. As well as the degradation, pain and terror caused at the time, the fear engendered remains long after. This fear is also experienced by other women who were not themselves attacked but are aware that they might have been, or might be in the future. Rape centred within a community undermines the well-being and secure existence of the community. For survivors, rape carries the risk of sexually-transmitted diseases, including of course AIDS. It also can result in pregnancy. Women have to face the prospect of bearing the child of the invader (of their State, their community and their bodies), or of seeking an abortion at a time of intense social dislocation and when scarce medical supplies are directed as a priority to military personnel.

This same factor reduces availability of treatment of sexually-transmitted diseases. Abortion is restricted under the teachings of a number of religions, or women have been forcibly detained to prevent abortion. Other women have been so badly internally injured that they will never be able to bear the children they would have chosen to have; infertility and loss of virginity make women unmarriageable in some societies. Still others have been unable to bear their shame and have committed suicide. Where the effects of conflict have caused shortages of food and shelter, and priority health care is directed towards the military, child bearing can impose an impossibly high additional material, as well as psychological, burden upon their mothers. This can be further exacerbated by the child-being seen by family or compatriots as `proof' of the woman's collaboration with the enemy, or of her immoral behaviour. Women fear they have become unacceptable to their families and communities, a fear which may be enhanced where the rape was committed publicly in the presence of members of these communities. Public rape terrorizes and traumatizes the civilian population. There is also only just beginning to be some understanding of the psychological damage caused by the trauma of violent sexual abuse.

INTERNATIONAL LEGAL RESPONSES

Substantive Law

One response has been to call municipal and international legal systems into play, which in turn raises the questions of the adequacy of legal norms and the effectiveness of their implementation.

A number of substantive international legal regimes are currently applicable. States are liable for harm done to individuals which constitutes violation of the laws and customs of war by troops under their authority and command, for violations of internationally guaranteed human rights, including genocide and torture, and for wrongdoing to aliens under the normal principles of State responsibility. These different legal regimes allow for analysis of rape through different lenses: violations of the laws of war, violence against women as a violation of women's human rights, and protection of ethnic groups against genocide. In addition to State responsibility there is individual criminal responsibility for the commission of war crimes and crimes against humanity. The plea of superior orders is not available as a defence to such actions.

Meron has demonstrated that rape has long been prohibited by the laws of war and has been incorporated into various modern Codes of Military Conduct. The currently applicable laws of war are contained within the 1949 Geneva Conventions, the 1977 supplementary Protocols, and in the body of law arising from the judgment of the Nuremberg Tribunal and the Military Tribunal for the Far East. Unfortunately, in these documents the position with respect to rape is ambiguous.

Rape was not included in the listed war crimes in Article 6 of the Nuremberg Charter, although the list was specifically stated not to be exhaustive. The Fourth Geneva Convention provides protection for civilians in international armed conflict and specifically provides that women should be protected against rape. This provision is almost exactly reiterated in Protocol I. It is noticeable that these provisions do not impose a blanket prohibition against sexual abuse, but rather oblige States to offer women protection against attacks on their honour and to accord them special respect. Article 4 of the Fourth Geneva Convention applies to those `who at a given moment and in any manner whatsoever find themselves, in case of a conflict or occupation, in the hands of a Party to the conflict or Occupying Power of which they are not nationals'. Article 76 of Protocol I enhances this protection by extending its scope to all women in the power of a Party to the conflict including a Party's own nationals.

In non-international armed conflict, Article 3 to the Geneva Conventions provides a minimum standard of behaviour that applies both to government and non-government forces. Prohibited actions include violence to life and the person, cruel treatment and torture, and humiliating and degrading treatment. It is easy to interpret these Articles so as to include rape, but it is nevertheless unfortunate that it is not spelled out as an explicit prohibition. For this reason the affirmation by the World Conference on Human Rights in Vienna in 1993 that `violations of the human rights of women in situations of armed conflict [with no distinction drawn between international and non-international armed conflict] are violations of the humanitarian principles of international human rights and humanitarian law' is to be welcomed. The Declaration and Programme of Action continues that violations, including systematic rape and sexual slavery `require a particularly effective response'.

The same is true of the enforcement provisions. States are under an obligation to make grave breaches of the Geneva Conventions and Protocols subject to the jurisdiction of their own courts and punishable by severe penalties. Rape is not however explicitly listed as a grave breach of the Convention, although acts wilfully committed and causing great suffering or causing injury to body or health do constitute grave breaches. Protocol I includes among its list of grave breaches `degrading practices involving outrages upon personal dignity based upon racial discrimination' but makes no reference to gender discrimination.

War crimes, that is violations of the laws or customs of war, are not the only possible legal regime for the prosecution of rape committed during international armed conflict. There is also the concept of a crime against humanity and, it has been argued in the context of the former Yugoslavia, genocide. A crime against humanity was defined in the Nuremberg Charter as:

> murder, extermination, enslavement, deportation, and other inhumane acts committed against any civilian population before or during the war, or persecutions on political, racial, or religious grounds in execution of or in connection with any crime within the jurisdiction of the Tribunal whether or not in violation of the domestic law of the country where perpetrated.

A number of points require special mention. First, although crimes against humanity were established as a separate category from war crimes, the crimes in question were inevitably associated with the occurrence of the Second World War. This association between armed conflict and crimes against humanity has been continued in the case of the former Yugoslavia. Second, despite the enormous incidence of rape of civilian populations during the Second World War, prosecutions of crimes against humanity were limited to persecutions on racial, political or religious grounds, in accordance with the wording of Article 6. These words import a requirement of discriminatory behaviour into the concept of crimes against humanity, which is equally well provided by the gender discrimination inherent in violent crimes against women. Thirdly, for actions to come within the category of crimes against humanity they had to be committed against a civilian population, not against individual civilians. Fourthly, in contrast to war crimes, it has been necessary to establish systematic government planning for crimes against humanity. Crimes against humanity are not easily established in light of these restrictive requirements. Nevertheless, when the four occupying powers in Germany adopted Control Council Law No. 10 they departed from the Nuremberg precedent and incorporated rape as a crime against humanity.

Genocide is defined in Article II of the Genocide Convention. There must be an intention to destroy, in whole or in part, a national, ethnic, racial or religious group through the commission of such acts as killing or causing serious bodily or mental harm to members of the group; deliberately inflicting on the group conditions of life calculated to bring about its physical destruction in whole or in part; imposing measures to prevent births within the group; or forcibly transferring children of the group to another group. At first sight rape does not appear to fall within this definition, but it has been forcefully argued that where it has been carried out on a massive and systematic basis for the purposes of producing babies of the ethnic class of the rapists, of destroying the family life of the victims and of cleansing the surrounding area of all other ethnic groups rape becomes genocidal. This categorization has been further supported by allegations that impregnated women were forcibly detained until it was too late to abort.

Despite this impressive body of formal prohibition, the incidence of rape in armed conflict has been widely ignored, underplayed or tolerated. Rape is too frequently regarded as an unfortunate but inevitable side-effect of conflict, or as an anticipated bonus for soldiers on all sides. Rape did not figure prominently at Nuremberg, `not because the Germans were not guilty of rape, but because the allied forces, especially the Russians and the Moroccan forces under French control, were also guilty of many rapes'. Rape was also largely invisible in the trials of the Japanese war criminals.

This silence by international law enforcement agencies denotes a double irony for women. Feminist writers have argued that the distinction drawn in international law between public acts of the State and private actions has been an important factor in its failure to address denial of human rights to women. Violence against women for example has not been readily viewed as torture, or as being imputable to the State, because of its widespread commission by private actors within the private arena of the home. Yet rape in international armed conflict, which is largely committed by military agents of the State under public authority, has also been ignored.

Law Enforcement

However, in the context of the former Yugoslavia there has been widespread pressure to ensure that this long silence is broken. The substantive law on rape in armed conflict has now become entangled with the question of arenas for its application. Condemnation of violations and calls for compliance have been made within international political fora, notably the Security Council, the Human Rights Commission, the Commission on the Status of Women, and the Committee on the Elimination of Discrimination Against Women. Proceedings have been commenced against Yugoslavia (Serbia-Montenegro) in the International Court of Justice by Bosnia-Herzegovina. Yugoslavia (Serbia-Montenegro) has counter-claimed in similar terms. Since under Article 34 of the Statute of the Court only States can be parties before it, this litigation will deal with the question of the responsibility of the State under the relevant treaties and customary international law. The options for the prosecution of individuals alleged to have committed such crimes are the domestic courts of any State, or an international war crimes tribunal on the precedent of Nuremberg.

Criminal proceedings have been commenced in domestic courts, for example in Germany, France and by a Bosnian military tribunal in Sarajevo. In the United States civil proceedings have been commenced under the Alien Torts Claims Act and the Torture Victim Protection Act against Radovan Karadzic, who has command authority over the Bosnian-Serb military forces. These claims rely upon the jurisprudence following the case of Filartiga v. Pena-Irala.

There Judge Kaufman accepted civil jurisdiction within the United States for offences violating the law of nations, in that instance torture, irrespective of where the offence had been committed and the nationalities of the accused and victim. While there may be concerns about the extension of United States' extra-territorial jurisdiction, there are advantages for the plaintiffs in such civil actions. Jurisdiction can be established for the violation of international law provided personal service can be achieved.

Amicus briefs from interested third parties, including non-governmental organizations, which set out many aspects of the issue can be admitted. A default judgment may be entered against an absent defendant on the basis of the burden of proof appropriate in civil cases. While it is highly unlikely that any award of damages would ever be forthcoming, the proceedings prevent free access to the United States for the defendant and allow a domestic court to assert its understanding of customary international law.

In Resolutions 808 and 827 the Security Council, acting under Chapter VII of the United Nations Charter, established an International Criminal Tribunal for the prosecution of persons responsible for serious violations of international humanitarian law committed in the territory of the former Yugoslavia since 1991. The Tribunal has been accorded jurisdiction over war crimes, genocide and crimes against humanity. Since a prevailing principle is that of nullum crimen sine lege, the definition of each offence relies upon pre-existing customary and conventional humanitarian law. In addition, all the parties to the conflict have largely accepted the application of the Geneva Conventions and Protocols to it. Thus the Tribunal can determine whether grave breaches of the Geneva Conventions have been committed. As already stated these do not explicitly include rape, although as a matter of interpretation it can be readily included.

The Tribunal also has jurisdiction over violations of the laws or customs of war. These include `employment of... weapons calculated to cause unnecessary suffering'. If rape is correctly regarded as a weapon of war in the way described above, it can readily be brought within this prohibition. The definition of crimes against humanity follows that of the Control Council Law No. 10 and therefore includes rape. The Secretary-General's report makes it clear that to constitute a crime against humanity the acts must be of a very serious nature and be committed as part of a widespread or systematic attack against any civilian population.

The purpose of the International Tribunal is to put an end to the commission of war crimes in the former Yugoslavia and to provide effective measures for bringing to justice those responsible for them. In accordance with the requirements for Chapter VII action, the Security Council has stated that the establishment of the International Tribunal will help to restore and maintain international peace in the area. There are enormous legal and practical questions relating, inter alia, to the identification, arrest and detention of accused persons, the collection and presentation of evidence, and the rules of evidence and procedure to be followed, which will have to be resolved for the Tribunal to become effective.

While the practical and deterrent effect of such a Tribunal may be questioned, the importance of an authoritative public articulation of the relevant norms of international law cannot be understated. In a decentralized legal system where principles of customary international law are generated through State practice and opinio juris, the conclusions of the Tribunal resting upon the authority of the Security Council will inevitably have normative and educative effect. It is for this reason that it is essential that rape is considered separately from the other charges and is explicitly condemned. It is not sufficient for it to be regarded as an add-on to other offences.

INTERNATIONAL LEGAL REMEDIES

Despite the importance of an affirmation of the illegality of rape in armed conflict, some reservations about the role of the Tribunal from the perspective of the survivors of rape must be expressed. Some of these can be addressed by sensitivity towards the process and procedures of the Tribunal, while others go directly to the inadequacies of international legal remedies in the case of rape.

The focus of the Tribunal is on punishing the wrongdoers, not on providing compensation and support to those who have suffered the harms described above. Admittedly this is a defect shared by municipal criminal legal systems, but these may be backed up by other domestic support services. A war crimes tribunal must be supplemented by long-term practical assistance from governments, such as medical care, shelter, support and counselling. Survivors of rape must be provided the space to specify their own needs within their own communities. Appropriate support must be made available to all concerned within the community to enable survivors to regain control of their own lives.

The health and emotional needs of those who were not themselves raped must also be given consideration. Indeed it has been argued that to concentrate only upon the survivors of rape can be `counter-productive by possibly stigmatizing and further traumatizing' those women. It cannot be assumed that all women will share the same needs. For example, some who feel that crimes committed against them have been disregarded may feel a sense of empowerment in the establishment of the Tribunal, while others may consider this a further intrusion into their lives, or fear the consequences of proceedings. Responses must take into account both individual preferences and the needs of the harmed society. The traditional exclusion of women from decision-making with respect to the use of force must not be here continued.

Those performing these tasks must receive adequate and relevant training, including psychological counselling. The international community must ensure that survivors do not become victims of, or become manipulated by, a well-meaning international reaction to the offences committed against them which fails to take account of their own concerns. It is important that fact-finding missions report their findings accurately and objectively and that research into the conflict reflects the complexities of its historical and ethnic origins. The fears of the Zagreb-based Centre for Women War Victims need to be taken seriously and responded to:

> ... we fear that the process of helping raped women is turning in a strange direction, being taken over by governmental institutions... and male gynaecologists in particular. We fear that the raped women could be used in political propaganda with the aim of spreading hatred and revenge, thus leading to further violence against women and to further victimization of survivors.

The pain of women raped and abused in armed conflict has often been appropriated by males for propaganda purposes. Suzanne Gibson discusses the examples of how rape of women in France during World War One became `transformed into a representation of France as an innocent female nation assaulted by a barbaric and brutishly male Germany' and British military conscriptors used the image of `the Hun' violating their sisters. She concludes with a warning that must be borne in mind throughout any criminal proceedings:

> ... rape has not throughout most of recorded history, been a crime against women. It has significantly however been a heinous crime against men: a humiliation inflicted upon a nation, an affront to a man's pride as guardian of his women,...

It is essential that prosecutions are brought against accused people from all sides. While the International Tribunal is unique in that it was established during the continuation of the conflict and is therefore untainted by notions of `victor's justice', it must not be used to prosecute offenders from only one side. Prosecutions must be brought against the alleged perpetrators and those higher up in the chain of command. It is essential that the message is made clear that rape of women is illegal and will be punished whoever is responsible for the commission of the offence.

There are various aspects of the Tribunal's composition and procedure that must be considered. Only two women judges have been nominated to it. While this is an advance on the composition of the International Court of Justice which has never had an elected woman judge, it is still far from the goal of 50% female judges sought by women's groups. Attention must be paid to gender distribution of all other personnel of the Tribunal, including prosecutors and investigators. Women may be fearful of retribution and publicity and thus be reluctant to testify before the Tribunal. The Special Rapporteur has pointed out that there are many reasons why survivors may be reluctant to testify as to their experiences. These include `severe traumatization, feelings of shame, lack of trust, fear of awakening bad memories as well as fear of reprisals against themselves and their families'.

A balance will have to be drawn between the rights of the accused to due process and the needs of the survivors. There has long been criticism in domestic criminal proceedings of the ways in which women in rape and other sexual abuse cases have been subject to intense and distressing personal questioning by investigators and defence lawyers. Procedural reforms have been introduced in some countries. The international tribunal should draw upon these experiences in determining its procedures. As a minimum, all people involved in the work of the tribunal, and especially those involved in judicial, investigatory or prosecutorial work should receive gender sensitivity training.

There are other still more fundamental questions that need to be addressed. The jurisdiction of the Tribunal is limited to offences in the former Yugoslavia; it will not assist women who have been raped or will in the future be raped in other conflicts all around the world, although its effectiveness is likely to impact upon its future precedential value. Further, rape and sexual violence against women occurs along a continuum of seriousness. The widespread and systematic nature of the offences committed in the former Yugoslavia place these offences at the far end of the spectrum, as is recognized by their inclusion as crimes against humanity in the Statute of the Tribunal. The focus on these rapes and the failure to make explicit that any rape committed in armed conflict is a war crime entails the risk of creating the assumption that `lesser' rapes may still be committed with impunity.

CONCLUSION

The measures here proposed are reactive, where what is primarily needed are positive steps to implement international humanitarian law in international and non-international armed conflict. The obligations incurred and learned in peacetime need to be sufficiently strongly imbued so that they hold fast in the social disruption of armed conflict. Even more urgently, commitment to preventing armed conflict and thus to eradicating the environment conducive to the occurrence of such offences is needed.

The maintenance of international peace and security relates to social and economic justice and the observance of human rights in peacetime, as well as to enforcement action in response to a breach of the peace or an act of aggression. This has been recognized by organs of the United Nations. The General Assembly has accepted it in the context of decolonization; nor has the Security Council limited its understanding of acts detrimental to international peace and security to external acts but has recognized the interlocking relationships between systemic oppression, deprivation, terrorism and breach of the peace. The Secretary-General has acknowledged the connection between armed conflict and sustained structural injustice in his analysis, `Agenda for Peace'.

Despite the willingness of United Nations' organs to move beyond a narrow concept of the causes of international conflict, and in particular the recognition of the threat to international peace caused by apartheid and racial discrimination policies, the global denial of basic rights to women has not been similarly recognized. This denial of rights has been largely ignored by mainstream human rights bodies which have failed to interpret their conventions in ways which are relevant to women's lives. Any rape of women in armed conflict is not the end of the spectrum, but it continues through to the constant attacks and sexual abuse of women in `normal' peacetime conditions. Physical, psychological and economic violence against women is manifested in many forms but is a constant fact of life for millions of women. It must be recognized that the climate of fear created through oppression and domination and the reality of violence is part of the patriarchal State structure and is a threat to international peace. Thus recent steps within the international community to ensure that women's rights are recognized as human rights and to enhance the accountability of governments for violence against women are as much an integral part of the overall counter-attack on the war against women as are the more publicized and dramatic responses to events in the former Yugoslavia.

18

The Task of Woman in the Modern World

"The important thing for a country is that the men should be manly, the women womanly." This comment of Chesterton's embodies a fundamental principle of social order. In society, as in any organism, unity and order are achieved through the cooperation of very different members, each fulfilling his own functions and contributing his special qualities to the common good.

The deepest difference among human beings--far more fundamental than any difference of intelligence or ability, nation or race--is the difference of sex. "And God created man to His own image: to the image of God He created him; male and female He created them." This basic difference is not merely physical but also psychological, coloring the total personality. In the whole range of her being--her mind, her senses, her emotions, her will, her interests and reactions--woman differs profoundly from man.

It is obviously of the greatest importance that this difference find its proper expression in the social functions of the two sexes. Each has unique qualities to contribute to the enrichment of human life. It is essential for the full and harmonious development of society, and especially for a Christian society, that "the men should be manly, the women womanly." Man and woman are made to complement each other at every point. Man's capacity for theory, for forming an abstract and comprehensive view, is matched by woman's practical sense and her gift for detail. Man's ambition and self-assertion which spur him on to great achievement must be balanced by the creative power of woman's spirit of sacrifice and self-surrender. Man's ability for leadership and desire for power must be tempered by woman's spirit of love and selfless devotion.

The undue predominance of either masculine or feminine qualities creates profound disturbances which reverberate throughout the entire social structure, as we can see in our own culture. Western European civilization under the influence of Protestantism, rationalism, liberalism, and other secularizing trends, has become progressively more masculine in the last four centuries. Ours is a culture of the self-assertion of man: of man's reason and scientific method in the intellectual sphere; of man's will to power and conquest in business and world affairs; of man's independence of God in all aspects of life. In our time we need women with a vision of their great task as women who will help to restore the social equilibrium by creating a vital current of the great womanly virtues: the spirit of love, compassion for the suffering, generous self-sacrifice. As women our fundamental contribution to the new order lies in finding our proper role in society. Our most urgent task in the work of reconstruction is to face this problem: What is the function of woman in the social order?

The Universal Mission of Woman

Woman's essential mission in the world is to be for mankind a living example of the spirit of total dedication to God. To love God with her whole heart, her whole mind, her whole strength, and to radiate that love to the world--this is the universal task of woman. It is true that every human being is made for the love of God and is meant to be totally consecrated to His praise. In what sense, then, can we say that it is the particular mission of woman to be both an example and guide of man along the way of dedication?

There are two poles, two principles in human nature. Father Gerald Vann, O. P., in his recent book, "The Heart of Man," distinguishes these two basic tendencies as "man the maker" and "man the lover." Both principles are present to some extent in every human being, but man the maker is realized most perfectly in man; man the lover in woman. It is the maker who asserts, who imposes his idea and his will on the surroundings. The race takes its forward motion along the way of organization and invention from him. It is man the lover who gives, who yields his own will and gladly surrenders not only his will but his very self to the beloved.

Mankind has always recognized that love plays a far greater role in woman's life than in man's. Every woman when she looks into her own heart finds there the deep desire to surrender herself completely in love. Woman is by nature total in her giving; love absorbs her whole being. Byron was expressing the common experience of mankind when he wrote:

"Man's love is of man's life a thing apart

'Tis Woman's whole existence."

In relation to God, we must all fulfill the role of the lover, awaiting the divine initiative, surrendering completely to the divine will. As C. S. Lewis writes so beautifully, "Our role must be always that of patient to agent, female to male, mirror to light, echo to voice. Our highest activity must be response, not initiative. To experience the love of God in a true and not an illusory form is therefore to experience it as our surrender to His demand, our conformity to His desire." Christian tradition has often expressed man's relation to God in the beautiful phrase: the soul is the bride of Christ. But woman's nature has the greater innate affinity for the bridal role, for the act of loving surrender. That is why woman has been throughout Christian history a symbol and example of the spirit of complete consecration to God. Woman's natural capacity for wholehearted giving of herself in love is the basis for her glorious supernatural vocation. It is her function to help to lead mankind to God by becoming herself a radiant example of total dedication to His will.

The lover's surrender opens the way for the action of God's grace in the world. "The world can be moved by the strength of man, but it can be blessed in the real sense of the word only in the sign of woman," writes Gertrude von Le Fort. It is first of all to Our Lady that these words apply. In her, the universal mission of woman, the lover, was fulfilled most completely. Her "fiat" is the perfect expression of the creature's wholesouled surrender to the creator, and through her surrender the fullness of blessing entered into the world. These words may be applied, too, to the universal task of womankind, for it is the function of every woman to re-echo the "fiat" of Mary and thus to become a source of blessing to humanity.

Woman as Mother of Mankind

Woman helps to lead society Godward by her direct service of mankind as well as by her example. Total dedication to God implies wholehearted service of man. A loving care for one's neighbor is but the necessary practical expression of a genuine love of God. In woman, the care for one's neighbor has the character of maternal love, with its warm personal devotion and generous sacrifice of self. Spiritually as well as physically, woman is the mother of mankind, the fountain and nurturer of life.

Through her relation to "man the maker" woman exercises a strong spiritual influence on the whole of a culture. Man leaves the imprint of his personality in the creations of his mind--works of science and art, monumental buildings and commercial empires. But woman's masterpiece is life itself. She is not interested in abstract or technical achievements but in persons, and in bringing persons to God. She stays in the background, the great inspirer, whose warm sympathy and encouragement spur man on.

Intuitively she perceives what is best and noblest in his proposals and helps to develop it. With her deep awareness of the sacramentality of life, she helps man to see matter as the image of spirit, inspiring him with her vision of the divine poetry of creation and the symbolism of human action.

In the life of every great man one finds this vital influence of a noble woman-Monica and Augustine, Paula and Jerome, Scholastica and Benedict, Clare and Francis, Blanche of Castile and King Louis, Clothilde and Clovis, Beatrice and Dante. Woman's influence is subtle and hard to define but nonetheless real. When she no longer fulfills her role as spiritual mother, culture becomes gross, materialistic, brutal, and loses grace and beauty.

The Three Spheres of Woman's Dedication

Woman must needs fulfill her universal mission of dedication to God and loving service of mankind in some concrete set of circumstances. There are three spheres in which she can carry out her primary task: religious life, marriage, and single life in the world. In the designs of God's

Providence, some women in every generation, the "first fruits," are meant to consecrate themselves to God in religion; most women are called to dedicate themselves to Him in marriage; and very few are intended for the life of the unmarried woman in the world. But whether she becomes a nun, a mother of a family, or a single woman in the world, her essential function remains the same: to be a living example of the spirit of surrender and love, the spiritual mother of mankind.

The virgin consecrated to God by her vow of chastity has always been regarded with highest honor in Christian civilization. Consecrated virginity diffuses a fragrant atmosphere of purity and spiritual integrity throughout society, which contributes to preserve the sanctity of marriage and the dignity of womanhood. The greater the respect and esteem shown to virginity in a society, the higher the position of all women will be. It is significant that the Protestant revolt which has had so many unfortunate consequences for the position of woman began with Luther's attacks on virginity and his liquidation of convents and monasteries.

The topic of woman's contribution to society through the religious life, however, demands a separate article for adequate treatment. The present discussion will be confined to the role of woman in marriage and in the single life in the world.

Woman in Marriage

Woman's nature is admirably adapted to her functions as wife and mother. The responsibilities of the family develop her powers and mature her spiritually, mentally. and physically.

Spiritually, a woman becomes mature through surrender, through finding the particular role in which she can accomplish her total dedication to God. The young woman who has found her vocation in life in marriage and is wholly given to her task of bringing her family to God is a mature person whatever her age. She will have that air of serenity and peace which are the sign of the basic fulfillment of her being.

The woman who has never surrendered wholeheartedly to any purpose outside herself remains immature all her life, like a bud which never unfolds itself. In marriage, woman can develop a spirit of selflessness which makes her dedication deeper and richer with the years. Her service to her family both expresses her love of God and increases her power of loving. The woman who has no outlet for her love, no one for whom she can spend herself, is apt to become hard, bitter, selfish, because she has no one but herself to consider. The woman who is constantly concerned with the needs of her family can unfold the qualities of love, tenderness, and unselfish devotion which make her truly great and truly happy.

Mentally, a woman's mind matures under the stimulus of the varied practical activities she performs for those she loves. In the concrete, living experience of the family, she can develop sound judgment and a keen insight into human nature. Lombroso's observation can readily be verified.

"The mother of a large family who has had no time to study, having been occupied with her children and her household, has more life, more breadth of ideas, than the old maid of the same age who has done nothing else than to potter about at universities and libraries." The responsibilities of her family life exercise all woman's mental powers. Her intuition and powers of observation are called into play constantly to discover the unexpressed desires of her family, particularly the needs of the helpless child. She has need of her intuition, too, as well as her tact, to help her solve the hundred problems of human relations and practical affairs that arise in the course of her day. Providing for the family helps to develop woman's natural ingenuity and inventiveness.

It is to the ingenuity of women intent on meeting the needs of their families that we owe the discovery of many of the most important arts: horticulture, for example; the creative arts of weaving, pottery, basketry; the domestic arts of food preparation and preservation; the uses of medicinal herbs in healing.

Physically, too, marriage and child bearing represent a development and completion for the normal woman, giving her new beauty and vitality. The mother of a large family experiences a physical fulfillment with the birth of each child which gives her fresh vigor and health.

Dr. Alexis Carrell observes that women attain their full development as a rule only after the birth of several children. He writes in "Man The Unknown": "Women who have no children are not so well balanced and become more nervous than the others. The importance to woman of the generative function has not been sufficiently recognized. Such function is indispensable to her optimum development. It is therefore absurd to turn women against maternity.

The Gigantic Task

In a well balanced society, where the family performs all its proper functions, the home is a society in microcosm, presenting all the problems of human relations, all the variety of human activities. The home is at once an economic and industrial center, preparing goods for family use; a school in which the young are introduced to the universe; a sanctuary for rest and relaxation; a temple dedicated to the praise of God. It is woman's function to organize and direct this complex undertaking, a role which demands intelligence talents and spiritual qualities of a high order. Chesterton describes the vastness of woman's task in the family in the following passage from "What's Wrong With the World":

"To be Queen Elizabeth within a definite area, deciding sales, banquets, labors, and holidays; to be Whiteley within a certain area, providing toys, boots, sheets, cakes and books; to be Aristotle within a certain area, teaching morals, manners, theology and hygiene: I can understand how this might exhaust the mind, but I cannot imagine how it could narrow it. How can it be a large career to tell other people's children about the Rule of Three and a small career to tell one's own children about the universe? How can it be broad to be the same thing to everyone, and narrow to be everything to someone? No; a woman's function is laborious but because it is gigantic, not because it is minute."

One of the greatest of woman's responsibilities is her task as educator, transmitting the fundamental heritage of civilization, the traditions of culture and religion, to the new generation. The child receives his first introduction to civilization from his mother. The first formation of his mind and character belong almost entirely to her. She gives the child his first concepts of reality, his basic acquaintance with his mother tongue.

The child's ideas of God, of right and wrong, of repentance for faults, his first meeting with God in prayer--all come through the mother's teaching. She socializes the young human being, training him to honesty, courage, generosity, developing self-control, responsibility, and all those other virtues without which society cannot exist. She molds the men and women of the future. No other influence is as strong as the mother's in forming and preparing human beings for life.

Woman not only transmits the foundation of culture to the child; she is the great keeper of tradition in society, the custodian of manners and morals, conserving the gracious customs and fundamental standards of the race. She inspires and enforces the code of social behavior as, for example, the great chatelaines of the middle ages upheld the noble code of chivalry, and the hostesses of the seventeenth century salons cultivated the refinement of taste and manner. She keeps alive those religious customs and traditions in the home and community which link the daily life of man to God by so many intimate bonds. She is the guardian of the moral standard, especially in all that concerns the family. In this respect, as in so many others, the modern woman has abrogated her traditional role with tragic consequences for society.

It is impossible to exaggerate the importance for society of woman's achievement in the family. The family is the foundation of all the larger social structures, the basic cell on which all other agencies depend for the very existence and first formation of their members. A nation can flourish only to the extent that it is composed of healthy, flourishing families. But the family can endure only if the woman spends herself wholeheartedly to create a real home. If the woman looks down upon her function and neglects her task in the family, nothing can take her place; the family will disintegrate and with it the whole society. This should be abundantly clear to us when we see how powerless the most elaborate schools and the most advanced methods of social work are in the face of the rising tide of juvenile delinquents from neglected and broken homes.

It is superficial to think as women that we must be in the forefront of public affairs, politics, or business to influence the course of the world. "Not in the branches of a tree but in its roots do force and power reside," writes Gertrude von Le Fort. Woman is at the very roots of social life. If she keeps the sources of life pure and healthy, the entire social order will be renewed and reinvigorated by her effort.

Woman in Single Life

The other sphere through which woman can carry out her mission is the state of single life in the world. In normal times, only a few women are called to this vocation. But in our time, due to the war and to other abnormal social conditions, many women will remain unmarried. We should realize that this circumstance falls within God's Providence, and that He has destined the single woman to fulfill an important role in the modern world.

The task of the unmarried woman is, by her whole hearted surrender to God, to make virginity spiritually fruitful in the world. In embracing virginity, she should radiate purity and nobility of soul. Her very existence, like that of the virgin consecrated in religion, should be a strong positive influence upholding the dignity of womanhood and the sanctity of marriage.

By developing her capacity for spiritual motherhood, she should become a source of strength and comfort and inspiration to mankind. Never has the world been so full of misery, so desperately in need of the healing influence of woman's love. The mission of the unmarried woman in this time is to give the full riches of her maternal love and devotion to alleviate the sufferings and renew the hope of mankind. In order to accomplish her vocation, the single woman must find an appropriate sphere in which she can carry out her dedication to God through loving service of human beings. She must strike out on new paths, searching for types of work in which she can use her womanly talents and develop her woman's nature. In the education and formation of the young; in agriculture, tending growing plants and animals; in the care of the sick, the weak, the poor, the helpless, woman finds fields of activity appropriate to her capacities as nurturer of life.

Unfortunately, work as it is carried on in these fields today often affords small opportunity for the use of woman's characteristic talents. In medicine, in education, in social work, we suffer from depersonalization, from too much large scale organization and mechanical routine, from too much concern with the physical aspects of the process. We need women to pioneer in these fields again, bringing with them their gift for warmly personal service and creating truly womanly occupations. We need women who will help to restore the emphasis on the spiritual, and who will make the work of healing, of teaching, of relieving the distressed a full expression of living charity between human persons.

How did We Lose the Concept of True Womanhood?

As we look over the modern world we may be tempted to echo King Solomon's cry: Who shall find a valiant woman? On every hand we see modern women turning away from this type of the greathearted woman. How does it happen that we have lost the concept of the woman of love and sacrifice and have accepted the ideal of the professional woman in its place?

Three major factors have contributed to the destruction of the womanly ideal: the Reformation, and the consequent secularization of western culture; the Industrial Revolution; the Feminist Movement. The Reformation was an ultra-masculine movement with small regard for woman's qualities and woman's functions. As society lost its Catholic sense, it lost also the concept of total dedication, the understanding of the sacramentality of life, the regard for the sanctity of marriage--all principles intimately connected with woman's mission and dignity. At the same time, "the masculine desire to dominate the woman found expression in the law." Public opinion looked down upon woman's sphere. "Kirche, kuche, and kinderstube" ("Church, kitchen, and nursery") were linked together and treated with scant respect as fit only for women.

Along with the intellectual devaluation of woman's activities came the profound economic and social changes created by the Industrial Revolution. Seventy-five years ago the woman in the home was still the center of a variety of economic enterprises of unquestioned value and importance. But one by one almost all the activities through which a woman served her family, developed herself, and earned the esteem of society, have been lifted out of her hands and transferred to the factory. The sphere in which most women had found their means of dedication was severely curtailed. At the same time, economic necessity forced many women into the labor market to help support their families and thus led them further away from a womanly pattern.

The third influence which has contributed to the loss of a true concept of woman's function is the feminist fallacy. Feminism was born of woman's natural reaction against the depressed condition in which she found herself in a secularized, masculine, industrial culture. The feminists vociferously demanded equality, but unfortunately they conceived equality on a masculine pattern. Their whole struggle for woman's rights has simply helped to destroy the difference between the sexes and has worked to make the woman a slavish imitation of the man. Feminism is an abject surrender to the masculine ideal as the only ideal. The feminist has completely lost faith in herself as a woman. Her effort to prove herself "just as good as a man" betrays her insecurity and is a tacit admission of inferiority.

Woman's struggle for freedom has led her deeper and deeper into a morass of conditions which frustrate her nature and her mission. Chesterton's bon mot is more than a witty pun: "Twenty million women rose to their feet with the cry: 'We will not be dictated to' and proceeded to become stenographers." It is a summary of woman's situation in the modern world. Women rebelled against the confinement of the home; they find themselves now confined to the mechanical routine of the typewriter and the assembly line, rendered all the more monotonous for a woman because of its exceedingly impersonal character. Woman is made for marriage and motherhood; the modern woman in the name of freedom urges easy divorce and artificial sterility. Woman is well adapted to the universal activity of the home; her demand for freedom leads her to a narrowly specialized education and still more narrowly specialized career. Woman is made for love, for the giving of herself in personal, devoted service. In the modern world she has found her way to a position of lonely and selfish independence.

Towards a Solution

The problem of woman's role is fundamental and no simple, facile solution will meet it. It is not surprising that a society which has lost its sense for divine things and for man's own nature should have lost also the true concept of woman. The unnatural position of woman in our society is but one aspect of the disintegration of modern culture. Nothing short of an intensive and all-embracing renewal of the modern world in the Christian spirit will restore woman to her proper functions. What can we do as women to restore a true concept of womanhood?

(1) *Know Thyself*: As women, our first task is to regain our self-respect in the light of a clear concept of our nature and our role. We must grasp the full splendor of the divine idea of woman as it is revealed to us in the sacred writings, climaxing in the figure of Our Lady. If we have the courage to be ourselves and to follow our spiritual mission, then the world will once again recognize and reverence the immeasurable dignity of womanhood.

(2) *Restore the Christian Family*: We must strive in all ways to restore the family to its rightful dignity and full vigor as the basic cell of the social organism. The family must regain the entire range of its functions, the full scope of its gigantic task--religious, educational, cultural, economic. As women it is our particular responsibility to develop a new pattern of integral Christian life in the family, in which common prayer, work, study and recreation will build the bonds of unity and draw the family heavenwards.

(3) *Create Womanly Work*: If woman is to give the full benefit of her special qualities to society, it is of the utmost importance that we create, especially for the unmarried woman, many types of womanly work. We need pioneers of vision and imagination to take the lead in developing occupations which give woman the opportunity to mature and use her distinctive gifts. We must be alert to discover appropriate spheres of activity in which woman may realize her dedication to God in loving service of humankind.

(4) *Become Radiant Examples of the Spirit of Total Dedication*: Most important of all we must fulfill our primary mission to radiate the spirit of dedication in the world. Never has there been a period in the history of the race when the need for woman's spiritual mission was so great. At the root of all the disorders of our sad, sick world lies man's attempt to assert his independence of God. To bring tranquillity and joy into the chaos of modern society, the first necessity is a profound renewal of spirit, a wholehearted surrender of man to God, a humble and joyful acknowledgment of our complete dependence on Him. To light the way to this surrender is the spiritual mission of the women of the twentieth century, the task of woman in the modern world.

FAITH AND FREEDOM

Muslim women around the world see their future in democracy-and in Islam. To veil or not to veil is hardly the question. The fate of women's rights throughout the Islamic world today hinges on matters of far greater substance, from reforms of family and penal codes to new understandings of Islamic law and teaching. In these best and worst of times for Muslim women, it is perhaps not surprising that every promising bit of news seems to come with a disturbing counterpoint.

Take Shirin Ebadi, an Iranian lawyer and former judge, who in mid-October won the Nobel Peace Prize for her unceasing efforts to promote women's rights and democracy in her native land. In response to the jubilant reaction of Iranians throughout the Islamic republic, President Mohammad Khatami--a reformist, no less--dismissed it as "not worth all that fuss!" Several days after the Nobel was announced, Morocco's King Mohammed VI, who claims descent from the prophet Mohammed, proposed reforms in family law that stand to improve the lot of women throughout the North African kingdom. But long before he presented the reforms to the national parliament, Islamists had taken to the streets to denounce them, dwarfing a pro-reform demonstration by roughly 3 to 1. Also in mid-October, in an unusual instance of Bedouin perestroika, authorities in Saudi Arabia announced that the kingdom would permit the holding of municipal elections within a year--though it's still unclear whether women will be able to run for office or even vote. And at the end of September, in one of a dozen Nigerian states that have adopted sharia (Islamic law), a religious appeals court overturned the death sentence of Amina Lawal, 32, a Muslim woman accused of adultery. Yet while Lawal was spared the gruesome fate of death by stoning, at least five other women in Nigeria still face the same sentence.

Women's rights face an uncertain future throughout much of the Islamic world--though nowhere more pointedly than in the constitution-making efforts now underway in both Afghanistan and Iraq. In two nations widely viewed as test cases of the compatibility of Islamic and universal values, it remains to be seen whether and how the principles of sharia, or even the more general spirit of Islamic traditions, will inform their future laws. And behind those uncertainties loom even broader questions facing Muslim women everywhere. In particular, rights activists wonder, are the foundations of Islamic law and theology compatible with international standards of human rights in general and women's right in particular? And if so, what must be done to surmount the practical hurdles--including the crucial matter of who interprets the law--that stand in the way of reconciling Islam with universal principles of women's rights?

Muslim women themselves are already actively engaged with these issues. "When I talk with educated women from Morocco to Pakistan," says Ann Mayer, a professor of legal studies at the University of Pennsylvania's Wharton School and author of Islam and Human Rights: Tradition and Politics, "I find that they are much more inclined to evaluate their condition in relation to international standards of human rights. And they say that international standards only reinforce Islamic standards."

Confidence. That underscores one notable development of the past decade: a new confidence among Muslim feminists and human-rights activists that Islamic teachings and sources can support their efforts. This represents a sea change, says Amina Wadud, professor of Islamic studies at Virginia Commonwealth University and author of Qu'ran and Woman: Rereading the Sacred Text From a Woman's Perspective. As late as 1995, at the Global Women's Conference in Beijing, many feminists from Islamic countries insisted women's equality could be attained only by jettisoning religion, including the outward trappings of the faith, such as the veil.

Since then, though, an expanding reform movement within Islam, driven largely by increased literacy and an explosion of new media outlets, has led more Muslims to explore the sacred writings on their own. While this has often reinforced the patriarchal viewpoint of militant Islamists, it has also supported progressive and feminist interpretations. Wadud insists that it is unnecessary and even constraining to argue only on the basis of historical precedent, but she finds there is more in the sacred texts and traditions to support notions of gender equality than there is to deny them. She notes, for example, that in the period after Mohammed's death, women, including the Prophet's favorite wife, Aisha, played "key roles in preserving traditions, disseminating knowledge, and challenging authority when it went against their understanding of the Koran or the prophetic legacy."

Referring to the decision of Iran's mullahs to remove Nobel winner Ebadi from her judgeship on religious grounds, Wadud notes, "Nowhere is it said that women cannot interpret the law." Ebadi herself, in a recent interview with Iranian emigre author Amir Taheri, makes the same point in her words of advice to Muslim women: "Don't believe that you are decreed to have an inferior position. Study the Koran carefully, so that the oppressors cannot impress you with citations and interpretations. Don't let individuals masquerading as theologians claim they have a monopoly on understanding Islam."

Fine words, but have they yet had any practical consequences? The answer, many activists say, is a qualified yes. In that widely followed adultery case in Nigeria, for example, Amina Lawal's attorney, Hauwa Ibrahim, got her client exonerated, but on several technicalities that may not work for other women. The real problem, says Mayer, is that Nigeria's version of sharia involves a "folkloric version" of Islamic adultery law. First of all, the rules of evidence spelled out in the Koran require either a freely gained confession from the accused or four eyewitnesses to the act of sexual penetration, neither of which was obtained in Nawal's case. Just as important, the maximum punishment for the crime is supposed to be 100 lashes, not stoning.

Illegal. Of course, even if the Nawal case and others did not involve a corrupted use of sharia, the punishments that Nawal faced would be in violation of both the spirit and letter of the U.N. Convention on the Elimination of All Forms of Discrimination Against Women (CEDAW), which Nigeria has signed and ratified. But appeals to international agreements have only limited effectiveness in advancing women's rights in the Islamic world. (Saudi Arabia is one of 50 out of the 57 Organization of Islamic Conference nations to sign and ratify CEDAW, but it explicitly stipulates that it will not observe any terms that contradict "norms of Islamic law.") In some cases, appeals might even backfire. According to Wadud, the defense attorneys involved in another Nigerian adultery case had to send out word that any additional international pressure might actually sway the jurists on a religious appeals court not to overturn the verdict.

In a more general way, says New York University law Prof. Noah Feldman, the former U.S. adviser to the Iraqi Governing Council on constitutional matters, the United States faces a similar challenge in its efforts to guide Afghanistan and Iraq toward becoming democratic and rights-respecting regimes. Feldman points out that as long as America is an occupying power, it can accomplish much "just by suggesting"--though, he promptly adds, the U.S.-led Coalition Provisional Authority had to insist on the appointment of several women to the 25-person Governing Council. "But at a certain point," Feldman cautions, "you cross the line to coercing people on how to run their lives."

Feldman prefers to stop short of that line, having disagreed openly with Sen. Sam Brownback and Rep. Frank Wolf's proposal for requiring explicit religious-freedom language in the Iraqi constitution. "Senator Brownback says if we allow the constitution to mention the word `Islam,' we'll have problems down the road, but I say if we don't, we'll have troubles immediately," Feldman explains. That does not mean that he has little hope for women's rights. To the contrary, says the author of After Jihad, an argument for the future of Islamic democracy, "I am for promoting women's rights by saying they are compatible with Islam."

In Iraq, there are good reasons for thinking that Islam and women's rights can go together. Before the U.S. invasion, says Khaled Abou el Fadl, a visiting professor at Yale Law School, Iraq was one of the most progressive of Muslim nations in relation to women. Not only were there female jurists and lawyers, but there was a civil code that blended the best of French and Islamic laws. Among the latter, he points out, was a law allowing a woman the right to divorce her husband and sue for alimony and child support if he decided to take another wife. (A similar expansion of women's prerogatives is one of the reforms that Morocco's king has just proposed.) Like Feldman, Abou el Fadl worries that attempts to expunge Islam from Iraq's laws will only trigger a stronger urge on the part of many Iraqis to put more of Islam in--and that might mean the most sexist and partriarchal versions of Islam.

Which raises the most important issue: How can Muslim feminists and rights activists win the interpretive struggle against those mullahs and muftis who confuse partriarchal codes and customs with the core principles of the faith? That is a major concern for Irshad Manji, a Canadian author and journalist. Like many other Muslim feminists, she sees the real problem of interpretation as one of overturning Arab traditions of honor that accompanied the spread of Islam and are now being recirculated throughout the world via the Saudi-funded Wahhabi religious establishment. As Manji explains, within the Arab honor code, individual rights are secondary to one's status within the family or tribe. Women are reduced to "communal or tribal property." In Pakistan or Nigeria, she says, a man from one tribe or family may rape a woman from another as an act of communal retribution.

For Manji, who develops her argument in her forthcoming book The Trouble With Islam, one of the best solutions lies in women's growing participation in trade, commerce, and capitalism, all of which have been valued since Islam's founding. (Mohammed's first wife, Khadija, was an astute businessperson.) And the economic empowerment of women in the Islamic world is not merely theoretical. It is already underway even in the most Arab of states, Saudi Arabia. In Jidda and Riyadh, respectively, women own a quarter and a third of all businesses. And it is no secret among foreigners working in Saudi Arabia that women are the most educated, able, and productive employees in the kingdom.

By consolidating and advancing their economic position, Manji says, and by becoming tax-paying citizens, women can assert their standing as individuals. This emerging reality is hard to ignore, whether in Saudi Arabia or Iran. Already in Malaysia, Amina Wadud notes, women working through Sisters in Islam and other groups have helped reform domestic violence law by promoting what she calls a "nice blend of sharia and civil law."

Still, it is one of the sad ironies of Islam, Manji says, that a religion originally intended to transcend tribalism has, at least in many parts of the world, allowed the tribalist codes to reassert themselves. But Manji refuses to accept that irony as the last word on women's fate within Islam. And she is far from alone.

19

Woman's Future Position in the World

To be strictly logical one should not treat of woman apart from the rest of the human race, for this is in a manner to admit that women are a distinct class, not affected by conditions, environment, etc., as men are. But we find a "woman question" actually existing. A great deal of discussion has been going on as to what is proper for woman, what her real nature is, and how many of the duties and privileges of man she should be admitted to. Women do not occupy the same position, socially, politically, economically, or intellectually that men do, and her powers are not equal to her brother's. She is daily reproached for trying to be other than she is, and reminded that her very nature forbids her presuming to climb out of the subserviency and inferiority which are now undeniably her portion. Thus a "woman question" is forced upon us whether we will or not. It is to discover, if possible, whether she may ever become equal to and like man without perverting her inherent nature, that this inquiry is made.

It is impossible to ascertain whether there ever was a time when woman stood an equally strong intellectual and physical being, on an equal footing with man, or not. If it ever existed, its memory is now very hazy. Yet there are writers who refer to it as a fact. August Bébel, in "Woman: Past, Present, and Future," refers to it thus: "We have no grounds for assuming that in this primitive state men were physically or mentally superior to women.... Certain savage tribes were governed by women instead of men owing to the superior strength of the former.... Primeval woman, although the equal of man in bodily and mental power, nevertheless became his inferior when periods of pregnancy, birth, and lactation forced her to look to him for assistance, support, and protection."

And in a more mystical sense Olive Schreiner refers to the time: "And he answered: 'Listen and I will tell you. Ages and ages long she has lain here, and the wind has blown over her. The oldest, oldest man living has never seen her move; the oldest book records that she lay here then as she lays here now. But listen! Older than the oldest book, older than the oldest recorded memory of man, on the rocks of language, on the hard baked clay of ancient custom, are found the marks of her footsteps. Side by side with him who stands beside her, you may trace them, and you may know that she who now lies here once wandered free over the rocks with him.'"

Matilda Joslyn Gage, in her "Woman, Church, and State," lays great emphasis upon the days of matriarchy, when women, as mothers of the race, ruled the people. But we have no evidence that any such period ever existed. Letourneau shows that cases have been where inheritances descended and relationships were determined through the women of the tribe. Accompanying this usage, a certain importance adhered to the mothers of the tribe. It is true, women attained powerful and prominent positions in the old civilizations that have come and gone. The mythical lost Atlantis was peopled with great women of divine aspect. There were queens in the days of Solomon; and the Helens, Cleopatras, and Hypatias of history dot the dark pages with glints of a glory to come. A matriarchy never existed; cases of matriarchy have been known. Woman never stood beside man his equal in all things; women have ruled in isolated instances.

Be that as it may, woman's subordination came to be complete. She was first knocked down, dragged away senseless, and made a slave. She was bought and sold, or traded; she became a thing, a piece of property, a bond slave. Her degraded position among men became a custom, then an institution, then a tradition. There were centuries of "dark ages for her, into whose gloom no ray of light ever pierced, and from whose depths little has come down to us to tell the sombre story."

Slowly, very slowly man developed in intellect and acquired a rude knowledge of art. The woman in his tents could not remain very far behind him, and in time arose to some degree of companionship. That he treated her with a little kindness, and even appealed to her in times of weariness or perplexity for sympathy or counsel, was due, not to his traditions and creeds conceived in another grade of civilization, but to changed conditions and his own developed nature. There might even have arisen a "woman's rights question" in those old Mosaic days, had not the priests, who feared any loosening of their control over the people, issued a "Thus saith the Lord," and so riveted her chains for another three thousand years. "Thy desire shall be unto thy husband, and he shall rule over thee," settled the problem for the time.

"Economic dependence is the basis of all slavery," Bébel says; and he is right. All forms of slavery had their inception in some kind of economic dependence, but the slavery often exists long after the dependent condition has passed away. A thing, once established, once made an institution, is very apt to outlast the economic phase which determined its existence, and become a very troublesome matter. Institutions are crystallized ideas; they stand still: people grow--grow beyond and outside of them. Yet there they remain, unwieldy, mischief-breeding; to get rid of them at all is to tear them out by the roots at great cost of life and suffering. The bonds made ages ago, by economic conditions prevailing at the time, have become sacred; they bear another strength than that which they possessed when first formed. Though no longer with any economical basis for existing, they are even more effective in power than when first established.

Individually men are not to blame for the inferior position of women. They accepted a condition, a chain of customs, as they found them. Though long past the time when constant danger from without rendered it necessary that his whole family give him implicit obedience, the habit of expecting filial deference is fixed. Though the days of absolute property in wives have gone by, the sense of proprietorship in and responsibility for wives still prevails. That sentiment which played upon the superstitious fears of woman, setting a sort of mental watchdog to guard the master's property in his absence as well as when present, still exists in a modified form in the demand for perfect chastity in woman not expected man. The old feeling of ownership, which led men to seclude their women, has softened into that modern sentiment which would keep women guarded from the public gaze in every respect. The stern commands of old are toned down into "what is expected of womanly women," but that expectation is as binding as any chain or title deed to person could be.

Thus, through ages of subserviency, of which there were many grades, women have come to be what they are: emotional, since any prominent display of other faculties has been unnecessary in that "sphere to which it has pleased God to call her;" deceitful, since deceit has been her only weapon; illogical, since the encouragement of her reasoning powers would have often placed her in direct opposition to her master; vain, since her personal charms were long the only qualities for which she was considered; weak-minded, since strong brains were not desirable in that function to which man wished to limit her. So from long persisting conditions woman has come to be the creature she is.

But the change in woman's position and in the manner in which woman is considered during the last fifty years has been a remarkable one. We scarcely realize its greatness until we begin to compare the prominent women of today with women of the last century. It is perhaps correct to say that Mary Wollstonecraft began the modern woman's-rights movement. Her work, "The Rights of Women," written toward the close of the last century, is read more widely now than at the time of publication. It was many years before an organized effort was made to secure political equality for women. The movement, which has lasted through the lifetime of some of America's noblest women, though a little too narrow for modern sociological students, has been a great element in the remarkable change. Unconsciously it has builded better than it knew, and helped to widen the field and elevate the aspirations of women far more than the originators ever intended.

The introduction of machinery has been the most potent factor in the transition. When the work of the world was done in the home, when the spinning-wheel, the loom, the soap vat, the "pig-killing," the bake oven, and the slender needle were institutions in every household, naturally "woman's place" was at home. But spinning-wheel and loom turned into great cotton and woollen mills; the pork-barrel became the vast packing-houses of our large cities; the needle was reserved for mending, and great clothing establishments took its place; the old lye barrel gave way to immense soap factories; and family ovens were relegated to the past, for the bakeries that now supply the staff of life.

It was no longer profitable to make these things in the seclusion of the home; and women followed the machines and went in great crowds to the factories. The demand for women's work came at a time when a new restlessness was pervading the inner sanctum of the home. Secluded and protected, kindly treated though they might happen to be, women began to feel that they were not living full, true lives. They felt that all their faculties were not being developed, that all their powers for giving and receiving happiness were not being called out. Though the duties of motherhood might for the time being occupy all their time and energies, it was also true that not all women were mothers of children, nor were the mothers always mothers of young children. A woman's life stretches over many periods, as does man's. In a lifetime she is capable of being much more than a mother, as man is expected to be much more than a father.

The restlessness was natural. Women came out into the world and became acquainted with each other and with their working brothers; they took a broader view of life; and something of that feeling of fraternity to which men had attained in their clubs, lodges, and unions, began to take lodgment in their breasts. For the "old" woman had no conception of the brotherhood of the human race. She loved her own passionately, and she loved her immediate friends; she loved her church and believed in a vague way that she "loved all men," as a good Christian should. But of the real solidarity of the human race, of the truth that "an injury to one is the concern of all," she had no conception. The "new woman" has a very fair realizing sense of this great social truth today. And therefore, though she may be more of a slave in the factory than she was in the narrow confines of home, she has come up higher. She has reached greater opportunities for full, well-developed existence; and though she makes some mistakes, she is far advanced in her evolutionary progress.

But as yet she is no happier, and men are not pleased. They think she has taken their places in the workshop, in the office, and at the business desk; they fear to lose the sweet, clinging, fragile, wheedling little creature they imagine they love; and they have not reached a conception of what the free, self-poised, capable, womanly woman of the future will be. They are not very well satisfied with the crude sample of the "new woman;" and they are in a manner drawing away from her in the consciousness of a lofty superiority which never needs a transitional stage.

Women themselves are not happy, because they are not yet accustomed to the new order--an order that is as yet chaotic and undefined. Just out from the unwholesome hothouse air of their old seclusion, the atmosphere of comparative freedom and independence strikes too harshly upon them, and they shiver. They cannot go back, and they cannot yet breathe easily. They can do wonders in adaptation, but they cannot find their equilibrium in half a generation of partial freedom. The adjusting process hurts; it always does.

What is it that woman wants? What is it she hopes to attain? What is it she lacks that men are not willing to give? It is no wonderful thing; nothing preposterous or presumptuous. She simply wants to be a human being, not a slave, not a toy, not a queen. She wants the equal personal liberty that every man demands in order to become a fully developed, well-balanced, happy, and useful being. Only this and nothing more.

With this emancipation--this "liberty to do whatsoever one wills so long as one [does not infringe] on the equal right of others to do as they will"--she needs not even the chivalry of old. Kindness, sympathy, love from equals she needs in common with man. She needs not that spirit of worship which some men who think they are "advanced" seem willing to pour out upon her; she needs not that undue devotion on account of her motherhood which many good people believe is right and just; she needs not that right which Robert Ingersoll declared she must possess when he said: "Women should have all the rights that men possess and one more--the right to be protected." The right to be a human being includes that right when necessary. If every individual in the world possesses an equal right to life, liberty, and the pursuit of happiness, the right of opportunity at nature's table, the right to develop to the highest she is capable of becoming, the rights of motherhood and womanhood are conceded. No better protection is needed than that which any enlightened human being will naturally give to another if circumstances make it imperative. A free woman will not choose to be "protected" in the old sense. Protection has ever been an implication of weakness and a willingness to occupy a subordinate position. Nations which call upon other nations for protection must needs give up for that protection some portion of their independence; and industries that can flourish only under "protection" create slaves in their turn.

A great fear seems to exist that if women were perfectly free to become whatever they see fit many dire calamities would happen. Woman would become "mannish;" she would lose her delicate sense of morality; and she might slight that one great duty to which she has been almost wholly consigned for so many ages. But why do we hesitate to trust woman free, when she has fulfilled so many precious trusts in bondage? I have no fear that motherhood and love is a great part of the sweetness of life, and free women are not likely to yield up any part of their happiness.

This one great fear seems to lie at the bottom of every objection to the full freedom and equality of woman--the fear that she will refuse to do her duty by the human race. It is the last prejudice, the last of the old traditions, that man is willing to let go. He will go so far as to admit the right of suffrage, to accept equal property rights, to grant equal opportunities in all the fields of human activity, but he cannot rid himself of that sacred old tenet: that a woman cannot be a good wife and mother if she have any other interest in life besides her home and children. Even very radical thinkers still at times declare that "woman's crowning glory is motherhood;" and only insist on equal opportunities and unequal consideration that she may be more fully and perfectly the mother. I am aware that I am proving myself a startling heretic to generally accepted ideas, but I most emphatically dissent.

I am aware that throughout the realm of nature the one blind impulse of every living thing is to reproduce itself. Everything else seems to be sacrificed to this one object. In the lowest living organisms individual identity is completely lost in the separation which creates two where one existed before. A little higher up in the scale extinction follows reproduction; and for many degrees in the ascending gamut the sole purpose of existence seems to be simply reproduction. But as the higher forms of life evolve, in both the animal and the vegetable kingdoms, more and more of life is utilized in other ways. Trees live to give shelter and shade, and they minister to our sense of beauty through many years; the higher animals have many uses, and many years of animal enjoyment, aside from the function of reproduction.

In the lower grades of human life the power of reproduction seems the most important part of existence. But as the race advances, develops, acquires knowledge, the existence of its members becomes rich and full with the wealth of life itself. The individual becomes an emphasized, distinct identity. It is something to the world that a bright, sound individual lives, acts, and thinks, even though it is never reproduced. The male portion of the race already feel as though fatherhood were a mere incident in their lives, and would be insulted were you to intimate that fatherhood should be the crowning glory of their lives. They know that they possess powers and capabilities that the world needs and appreciates, and that fatherhood, blessed though it be, is not the fullest and best manifestation of their existence. The idea is in every way as applicable to woman as to man. Why should all the faculties and energies of woman be turned to the fulfilment of this one function of her being?

It is flattering to man to think that it takes all of a woman's whole life to carry out her duty to him and his children. But if he only knew it, the entire devotion of her powers to this one purpose is the poorest preparation for wifehood and motherhood that can be made. Even the man himself feels a sort of undefined contempt for the woman who is nothing but wife and mother. A woman becomes morbid who simply retires within herself to brood over her fitness or unfitness for her "crowning glory." It is distorting, dwarfish, narrowing. Her child is unfavorably affected by this intensity of thought centred upon its embryonic existence. It is like that unwholesome "self-analysis" which has ever made up so great a part of the old religious creeds, and which still crops up in modified forms in the "new philosophies."

Let the woman live for herself, not for unborn children. Let her fill her life to the brim with happiness, knowledge, mental and physical activity; let lofty emotions and vigorous thoughts fill her being; let her whole existence expand to its fullest extent; let her forget her motherhood; she will be the better mother for first being a perfect woman. And to be this she must first be free. It will not do to ask what she will do with her freedom, to criticise, to judge; one must only wait. "The cure for the evils of liberty is more liberty."

Do not fear for the result. The trend of human evolution is upward and onward. The plant allowed to grow freely, in the sunlight, with warm rich soil and pure fresh air, will develop to its very highest possibilities. Cramp it, interfere with it, abstract either light or warmth, and it becomes a stunted, pale, sickly growth. Looking upon it, no one could tell what it might have become under proper conditions.

Do not fear that woman thus freed would become a poor mimicry of a poor sample of a man. To become "mannish" is in the eyes of conventional society worse than to commit a crime. But what do we mean by this term? If it is anything reprehensible, believe me, it is as bad in man as in woman. Does it apply to the manners, morals, or the intellect? It is very vague at best. For those qualities which we call "good" are as beautiful in man as in woman. We love bravery, self-poise, strength, honor, truthfulness in one as well as in the other. We love gentleness, kindness, sympathy, tact in both sexes. We see today timid men and brave women; weak-minded men and strong-minded women; deceitful men and truthful women; vain men and self-forgetful women. Under equal and similar conditions the virtues and vices would be diffused much more equally. For I hold another heresy: that there is no sex in intellect, sentiment, or morals. The same environment, the same treatment, the same teachings would result in a similarity of characteristics. There will never cease to be variety, but we should not find a greater tendency toward any particular group of faculties in one sex over the other.

True, some scientific scholars declare that it is a physical impossibility for woman under any condition to become man's equal in physical and mental strength, or to become free from her emotional disturbances and sensitiveness of nerves. The shape, size, and quality of the brain, they say, preclude this; her peculiar functions, the time and energy necessary to the bearing of children and the nourishing of them, prevent a change from her present nature. Nevertheless this is not a demonstrated truth; no one knows by actual experiment whether it is true or not. The fact that all human creatures are the subject of environment and of hereditary conditions signifies that woman is no exception. There is every reason to suppose that under like conditions with men, women would develop in a manner as men do. Woman's peculiar functions should not create the sharp distinctions now seen. Weakness, dependence, emotionalism, vanity, deceitfulness have been cultivated in woman; these traits have been considered her greatest attractions; tradition, custom, public opinion have fixed them upon her, and it will take long to eliminate them.

There is no reason why woman should devote more of her time and energies to motherhood than man does to fatherhood. Work, activity, interest in other things, both while carrying and nourishing children, are better than idleness. No special training, no particular occupation or exercise of one's faculties, or the cessation of activities, are necessary as a preparation for motherhood. The life which makes a woman all she is capable of being as a human being is the only one essential to the rearing of good children. So little is required of a mother that need interfere with ordinary duties and occupations, that it is difficult to see how motherhood should have, in itself, such a wonderful differentiating effect.

Woman has been considered too much as woman, and not enough as a human being. The constant reference to her sex has been neither ennobling, complimentary, nor agreeable. Either as slave, toy, pet, or queen, this ceaseless thinking of her sex instead of herself has been degrading. To finally arrive at her best she simply needs consideration as a fellow member of society.

Do not fear liberty. Just now the results of the beginnings of freedom do not seem very satisfactory. Woman seems to be an intruder; she cannot overcome at once the prejudices that had their inception in the time of her complete economic dependence. She herself is dissatisfied. She is not as lovable perhaps. She has lost some of the charm of clinging womanhood which at best man only heeded in his leisure moments, and has not yet gained the poise and individuality that will draw him to her as a companion. She is dissatisfied with the old gallantry, and has not yet attained the spontaneous recognition and respectful love she longs for. But this will come. There will be a time when men and women, equal human beings, clasping hands and looking each other in the eyes on a level--not leaning on each other, but upright--will feel a true fellowship; and mutual admiration and respect will exist between them. Then will love be sweeter, purer, more beautiful than the world has ever known.

20

Women's Empowerment

Wives are lonelier now than they ever used to be. In older, gentler times, when age still had its privileges, the old folks never harbored any guilt feelings about being a drag on the young. They either moved in, reasoning that it was high time they were supported for a change, or else they lived nearby. People moved less, and families stuck closer together. Grandma, never having become emancipated, was always around for advice and help. (Today grandma is likely to be off fund raising or taking courses at Columbia.) I know a Polish area in Chicago where everyone in the family lives within a few blocks of the others, and there are usually two generations in each house. They may have other problems, but loneliness isn't one of them.

The young college-educated mother with a medium amount of money is the one who reflects all the problems at once. In spite of her hopes for fulfillment through her children and contentment with woman's great career, she vaguely feels that she is frittering away her days and that a half-defined but important part of her ability is lying about unused; she is guilty about her feeling of futility because of her belief in the magic medicine of love. This is the housewife's syndrome, the vicious circle, the feeling of emptiness in the gap between what she thought marriage was going to be like and what it is really like.

Let's take a look at a fairly typical young mother. She married her husband because she loved him, and she still does. She has two children and is pregnant with a third. Whether in city or country, she is more or less surrounded by gadgets which free her from drudgery. If she is lucky, she has a cleaning woman once a week. She and her husband have enough money for a fairly comfortable life, but for time alone together are dependent on baby sitters and possibly a grandma who will help out in a pinch. If the young mother is in the country, the children play in the yard, and she watches them from the window; if she is in the city, she takes them out once or twice a day, pushing a carriage and pulling a tricycle. Talking to her friends on these outings is her solution to loneliness. Her day is full of a thousand pressures, some miniature, some large. Two of the main worries are illness and money. If everyone in the family is healthy for two weeks at a stretch, she counts herself fortunate. Every cold goes the rounds of the family, and she sometimes feels that she supports the pediatrician singlehandedly.

During the healthy periods she strives to improve her home, cook a new dish, do something about her looks, give a dinner party and a children's birthday party, go to the theater with her husband, catch up on her reading, have coffee with a friend. Her life vacillates between being very organized and completely disorganized, because she has the struggle of all women: to keep the house clean and in repair without being a shrew about people's messing it up. Because children are natural makers of havoc, she constantly strives to maintain the delicate line of balance. Usually, when the first child starts school, she is drawn into community or P.T.A. work of some kind. If she is normally conscientious, she feels she should do something, but if she is normally realistic, she knows she doesn't have time. So she does it anyway. Joining things as a virtue is a hangover from college, where well-roundedness and abundant interests were considered rungs on the ladder to heaven.

The demands of her family and community cause her to feel, as one woman put it, like a pie with not enough pieces to go around. Depending on whether or not she is gregarious, she longs for time to talk to her friends or time to be alone; I should say, the busier she is, the greater her urge to be by herself, to feel unique and separate again. Great numbers of friends are a luxury she can no longer afford; old friends often diminish in importance, which she is sorry about. But there is a limit to her capacity for giving affection, and maintaining old friendships at their original intensity requires an effort she hardly has the energy for. Besides, she is often forced into unwanted and demanding friendships with the next-door neighbor, the boss's wife, or the ladies' club chairman, and she must learn to cover up her real feelings. (To her surprise, she often ends by liking these women.) Another group of demanding relationships is required with her in-laws, and if she gets along well with them, she is lucky. If her husband now lacks the mystery and fascination of the wedding night, he is now more loved and appreciated. The occasions when they have time alone together are among her precious jewels.

In spite of this full life, the old illusions of what life was supposed to hold, the restless remnants, the undefined dreams do not die as they were supposed to. Probably every educated wife has found herself staring at a mountain of dirty diapers and asking herself desperately, "Is this all there is?" And at the same time she is embarrassed by her dissatisfaction; she, of all people, with her intelligence and realistic view of life, should be able to rise above it. But the paradox is that it is she who is least able to. She lives for a better day. Things will be easier when this baby is born, or that one toilet-trained, or the children are all in school; and she will have time to be pretty and intelligent and young again. The mistake is in thinking that everything is going to solve itself by magic. What our girl must do, as she stares at the diapers, is to accept some of the truths about marriage and motherhood that her education and society conspired to keep from her, and go on from there. And if she would appreciate what she has, she must do it now, not next year or five years from now.

The first truth is that marriage does not automatically equal security and contentment. An unmarried friend of mine told me once that she did not see how any problem in marriage could be as bad as one outside of it, because if you had your man, anything else could be easily straightened out. We had a long argument about whether the heart sank more over a sick child or a departed boy friend, and neither of us won. She is one of a good many girls who think that three dates a week, secretarial jobs, and the responsibility of keeping themselves clothed are a nerve-shattering, frantic business, and who look forward to marriage and motherhood as a long, relaxing rest cure. "Getting married and settling down" is a valid notion for men, as it has been throughout history, but not for potential mothers. The day the doctor confirms one's pregnancy is the day to start bracing oneself for the really hard work. (I cannot convince my unmarried friends of this, but, of course, that is as it should be, or many babies might never be born.)

The truth is that, with the birth of the first child, marvelous changes take place. From that moment on, mama is no longer the center of attention; the baby is. Mama and papa will give-and willingly-and the baby will take. They will assume responsibility, earn money, employ their energy, change their lives, if necessary-all for the baby.

This is no light undertaking, but the business of life is starting now, and every day of mama's life proves it to be so. And here her struggle starts. She wants to give everything to the baby; she wants equally to hold on to herself, her intelligence and uniqueness, while the baby con-stantly tries her patience, her strength, her nerves, and roots out of her the deepest emotions she has ever known in her life. This is a whole new process, and not one that provides built-in security. It is a mistake to assume that marriage is a cure-all, a miraculous bit of psychiatry that is going to banish all the old problems overnight and, like phenobarbital, put disturbingly violent instincts to sleep. The benediction of church and state is not enough to still the quality of excitement that comes from strangeness and the idealization of a still-unknown experience.

These things, after all, were part and parcel of sex before marriage, and half its value. Sex in marriage makes up in intimacy what it loses in mystery, but this does not mean that mystery is no longer attractive. The most embarrassing lust for the least likely person can exist in the best-adjusted P.T.A. member in town. Whether or not anything is done about it is another story, but probably most of the time nothing is. We take marriage very seriously; our Puritan heritage is still very much with us; and we fear the wages of sin. Besides, the communities of young married couples are built for decency and togetherness, and the woman who considers taking a lover simply has no place to go.

All of the notions about peace being intrinsic in the state of marriage have to do with the happiness-togetherness cult, the great American dream, the return to the hearth. The peak of all earthly satisfaction is said to be found in the family, popping corn together in matching pajamas, not in hard work and self-denial, or even in the self-knowledge that came with the Freudian age. In our unending search for panaceas, we believe that happiness and "success"-which, loosely translated, means money-are the things to strive for. People are constantly surprised that, even though they have acquired material things, discontent still gnaws.

An Englishman said to me recently, "You Americans live on a much higher plane of expectancy than we do. You constantly work toward some impossible goal of happiness and perfection, and you unfortunately don't have our ability just to give up. Really, it's much easier to accept the fact that some things can't be solved." He is right; we never accept it, and we kill ourselves trying. The feeling of futility of the housewife is based on a history of high expectancy, a faith in external things, and an inability to see that the rewards are found within oneself. It is a paradox that the achievement of a home and family is so often regarded by women as the consummate solution for human ills, when actually the responsibilities it entails are enough to reduce some people to nervous wrecks. Marriage, entered upon maturely, is the only life for most women. But it is a way of life, not a magic bag of goodies at the end of the road.

The fact is that marriage and motherhood bring forth deeper and more staggering emotions than any experience before marriage. There is nothing soothing or secure about the feeling, familiar to all mothers, of wanting to murder one's child and really feeling capable of it, and then the next moment dissolving into the deepest love and repentance. There is nothing soothing about the insane annoyance that one can feel at some irritating habit of a loved one, or at loathing the knowledge of what he or she is going to say; one feels trapped by a total ability to see-mystery gone forever. It can be painful to find oneself isolated, in marriage, with problems that have always been shared with mother or girl friends, and to realize that there are some things that even one's husband cannot be told. This is the hard lesson of discretion. And there is nothing soothing to participants or onlookers about the spine-chilling habit of some couples who goad each other to a fever pitch of irritation, with repeated fingernail rasps on each other's well-known sensitive spots-all in the name of playful affection. It is frightening to see how close emotions are to the surface and how little it takes to make destruction.

And it is equally frightening to know suddenly how complete love is and how much one gives to it, to see how little one can really stand when someone in the family is sick, and to know how quickly one can be torn apart by nothing at all. A young mother said the other day, speaking of young mothers in general, "It always amazes me how vulnerable we are and how we, who are supposed to be so responsible, are such preys of our own feelings." In a family of love, one must become infinitely flexible to withstand the continuous jounce of emotion. This is the muscle that develops, not superefficiency or physical strength, and it is the weariness of this muscle that causes young mothers to want to run away and hide in a solitary place where nothing can jar the heart. The second truth is that a girl does not need a college education to take care of babies and keep house. I recall a lot of talk at college among engaged girls that bringing up children is a vastly complicated business which makes full use of a mother's brains and energy, and that no man on earth has a position as responsible and delicate as that of being totally in charge of the education of minds, souls, and bodies of two or three important human beings.

Well, for one thing, mother is not totally in charge, though she may like to think so. The influences of father, school, doctor, friends, neighborhood, city, or country are equally important. Besides, mother is not really in charge of herself enough to be in charge of her children. What the children learn is what mother is, not what she thinks she is. For another thing, the job is hardly complicated and delicate, at least at first. It is the simple, nerve-wracking, mindless, battering-ram process of trying to teach a savage to use a fork. It requires bloodless patience, a deadly will, enormous physical stamina, and a stable disposition, but no precision instruments. It takes strength and determination. For the fact is that motherhood makes the heaviest demands in what might be called the areas of least experience. I would be surprised if there were a single college-educated mother who has not been struck by the total uselessness of her liberal education when it comes to housewifery.

Instead of distilling pearls of knowledge from a large body of facts, she must now master a whole new set of domestic facts: how to roast a chicken, remove gum from the rug, take a child's temperature, keep the shine on the Sheraton table, iron a blouse, or even change a tire or build a bookcase. Some of these necessities are positively shocking. The care of dirty diapers and the job of keeping the oven clean call for a strong-minded unfastidiousness; even more does the whole process of having a baby, which is certainly nature at its rawest. Learning all of these things calls for a day-to-day resourcefulness and is a new and rather frightening responsibility.

Choosing a house and everything that goes into it, and a school, and a competent doctor are decisions that the young mother makes without adequate knowledge, and she can ill afford mistakes. If her husband is sympathetic, he helps her with these decisions. If not, she gropes her way along and takes the blame when that lovely color for the living-room walls turns out to be bilious salmon pink in the sunlight. And this calls for a brand-new virtue, too; the ability to adapt oneself completely, in about thirty seconds flat, to an entirely new viewpoint. Around a house, no achievement is very permanent, and the day can turn inside out before one's eyes. The salmon-pink walls must suddenly be repainted, the baby sitter suddenly fails, the clean living room is no longer clean, the elevator in the apartment building breaks down, and mother and baby carriage are trapped for the day on the seventh floor.

BACKGROUND

The National Commission on Population which was set up to review, monitor and give directions for the implementation of the National Population Policy with a view to meeting the goals set out in the Policy constituted eight Working Groups on the following subjects related to population stabilization in the country:

I. Strategies to Meet Unmet Needs;

II. Primary and Secondary Education in relation to Population and Civilization;

III. Registration of Births, Deaths and Marriages;

IV. Media for Information, Education and Communication and Motivation;

V. Role of Panchayati Raj Institutions and Self-Help Groups;

VI. Mainstreaming of Indian System of Medicine and Homeopathy into the Health System;

VII. Task Force on Monitoring;

VIII. Advisory Group on Tribal Communities.

Four Sub-Groups have been constituted under the first Working Group on Strategies to meet the following specific unmet needs:

a) Sub-Group on Strategies to Address Unmet Needs of Contraception;

b) Sub-Group on Unmet Needs on Maternal and Child Health;

c) Sub-Group on Strategies for Unmet Needs for Public Health, Drinking Water, Sanitation and Nutrition; and

d) Sub-Group on Empowerment of Women, Development of Children and issues for Adolescents.

The Sub-Group met twice under the Chairpersonship of Smt. Margaret Alva, Member of Parliament and Chairperson of Parliamentary Standing Committee on Empowerment of Women. During the course of the deliberations of the Sub Group, two important developments took place-first, the provisional results of Census 2001 were published and National Policy for Empowerment of Women was approved by the Government. The Sub Group considered both the developments and deliberated on various issues of empowerment of women and development of children and adolescents in the context of the National population Policy.

The Sub-Group felt that the 'unmet needs' of empowerment of women and development of children and adolescents cover a whole gamut of issues which cut through the terms of references of all the Sub Groups and of the Working Groups and, therefore, there is bound to be considerable degree of overlapping in the terms of reference and deliberations of this Sub-Group. The issue of empowerment of women and development of children and adolescents is not a side or peripheral but a core issue for stabilizing the population growth of the country.

DEMOGRAPHIC TRANSITION

The demographic transition of the country in the recent years has brought the issues of women and children into the forefront of the country's development strategy. From a "high birth rate-high death rate" country of the pre Independence era, which provided fodder for the theory of Malthus, India had reached the stage of " high birth rate-low death rate" in the early fifties, which contributed to the high rate of growth of population. This continued till the beginning of the eighties, with a decadal growth rising to 21.51% in the fifties, from 13.31% in the previous decade, followed by 24.80% in the sixties and 24.66% in the seventies, despite all the national efforts made to contain this growth. The transition to the phase of "low birth rate-low death rate" has started at a very slow pace, with population growth sliding to 23.85% in the eighties and 21.34% in the nineties. If the goal of National population Policy of bringing TFR to the replacement level has to be achieved by 2010, the growth rate of population has to be brought down to 10.7% during the current decade, which is a very tall order and can not be achieved unless the issues of women, adolescents and children are brought to the centre stage of our development planning.

The changing demographic profile of the country indicate a few important trends which will have significant bearing on the position of women and children of the country. First, although the percentage of child population below the age of 14 has declined from 37.76% in 1991 to 34.33% in 2001, the absolute numbers of children are still on the rise. The population of children in the age group of 0-6 has increased from 150.42 million in 1991 to 157.86 million in 2001. Likewise the population in the age group of 7-14 is projected to be 170.34 million today as compared to 161.94 million in 1991. Together they constitute 31.9% of the country's population-a huge 328.20 million out of 1.02 billion-the largest number of children in any country anywhere in the world. The adolescents in the age group of 15 to 19 constitute another nearly 10% of the population. Together they constitute the most important potential human resource and it is the health, nutrition, education and well being of these children and adolescents that will determine the future of the country.

The second trend in the country's demography is the declining sex ratio. The overall sex ratio has declined almost consistently over the years-from 972 females per 1000 males in 1901 to 933 in 2001-although the numbers had improved marginally by 1 point in 1951, 3 points in 1981 and 6 points in 2001, but sliding by 5 points in 1961, 9 points in 1971 and 7 points in 1991. The decline of sex ratio have been particularly striking in the age group of 0 to 6 years in recent years. Census 2001 has registered this decline by 18 points-from 927 in 1991 to 945. This decline has been registered in all the States and Union Territories except Kerala, Mizoram, Sikkim, Tripura and Lakshadeep. The decline has been very sharp in prosperous States like Punjab, Haryana, Maharastra and Gujrat. In Punjab the gap in the sex ratio has widened to more than 200 per 1000 children. Unfortunately, the trend could not be arrested by rising female literacy during the decade. This is reflective of a deep seated prejudice against the girl child in the country. Countering this trend should be one of the priorities in the National Socio Economic Goals of the country.

While the female sex ratio among the children is declining, it is increasing among the aged, due to increased life expectancy among the females, leading to a strange gender asymmetry in the population pyramid of the country. With the gradual weakening of family based social security and absence of any strong alternate system, the care of the aged and particularly of the widows, is increasingly assuming the shape of a national problem to be reckoned with in the coming years.

The age pyramid of Indian population will swell in the centre in the years to come. At present 58% of Indians are in the age group of 15-59 years. This will increase to nearly 64% during the next ten years-from 596 million at present to 708 million by 2010, even if TFR reaches its replacement level. The implication of this transition in terms of additional needs of food, water, energy, health care, education and employment will be enormous. At the same time, the gradual increase in literacy particularly among the females on the one hand and the rise in the mean age of marriage of girls on the other, would mean that more and more girls will demand employment, particularly in the organized sector. New types of demands will be placed on the country's educational and training institutions for building capacity and skill of the workers and particularly of the female workers and of those who will be employed in the self employed and informal sectors.

The national demographic features often conceal substantial differences between States and between regions and sub regions within the same State in the achievement of basic demographic indices. These differences are conditioned by factors such as illiteracy, poverty, inadequate access to health and family welfare services etc, which often coexist and reinforce each other. At one end of the spectrum is Kerala with IMR and TFR comparable to many developed countries, but there are districts within the same State like ldukki and Malappuram where IMR and CBR are higher than the national average. At the other end are the States like Bihar and Uttar Pradesh (including newly created Uttaranchal an Jharkhand) which have the worst HDI indices in the world, but with districts like Almora and Ranchi with IMR and CBR much lower than the national level.

The co-relationship between various indices have also been conditioned by a complex web of 'other' factors which need to be studied in depth. Kerala and Tamil Nadu, for example, have achieved replacement level of fertility well before CPR of 60% was reached, whereas, in spite of a developed health infrastructure and CPR much above 60% Punjab is yet to reach that level. Inspite of low female literacy, Andhra Pradesh will be achieving replacement level of fertility much ahead of States with higher literacy rates. Maharastra, Haryana and Punjab have higher SDP than Kerala and Tamil Nadu, but are much behind the southern States in the rates of female literacy, infant mortality and fertility. These suggest that different strategic interventions are required in different States and in different regions and sub regions within the same States for reaching the desired goals of population stabilization. The Sub Group felt that concerted attention should be paid on 5 BIMARU States (Bihar, Madhya Pradesh, Rajasthan and Uttar Pradesh) plus Orissa which account for nearly 44% of the total population of India and which are anticipated to contribute 55% of the population growth in the next decade. Here again district and sub-district specific strategies and action plan should be worked out.

CONCEPTUAL ISSUES

National Population Policy has rightly looked at the issue of population stabilization not as a technical issue that has a technical fix. Population stabilization cannot be achieved by mere physical provisioning of contraception mix or emergency obstetric care. It is critical to involve people-and enable women in particular-to have a say in decisions relating to reproduction and livelihood. This brings in the issues of reproductive rights of women and of the larger conceptual issues of gender equality and of empowerment of women within and outside the household.

The linking of the issue of reproductive health with women's empowerment recognizes that underlying the issue of good health and nutrition for women, we need to examine the issue of power and the nature of gender relations between men and women within the family and community. Here the following conceptual issues need to be highlighted.

Defining Women's Health and Meeting Women's Health Needs: While there have been intense debates attempting to distinguish "women's health" as a more holistic concept than "reproductive health", the issue perhaps is to clearly define what is meant, for our purposes, by women's health and to locate the discourse within a framework of rights. While decision making linked to reproduction and regulation of fertility is important, meeting health needs of women through a system that is sensitive to the differential needs of men and women and their differential access to health care also needs to be taken into account. There are some aspects regarding organizational issues of health delivery which need to be specifically addressed. The division of the health delivery system in terms of two structures-family welfare and health-is not very conducive to a holistic approach to women's health.

Enhanced Awareness and Information: Linked to women's empowerment is the issue of raising awareness about rights-legal literacy, rights to education and health and enhancing information sharing about basic issues. Various studies have indicated that the knowledge of women and adolescent girls about their bodies, and reproductive functions is very limited. Substantial systematic efforts need to be made for enhancing women's and adolescent girls understanding and awareness about various issues.

Linking Health and Reproductive Rights to Other Issues Related to Human Rights: It is essential to recognize the connection between women's health and food security and other economic and environmental conditions. For example, lack of access to water impacts on hygiene, heavy load bearing leads to occupational diseases, lack of nutrition impairs productivity and so on. Therefore the issue of access to safe contraception cannot be delinked from the larger issue of access to food, water, shelter and the issues of sustainable livelihood and a safe environment.

Involvement of Men and Changing Power Relations in Family and Society: In view of the fact that we are laying emphasis on reproductive rights, informed choice and autonomy, it is important that attention is given to underlying social issues which relate to decision making and lack of choices at the level of the family. This involves the social conditioning of roles and responsibilities which one learns from one's 'culture'. It also means trying to address the structural/fundamental inequalities that exist and give rise to certain situations. For example, it is important that solution to anemia etc. is not viewed as a problem, which can be solved by distributing folic acid, but also as an issue of inadequate nutrition, which also has socio-cultural determinants.

Women's Participation: For an empowerment approach to be well integrated into health programmes it is important that women's participation is incorporated at each stage of the programme and issues regarding power structures are also dealt with. The entire conceptual shift from targeted family planning to reproductive health, which is based on informed choice, is to allow women to voice their preference and needs. However, for women to be able to speak out within the family and community social factors have to be taken into account and conditions create for an enabling environment which would allow this to happen.

STATUS OF WOMEN'S HEALTH

The experience of economic progress, political developments and social transformation of the last 50 years, indicate that although women of India have made major gains in terms of decline in maternal mortality and rise in life expectancy, increase in female literacy and employment, mobilization through self help groups and representation at the grassroots level democracy etc., large gender gaps still exist in almost every sphere of life, which do not empower women to have informed choices on their health and nutrition. India accounts for nearly 25% of the world's maternal deaths. Every year about 1,25,000 Indian women die from pregnancy-related causes many of which are preventable. Poor maternal health results in low birth weight and premature babies. More than 7% of the new born babies perish every year. Nearly 2.3% of the babies who survive the first year perish before they complete five years. The number is more in case of female babies.

The mean age of marriage at the national level is 19.5 years, but about 17.4 percent of girls are married below the age of 18 years. Corresponding rates show marked rural (20.3%) and urban (7.4%) difference. 8.3% of fertility in India is contributed by mothers below 19 years of age and this is also linked with pregnancy wastages ranging form premature death, still birth, neonatal deaths, low birth weight babies and maternal morbidity.

Micro Studies have indicated that women do not get adequate nutrition during pregnancy and lactation. The dietary intake of women in the lower economic group is deficient by 500 to 600 calories. In the above 7 years age group there are gender differences in consumption of cereals, pulses, and milk products. In the above 18 years groups, gender difference is quite prominent in the intake of energy rich food. According to an assessment of underweight and stunted growth of children (1997), in the age group of 1-5 years, almost half (49.1 %) of the girls were underweight and 20.3 per cent were severely underweight. Stunting was observed in 56 % percent of girls. The Body Mass Index (BMI) indicates that more women (36.1 %) than male (28.6%) are affected by various stages of Chronic Energy Deficiency. Research has provided enough information on women's morbidity linked with the environment like indoor air pollution, iodine deficiency of soil/water, flurosis and arsenic related disorder, use of fossil fuels etc. The spread of Tetanus, Pneumonia, Dysentery, Typhoid, Cholera, Plague do not need any further research to prove their relationship with environment and sanitation. The brunt of all these fall disproportionately on women. Several domestic chores as also occupational work of many kinds affects the women and leads to an incurable state of health. This is true both at household level and at the work place specially in the unorganised industry sector where maximum number of women earn their livelihood.

Chronic Mental depression and neurosis in girls and adult females is quite wide spread, but the present health care delivery system and social attitude are ill equipped to tackle them especially in rural areas.

Studies have indicated that women are biologically and epidemiologically more vulnerable to AIDS. Male to female transmission of HIV is twice as efficient than female to male. Moreover, majority of Indian women being anemic, transfusion of blood during child birth is quite common making the women more susceptible to the contact. Besides social factors like lack of control over their own body, early marriage and repeated pregnancies, lack of information, poverty induced/forced prostitution, promiscuity of husbands etc. make them more vulnerable to this disease. The impact of HIV and Aids on women is also much more severe and critical. First, inter-generational transmission of the disease takes place through women. Secondly, the rejection and ostracisation of women and girls are much more than for males. Further, women and girls suffer disproportionately from the burden of the disease. The traditional gender role of women in caring for the sick make them more susceptible to the disease. Girls of AIDS affected families often have to leave the school to care for the sick.

Women are the victims of a whole plethora of violence committed against them-infanticide, torture, rape, molestation, battering, trafficking, prostitution, forced marriage, dowry death, custodial violence and so on. This is a reflection of the deep rooted 'gender ideology' of society. Often the crimes are committed by people who are close to the victims and are traditionally supposed to be their protectors. But the victims, especially the sexually abused girls and women, face the brunt of the act more than the abuser. Only a miniscule of the acts of violence committed against women are covered under legal provisions and the bulk of them go unreported. Complex and lengthy legal procedures, often involving substantial expenditure, poor rate of conviction and lack of support from relatives and community are the important reasons for under reporting of crimes against women. Even then the crimes committed against women in relation to the total crimes, has increased from 11% in 1996 to 13.5% in 1998.

Poverty in general, and extreme poverty in particular, has a significant gender dimension. Studies has been revealed that (i) the percentage of adult women exceeds the percentage of adult men below the poverty line, both in rural and urban areas; (ii) the percentage of children in the 0-4 age group in poor households exceeds that of non-poor households, and (iii) in both urban and rural areas, disadvantaged groups of women from Scheduled Castes and Tribes constitute a high proportion of the poor. Incidence of poverty is positively co-related with IMR-a poor couple perceives an additional child to be an investment, both as security against probable mortality of the surviving child and as a potential wage earner. Significant co-relation between spread of female literacy and decline of fertility has been observed throughout the country although there are regions where fertility has declined despite prevalence of illiteracy. A lot of gains have been made in the recent years in female illiteracy. For the first time the number of absolute illiterates has declined and rate of growth of female literacy has outpaced that of males. But still 45.84% of females in the age group of 6 to 50 are illiterates. The gap between male and female literacy is still as wide as 22 percentage points.

THE STATE OF INDIAN CHILDREN

India is to home the largest number of children in the world. Nearly one third of its population-328.20 million in absolute terms- is children below the age of 15 years. About 45% of its population are minors i.e, below the age of 18 years. The country had formulated a National Policy for Children in 1974 and ratified the United Nations Convention on the Rights of the Child in 1992. A National Plan of Action for Children (NPAC) was also drawn up in 1992, which had set goals for various indicators to be achieved by the year 2000. But most of these goals have remained unfulfilled, although significant improvements have taken place in all the crucial indicators like infant and child mortality rates, school enrolment ratios, drop-out rates, levels of mal-nutrition etc.

Infant mortality has remained around 72 per 1000 live births with no significant improvement in the nineties unlike in the eighties. This is much below the average of 6 in developed countries, 64 in developing countries and the world average of 59. There are significant disparities across States, within the States and among castes, communities and other ethnic groups. Kerala for instance, has IMR of 13 per 1000 live births against 94 in Madhya Pradesh: The Infant mortality rate among Scheduled Castes is 24% higher than the national average. Like-wise, the rural and urban differentials also continue to be very high-46 in urban areas as compared to 78 in rural areas. The underlying reasons of high infant mortality are early marriage and childbearing, lack of birth spacing, inadequate maternal nutrition, inadequate antenatal care, and large proportion of deliveries lacking supervision by trained birth attendants.

The Child Mortality Rate (CMR) of India is also very high 25 children out of every 1000 who survive the first year die before they complete 5 years. India ranks 49 out of 189 countries in CMR i.e, if the worst is ranked 1, India is 49th. This reflects the inability of families to look after their young children.

Despite efforts being made under the Integrated Child Development Services programme, malnutrition continues to remain a principal underlying cause of morbidity and mortality in under-5 children. This is because intrauterine growth retardation caused by inadequate nutrition during pregnancy cannot be corrected later on. It is an alarming fact that one out of three children are born in India with low birth weight (<2500 g). Coupled with unsupervised delivery and delayed complementary feeding, unhygienic sanitary practices and lack of access to safe drinking water, the average child succumbs to acute respiratory infections and diarrhea.

Malnutrition constitutes a major threat to the development potential of young children. Although surveys conducted by the National Nutrition Monitoring Bureau, Hyderabad have confirmed that there has been a declining trend in severe and moderate degrees of malnutrition amongst children, the micro-nutrient deficiencies, viz. Vitamin A, iron and iodine have been affecting children in various degrees. The national data indicates that although the proportion of nutritional blindness has reduced drastically, yet the sub-clinical deficiency of vitamin A still continues. Other health concerns of the children are vaccine preventable diseases, birth asphyxia, injury and disability, Mother to Child Transmission (MTCT) of HIV and iodine deficiency disorders. While India has achieved great success with the Pulse Polio Campaign, reports indicate that this has affected routine immunization under the Universal Immunization Programme where the coverage has slipped in recent times. Birth asphyxia is linked to lack of resuscitation facilities during delivery. Many cases of congenital birth defects and mental retardation are caused due to neglect at the time of birth, which are preventable.

A growing incidence of HIV positive mothers in the general population suggests that problem of HIV infected children may soon emerge as a serious problem to be reckoned with. The rate of transmission from a HIV positive mother to her child varies between 15 to 40% with increased risk if the child is breastfed. A child infected at birth, unlike in the case of adults with HIV has a short window period of 3-5 years before the infection overwhelms the developing immune system of the child.

Education is a right of every child. The Directive Principles of State Policy enshrined in the Constitution of India require the State to provide free and compulsory elementary education to all children up to the age of 14 years. Although there has been a substantial increase in the enrolment of children at all levels of schooling, yet 100 million children are estimated to be out of school. Most of these children are vulnerable to neglect. The NSS survey of 1977 has indicated that child labour in the country has increased to 17 million as compared to 13.6 million in 1981 and 11.3 million in 1991. As many as 4.15 lakh children live on the streets in the mega cities of Bangalore, Mumbai, Calcutta, Delhi, Hyderabad and Chennai and are exposed to all types of exploitation.

ISSUES OF THE ADOLESCENTS

Adolescents comprise about a fifth of India's population, but they have so far not been recognized as a target of any strategy for development in the country. They are important human resource material, which can be effectively moulded and channelised for nation building. A bulk of population in this age group, particularly in the rural areas, are drop outs from schools and are vulnerable to exploitation of various sorts. The adolescent girls particularly are at high risk of anemia and mental and behavioral disorder. A three-fold strategy must be adopted for helping adolescents in the country. First, efforts should be made to retain them in the education system by progressively reducing the rate of dropouts from schools and colleges through improvement in educational facilities.

Secondly, vocational training and skill development for the drop outs should be organized in various traditional and non traditional trades, depending on their aptitudes and job opportunities, to prepare them to become self sufficient economically and responsible citizens of the country. Thirdly, the nutritional requirement of the adolescents, particularly of the adolescent girls, should be a matter of special concern, since they are the potential mothers and any investment in their health and nutrition shall not only empower them to be better women, but also be an insurance against the underweight and under nourished children of the future.

Improvement of health of the adolescent girl is a definite way of breaking the inter generational cycle of malnutrition in the population. The adolescent girls need also to be protected from unwanted pregnancies and sexually transmitted diseases. Reproductive health services for adolescent boys and girls is particularly needed in rural areas where adolescent marriages and pregnancies are widely prevalent.

STRATEGIES FOR INTERVENTION

The intervention strategy for empowering women to have informed and effective choices on their health and nutrition and for the development of children and adolescents has to be multi-pronged.

Convergence of Service Delivery at Village Levels

There are two main programmes in the Department of Women and Child Development, which aim at convergence of services delivery at the village level, namely, Integrated Child Development Scheme (ICDS) and Integrated Women.'s Empowennent Programme (IWEP). The ICDS network through Anganwadi Centres reaches 85% of the villages and hamlets in the country. The IWEP (erstwhile Indira Mahila Yojana) which extends to 650 blocks operates through the self help groups of women. Both these programmes can be effective vehicles for the implementation of the National Population Policy. It is therefore critical that both the schemes are universalized.

Nutrition

The Supplementary Nutrition provided under the ICDS Scheme is one of the most vital components under Basic Minimum Service Programme aimed at eradication of the menace of malnutrition of children and women. The success of the programme however depends largely on adequate provision of funds to the States and UTs. An Action plan needs to be drawn up for taking up nutrition in a mission mode to cover infants, adolescent girls, pregnant and lactating mothers-the three critical links in the inter-generational cycle of malnutrition. One intervention that has successfully worked in improving nutrition levels as well as impacting favourably on retention of children in schools is the mid-day meal scheme. This has shown positive results in programmes like TINP and needs to be replicated widely.

Formation of Self-Help Groups

The formation of self-help groups as a basis for the social and economic empowerment of deprived and disadvantaged women has been found to be a successful mechanism for the organization, mobilization and self development of women. This has been tested through the IMY and Swa Shakti projects of the Department of Women and Child Development and is being replicated in a number of programmes of other Departments. These groups can facilitate the process of economic empowerment through thrift and savings, training and skill upgradation and access to credit and other productive resources. They can also be instruments of social empowerment through awareness generation and convergence of delivery of schemes. With the feeling of ownership and management of their own resources and savings, poor women have been able to choose their priorities and have even been found to cover the cost of additional nutrition and health gaps. The success of this approach has resulted in universalization of this mode of organization in all the southern States. There is a need to replicate this mode throughout the country.

Access to Resources

The issue of improved health and nutrition is intimately linked to access to and control over local, social, and economic structures. For women to be empowered we need to ensure

(a) equitable access and distribution of resources like land, credit etc.

(b) access to education.

(c) access to health/nutrition

(d) access to water and sanitation

This implies that resources should flow into these areas to bridge the gender gap and that systems be developed to plan, implement and monitor the 'bridging' of the gap. Various studies have shown that ownership of land tends to reduce fertility by providing an alternate means of security. Similarly education has its own impact on reproductive behaviour of both men and women. Improving the access of women/households in rural areas and urban slums to safe sources of drinking water will free them from the drudgery of fetching water and in decreasing the morbidity resulting from water-borne diseases such as diarrhoea and cholera. This will impact positively on the health and energy levels of women. Access to technologies which can reduce the drudgery of women on the various works performed by them both within and outside the household is also a very useful intervention for empowering the women.

Women's Component Plan

While the Planning Commission has already incorporated the concept of Women's Component Plan in the 9th Five Year Plan whereby 30% of funds/benefit on every women related sector actually flow to women, it is important that guidelines are finalized early so that this could be implemented effectively.

Development of Gender Disaggregated Data System

One of the constraints in the preparation, implementation and monitoring of plans for the development of women is the absence of gender segregated data on various indices of development at the State, district and sub district levels. This lacunae in our statistical system should be addressed on a priority basis.

Legislation

Laws should be gender sensitive and ensure equal provision and access to resources for men and women. Also there needs to be a much broader focus on implementation issues. Many of the existing statutes such as Indecent Representation of Women's Act, Minimum Wages Act, Equal Remuneration Act, and Pre-natal Diagnostic Act, Maternity Benefit Act, etc., are implemented more in their violation. A number of these Acts are under review in order to strengthen their provisions. The Maternity Benefit Act needs to be strictly implemented and expanded to cover women in the informal sector, along with provision of paid leave for a longer period.

Freedom from Violence

Women and girls face violence in various forms at various stages of their life cycle. This takes the form of female foeticide and infanticide, rape, dowry death and more indirect forms such as desertion or abandonment of older women. This calls for a multipronged strategy of implementation of laws, awareness, community sanctions etc.

Participation in Political Life

For empowerment, women need to have a voice in decision making and planning through adequate representation. Reservation of women in the rural and urban local bodies had enabled representation of nearly a million women at the grassroots who play a very important catalytic role in transforming the society. Similar representation in State Legislature and Parliament would further strengthen the process of empowerment of women.

Sustained Media Campaign

One of the most effective interventions that can take place to address the issues of attitude and mind sets of men and women, of the community and also of the functionaries of the government-the bureaucracy, police and judiciary is media campaigns. A sustained campaign through the print, electronic and folk media is necessary on various issues related to empowerment of women, health and nutrition, laws, value of the girl child, violence against women etc. As the Sub Group was deliberating on the issue of empowerment of women, the National Policy for Empowerment of Women (NPEW) was approved by the Government. The Policy makes a series of prescriptions for the economic and social empowerment of women and for mainstreaming the gender perspective in the development process. The policy has also enjoined upon all Central and State Ministries to draw up time bound Action Plan for translating the Policy into a set of concrete actions and measurable goals to be achieved by 2010.

The Policy has also talked about identification and commitment of resources and responsibilities for implementation of the action plans and of development of suitable structures and mechanisms to ensure efficient monitoring, review and gender impact assessment of plans and policies.

NATIONAL SOCIO ECONOMIC GOALS

The objectives of National Population Policy have been conceptualised into three stages:

(a) *Immediate*-to address the unmet needs for contraception, health care infrastructure, and health personnel, and to provide integrated service delivery for basic reproductive and child health care.

(b) *Medium-term*-to bring the TFR to replacement levels by 2010, through vigorous implementation of inter-sectoral operational strategies.

(c) *Long-term*-to achieve a stable population by 2045, at a level consistent with the requirements of sustainable economic growth, social development, and environmental protection.

In pursuance of these objectives, the NPP has fixed a set of fourteen National Socio Demographic Goals to be achieved in each case by 2010. The NPEW has also urged that measurable goals to be achieved by 2010 have to be fixed in the Action Plan although these goals have not been stated in the Policy itself. Both the Action Plans of NPEW and of the medium term objectives of the NPP have taken the year 2010 as their time frame.

There is urgent need therefore for operationalisation of the convergence of the two Policies through the Action Plans of the Governments at the national and State levels. In other words, the fourteen National Socio Demographic Goals should inform the preparation of the Action Plans under NPEW and to that extent guidelines should be issued by the Department of Women and Child Development to all the State Governments and Union Territories. These fourteen National Socio Demographic Goals of NPP are:

(a) Address the unmet needs for basic reproductive and child health services, supplies and infrastructure.

(b) Make school education up to age 14 free and compulsory, and reduce drop outs at primary and secondary school levels to below 20 percent for both boys and girls.

(c) Reduce infant mortality rate to below 30 per 1000 live births.

(d) Reduce maternal mortality ratio to below 100 per 100,000 live births.

(e) Achieve universal immunization of children against all vaccine preventable diseases.

(f) Promote delayed marriage for girls, not earlier than age 18 and preferably after 20 years of age.

(g) Achieve 80 percent institutional deliveries and 100 percent deliveries by trained persons.

(h) Achieve universal access to information/counseling, and services for fertility regulation and contraception with a wide basket of choices.

(i) Achieve 100 per cent registration of births, deaths, marriage and pregnancy.

(j) Contain the spread of Acquired Immunodeficiency Syndrome (AIDS), and promote greater integration between the management of reproductive tract infections (RTI) and sexually transmitted infections (STI) and the National AIDS Control Organisation.

(k) Prevent and control communicable diseases.

(l) Integrate Indian Systems of Medicine (ISM) in the provision of reproductive and child health services, and in reaching out to households.

(m) Promote vigorously the small family norm to achieve replacement levels of TFR.

(n) Bring about convergence in implementation of related social sector programs so that family welfare becomes a people centred programme.

It may be seen that out of these fourteen goals the first seven relate directly to the women and children and the remaining seven concern them indirectly, although vitally. The Sub Group deliberated on each of these goals. Judging by the pace of progress achieved in the social sectors in the last fifty years, the Sub group felt that implementation of these goals during the course of a decade may become extremely difficult and challenging unless there is commitment of adequate resources by the Central and State Governments on the social sector, particularly in the fields of health, education and nutrition and unless there is strong and effective convergence of services at the grassroot level involving all the stakeholders and the functionaries of all the related Government agencies.

Reduction of IMR to below 30 per 1000 and of MMR to below 100 per 100,000 live births from 72 and 408 at present would require identification of the blocks (i) where IMR has already reached below 30 level, (ii) where it has reached a threshold level, (iii) where it would reach the mark during the decade given the normal rate of progress already achieved, (iv) where it would need additional input and (v) where it would require substantially additional input of both child and maternal care services. At present no scientific system of continuous grading and monitoring of ICDS services, according to the level of achievements of IMR and MMR, exists at the national level. Uniform guidelines and criteria are applied to all the ICDS blocks throughout the country, irrespective of the levels of achievement. This must be replaced by a block specific flexible approach with additional anganwadi centers and additional supplementary nutrition wherever required. This should be put in place immediately in consultation with the State Governments and other stakeholders.

Although there are marked differences in the level of IMR/ MMR between ICDS and non-ICDS blocks, such differences are very marginal in many blocks. In Uttar Pradesh, for example, average IMR in ICDS blocks is 86 per 1000 live births against 86.5 in non-ICDS blocks. This strongly suggests that the programme has not been properly implemented in certain States of the country. There is an urgent need for analyzing the causes of poor performance in some blocks and to take effective remedial steps for improving the level of performance in a time bound manner.

It is unfortunate that in the division of responsibilities between the Central and State Governments, Government of India have chosen the 'easy to manage' task of providing the cost administrative services and of medicines and learning materials, while entrusting the job of funding and arranging the nutrition items to the State Governments. Given the critical resource position of most of the State Governments, nutrition always remains a neglected priority for them. There are reports that the supplementary feeding programme in the States was not taken up for months together. Even the Additional Plan Assistance under Prime Minister's Gramodaya Yojana (PMGY) was not utilized for supplementary nutrition in many States. It is unfortunate that when the country is facing the problem of storage of surplus food grains procured by the Food Corporation of India, there are large number of infants and mothers who die every year due to lack of nutrition. The country's achievement in food security must be converted into nutritional security by effectively distributing the surplus food grains at least to infants and mothers through the network of ICDS centers. This should be taken up in a mission mode, if the targets of IMR/MMR are to be achieved within the given time frame.

It is also unfortunate that the most backward areas of Bihar, Jharkhand and Uttar Pradesh, which have the highest incidence of infant and maternal mortality, have not yet been covered under the ICDS. These 450 blocks, which should have been the first charge on the programme, have been kept last in the priorities of the Government. The ICDS must immediately be extended to all the remaining blocks of the country and the unusual time lag between the sanctioning of the projects and the actual operationalisation must be reduced to a minimum. It is seen that the time lag is sometimes as high as two years, which cannot be justified by any means whatsoever.

The ICDS programme must also be effectively converged with the grassroot level programmes and infrastructure of Health and Family Welfare Departments, if the desired goals of IMR/MMR and of universal immunization of children against all vaccine preventable diseases are to be achieved. The States like Orissa and Gujrat, where such convergence has taken place, have done remarkably well, in a relatively short period of time. In most of the States the programmes suffer due to the lack of effective co ordination between the Department of Women and Child development and the Department of Health and Family Welfare. The village Panchayats and the community should also be involved more effectively with the functioning of the ICDS centers.

It is a matter of national shame that despite the Constitutional directive to the State to endeavour to provide within a period of ten years from the commencement of the Constitution, free and compulsory education for all children until they complete the age of fourteen years, more than 100 million Indian children either do not get admitted to schools or drop out.

It is high time that the Directive Principle is converted into justifiable Fundamental Right of citizens and a comprehensive package of incentives and disincentives are built into our national education system to make it a reality. The Balika Samriddhi Yojana, which links payment of scholarship to girls to duration of school attendance should be implemented more vigorously and provided with adequate funds.

The average age of marriage at the national level has already reached 19.5 years and therefore achieving the target of 20 years by 2010 would seem to be an easily achievable task. But the average conceals significant regional differences. Child marriage is still a practice in many States.

About 20.3% percent of girls in the rural areas are married before 18 years. 8.3% percent of fertility in India is contributed by mothers below 19 years of age and this is closely linked with pregnancy wastages ranging form pre-mature death, stillbirth, neonatal deaths, low birth weight and maternal morbidity. Therefore, region specific strategies and action plans need to be worked out to achieve this national goal.

OPERATIONAL STRATEGIES

The Action Plan under NPP 2000 has outlined operational strategies for (i) empowering women for health and nutrition, (ii) child health and survival and (iii) adolescents. The Sub Group considered these strategies, but while broadly agreeing with them felt that the overwhelming emphasis placed on maternity and childcare services can not be taken as 'stand alone strategies'. Rather these should be effectively integrated with the overall perspectives, strategies and programmes for empowerment of women and of development of children and adolescents, as outlined in this report.

RECOMMENDATIONS

The Sub Group makes the following recommendations for the consideration of the National Commission on Population: The task of stabilization of population is not simply a question of birth control or contraceptives. It is intrinsically connected with the larger issues of alleviation of poverty, empowerment of women, changing mind set of men, women and community and of creation of opportunities and enabling environment of all round development of women, children and adolescents. There is a tendency to marginalize these 'strategic' issues in the belief that 'practical' needs are in some sense more immediate, urgent and easier to manage. Unless these practical needs of women are conceived within a long run and 'strategic' framework, there is a danger of losing sight of the essential inter connections between the two. In principle a long-run goal may well be achieved through a series of co-ordinated short-term strategies, but in practice these may turn out to be stand-alone pieces, which could be symptoms of a long run structural malaise. Defining 'short term' goals simply in terms of combating such symptoms would be tantamount to treating the symptom of the disease rather than treating the disease itself. Therefore, it is extremely important to design strategies for empowerment of women and for development of children and adolescents, keeping this disease in mind.

The long awaited approval of National Policy for Empowerment of Women which has closely followed the National Population Policy is a welcome development. It is understood that a new National Policy on Health and a National Policy on Youth are under consideration. The Government is also seized with the idea of declaring basic education as a Fundamental Right of citizens and formulating a Charter of Rights of Children. All these efforts should be integrated and the National and State Action Plans to be framed under each of these Policies should be effectively converged for the effective delivery of services at the grassroot level. The broad National Socio Economic Goals of NPP should inform the process of preparation of the Action Plans under NPEW.

The Planning Commission should make a commitment of adequate resources for the effective implementation of Plans to achieve the National Socio Economic Goals. At present less than 10% of the Annual Budget is spent on the social sector. There is a strong need and justification to substantially step up allocation to all these sectors, such as health, education, women and child development, rural development, social welfare etc.

Both the programmes on Integrated Child Development Services (ICDS) and Integrated Women's Empowerment Programme (IWEP) should be universalized covering all the development blocks of the country, but the design, content and guidelines of the projects under both the programmes should be flexible enough to meet the specific requirement of the blocks so that they are in a position to achieve the National Socio Economic Goals within the time frame prescribed in the NPP.

Larger number of creches/day care centers should be opened to encourage female participation in the economy and also to create a positive impact on enrolment and drop out rates of girl children.

The Kishori Shakti Yojana as a component of ICDS, which has been taken up in 2000 blocks needs to be reworked and restructured to have a developmental approach rather sectoral approach. It should have a gender centred adolescent nutrition and development programme and should aim at a high level of adolescent participation. It should meet the requirements of nutrition, training and education of the adolescent girls so that they can gain the knowledge and self-confidence to be informed and capable members of society. The restructured programme should be universalized to cover all the blocks in the country.

A strong focus on the adolescents should be built in various programmes and schemes to address their concerns related to health, nutrition, sexual activity and behivour, vulnerability to HIV/AIDS etc. Sex education is an area which needs to be specifically addressed.

The gains made by the country in food security should be converted into nutritional security of children and the mothers below the poverty line to completely eliminate nutrition related deaths within a given time frame. Here again block specific strategies need to be worked out in consultation with all the stakeholders.

The constitutionally mandated country wide Panchayat Raj Institutions with one third of its Members and Chairpersons from among the women, has the potential to co-ordinate various programmes of the government on women and children according to the needs and requirements of the micro level realities and to monitor the services to the community. If properly constituted and adequately empowered, they have the potential to ensure the highest degree of transparency and accountability at the grassroot level. Panchayats can also be used for initiating popular movements, as has been done in the context of the National Literacy Mission in a number of States. A nation wide movement on informed fertility control through the Panchayats can very well be initiated under the auspices of the National Commission on Population. Village Panchayats can become regular forums for discussions on village health issues, including issues of reproductive health and fertility control.

Capacity of elected representatives at the grass roots should be developed so that they will be in a position to design projects on health and related areas as appropriate to the needs and requirements of local areas.

Given the size and heterogeneity of our population and the power structure within the Panchayats, even the Gram Panchayats may still be far away from the community. Some NGOs have found it expedient to create intermediate structures between the Panchatyats and the village communities for more efficient processes of information and dissemination and better service delivery. But these local elected bodies are by and large the best instruments for implementing community programmes.

The self help groups of women have been found very effective in organizing and sensitizing women to various issues and empowering them socially and economically. The collaboration of Panchayats, NGOs and Self Help Groups at the grassroots level could become very effective for implementation of grassroot level initiatives in the social sectors. Depending on the strength of the stakeholders at the field level, different models of collaboration can be worked out for effective synergy of these initiatives, to transform the situation at the ground level.

The districts and blocks should be graded according to the level of achievements in the social sectors and block specific action plans should be framed for achieving the National Socio Economic Goals within the given time frame. Instead of uniform allocation of resources to blocks as is currently the practice in almost all the programmes, a more flexible and need-based approach should be taken. The segment of population and areas which have lagged behind in national development efforts, should be positively discriminated, so that they can be helped as quickly as possible to reach the minimum desired levels of standards and goals. But care should be taken to ensure that those blocks which have shown results do not feel discriminated against.

In order that district or block specific plans and projects can be prepared, implemented and monitored it is necessary to develop a system of gender segregated data on various indices of development at the district and sub district level at regular intervals. The absence of such data constraints the preparation of sound Women Development Plans at the field level.

The Medium Term perspective of 10 years should be adopted for the empowerment of women and development of children and adolescents. To that extent the National Socio Economic Goals of NPP should be accepted in the Action Plans for the Empowerment of Women and Development of Children and Adolescents. The achievement of these goals should be monitored on a quarterly basis and appraised on a bi-annual basis.

Involving the male is equally important for the empowerment of women and for stabilization of population. Reproductive decisions are typically taken within the family and hence promoting gender equality within the family has to be based on partnership and not on relationship of domination or subordination within the family. To achieve better understanding, every effort must be made to involve men in the promotion of reproductive rights. This is vital in order to change the societal perceptions about the contribution of women. This can happen only when women are seen by men-and by society-not as 'better halves' but as 'equal halves'.

There is a large unmet need for contraceptives and comprehensive information regarding their efficacy and usage. There has to be greater focus on male contraceptives as they are safer and easier to use. New contraceptives for women need to be carefully introduced with the fully informed participation of women.

A system of incentives/disincentive for the functionaries as also the beneficiaries of various programmes should be developed to convey clear messages about the priorities of the Government regarding population stabilization of the country. However, in order to ensure that disincentives do not become a tool for harassing the disadvantaged, it is necessary to create an environment enabling the women to have self-determination in terms of their reproductive life.

The target of achieving 80% institutional deliveries by 2010 is a tall order, considering that more than half of the deliveries still take place at home at present. The idea of maternity hut in each village to be used as the village delivery room, with storage space for supplies and medicine, and equipped adequately with kits for midwifery, antenatal care and delivery and basic medicines, contraceptives and drugs and medicines for common ailments, is conceptually very sound but may be difficult to implement within the given time frame. A more realistic and practical alternative is to train and equip the village midwives to ensure 100% safe deliveries. This must be taken up immediately as a time bound national programme, to upgrade their skills.

In view of the shortage of trained medical personnel at the PHCs and dispensaries, it should be made mandatory for medical students in both Government and private medical colleges to go to designated rural areas for service for a period of 12 months after they complete one year of residency but before their final degree is awarded. Posting to rural areas for a minimum period of two years at a time should be legally binding for medical officers. Similar arrangements should also be made mandatory for nurses, pharmacists and other paramedical staff.

A Core Group of Women Functionaries at the village level such as ANM, AWW, lady school teacher and elected women Panchayat members could co-ordinate the various programmes on women and children at the village or hamlet level. They should meet once in a fortnight at a fixed place and date to discuss among themselves the progress of the implementation of the programmes and to sort out the problems and difficulties at the purely local level. Coordinating and an integrated approach rather than competition among the local functionaries is essential to ensure positive results. Common training and parity in salaries could ensure this.

Training and capacity building of field level functionaries, NGOs, SHG workers and PRI members are extremely important if they are to perform their desired roles for the achievement of National Socio Economic Goals. Role of Angan Wadi Workers (AWW) is very crucial for the success of the various grassroot level initiatives of the Government. Today the contribution of AWW is not limited to the ICDS only. Her services are required in other programmes also. But she is paid very little-even less than the minimum wage prescribed by the Government itself. Therefore, the honorarium of the AWWs should be enhanced suitably with incentives for results shown. But the AWW must be a local person who stays in the villages.

In view of unacceptable high neonatal and perinatal mortality a comprehensive package needs to be developed at block level concentrating on improving home based care through trained personnel, with adequate referral linkages.

Every infant and maternal death must be compulsorily audited, to have better understanding of the underlying factors for such deaths. Simultaneously, a system of accountability of every functionary must be put in place to fix responsibility for every action or inaction for causing or precipitating such deaths.

Certain clinical and medical interventions can result in immediate and significant improvement in the maternal mortality. Such interventions can also be very cost effective. For example, Tetanus Toxoid injections can prevent a significant percentage of maternal deaths. Such interventions can be taken as a campaign on fixed dates throughout the country, for which nation wide publicity can be given. The same occasion can also be utilized for the health check up of pregnant mothers.

The provisions of Pre-natal Diagnostic Act is not at all be effective in checking the practice of female foeticide, which have become rampant in many States. The requirement of prior permission of 'competent authority' before a case for violation of the provisions of the Act can be challaned before the court, has been found to be a hindrance for booking the offenders, since most of the States have designated the Director of Health Services as the competent authority and they have been found to be reluctant to take action against their colleague doctors. The Act needs to be reviewed thoroughly. More than that a concerted public opinion involving religious leaders and opinion makers from every field should be built up against this highly undesirable social practice.

A sustained, systematic, concerted and pervasive campaign in the print, electronic and folk media should be built up in support of the National Socio Economic Goals of NPP and on various issues related to empowerment of women, health related issues, value of girl child, rights of women, violence against women etc. Village melas and festivals, which bring people together, should be used to popularize these messages. The media budget of the entire social sector Ministries/departments should be pooled together for this campaign.

Bibliography

Alamgir, Mohiuddin Khan: 1988, *Development Strategies for Bangladesh*, Dhaka, Bangladesh.

Ali, Tariq: *An Indian Dynasty: The Story of the Nehru-Gandhi Family*, New York, Putnam, 1985.

Arvind, Sharma : *Women in World Religion*, New York Press, New York, 1990.

Baker, Christopher J.: *An Indian Rural Economy: The Tamiland Countryside*, Oxford, Clarendon Press, 1984.

Benjamin, J.: *Socio-religious Status of Girl Child in India*, New Delhi, Ashish Publishing, 1991.

Bhai, N.: *Harijan Women in Independent India*, Delhi, BR Publishing 1986

Burton, Antoinette: *Burdens of History: British Feminists, Indian Women, and Imperial Culture, 1865-1915*, Chapel Hill, University of North Carolina, 1994.

Calman, J.: *Toward Empowerment: Women and Politics in India*, Colorado, Westview Press, 1992.

Chandra Mowli, V.: *'Jogin'. Girl-Child Labour Studies*, New Delhi, Sterling 1992

Dak, T.M.: *Women and Work in Indian Society*, Delhi, Discovery, 1988.

Datta, V.N.: *Sati: Widow Burning in India*, New Delhi, Manohar, 1990.

Dikshit, D.P.: *Political History of the Chalukyas of Badami*, New Delhi, Abhinav, 1980.

Erikson, E. H.: *Childhood and Society*, New York, W. W. Norton, 1993.

Fine, M.: *Women with Disabilities: Essays in Psychology, Culture, and Politics*, Philadelphia, Temple University Press, 1988.

Gilligan, C.: *In a Different Voice: Psychological Theory and Women's Development*, Cambridge, Harvard University Press, 1993.

Heinsath, Charles: *Indian Nationalism and Hindu Social Reform*, Princeton, Princeton University Press, 1964.

Jain, D.: *Women's Quest for Power*, Sahibabad, Vikas, 1980.

Jordan, J. V.: *Women's Growth in Diversity*, New York, Guilford Press, 1997.

Karl Marilee: 1995, *Women and Empowerment: Participation and Decision-Making*, Zed Books Limited, London.

Kelles-Viitanen, A.: *Invisible Hands. Women in Home-based Production*, New Delhi, Sage, 1987.

Mathur, B.B.: *Women and Depressed Class Population in India*, Allahabad, Chugh, 1994.

Minakshi, C.: *Administration and Social Life under the Pallavas*, Madras, University of Madras, 1977.

Mueller, R.: *Women's Work in Third World Agriculture*, Geneva, ILO, 1985.

Nair, Janaki: *Women and Law in Colonial India*, New Delhi, Kali, 1996.

Palriwala, R.: *Structures and Strategies. Women, Work and Family*, New Delhi, Sage 1990.

Panini, M.N.: *From the Female Eye. Accounts of Women Fieldworkers Studying their Own Communities*, Delhi, Hindustan, 1991.

Selliah, S.: *The Self-Employed Women's Association, Ahmedabad*, Geneva, ILO, 1989.

Stern, R.: *Changing India*, Cambridge University Press, Cambridge, 1993.

Tinker, I.: *Persistent Inequalities: Women and World Development*, New York, OUP, 1990.

Viitanen, A.: *Invisible Hands. Women in Home-based Production*, New Delhi, Sage, 1987.

Vyas, A. & Singh, S.: *Women's Studies in India. Information Sources, Services and Programmes*, New Delhi, Sage, 1993.

Index

♦♦♦